MW00425023

"There is an incredibly powerful move
partner to help energize the faith of
implanted, it works very well. *Owning*
finest experts in the field. This book is filled with what I think is the most effective
strategy to impact kids' faith, as well as practical ideas on just how to do it. I loved
every chapter."

> —**Jim Burns**, PhD, President, HomeWord, Author of *Faith Conversations for Families,*
> *Pass it On, and Confident Parenting*

"Nothing advances the faith more than passing it on to the next generation. These
authors remind us that it takes all of the older generation to pass the faith on to the
next one. We never take early retirement from Christianity. Young people must see
us model the faith, hear us teach them about the love of God, learn that affluence
and the problems of life create a crisis for faith, and learn that faith rests on grace.
These authors remind us that children mean the world to God."

> —**Harold Shank**, PhD, President of Ohio Valley University, Author of *Children Mean*
> *the World to God*

"Everything changes when you really, truly own 'it'—whether that 'it' is some thing
or your faith. And, what changes the most, is you. Dudley Chancey and Ron Bruner
have pulled together experts and insights that we, and our young people, need."

> —**John deSteiguer**, President, Oklahoma Christian University

"For years, most churches have recognized that Youth Ministry is a vital component
for any church that even grudgingly cares about ministry to emerging generations.
But all too often, the work has been relegated to quasi-professionals with lofty
expectations and programmatic job descriptions. *Owning Faith* is a comprehensive,
thoughtful, and clear roadmap for a whole church's commitment to the young. As
parents are equipped and encouraged, and congregations take on a greater degree
of ownership, youth ministry leaders on the front-line are less alone and more
empowered as the body of Christ leads kids to lifelong faith."

> —**Chap Clark, PhD**, Author of *Adoptive Young Ministry: Integrating Emerging*
> *Generations into the Family of Faith*, Professor of Youth, Family, and Culture,
> Fuller Theological Seminary

"*Owning Faith* is a must read for every youth minister, church leader, and parent
who care about adolescent spiritual formation. Each author thoughtfully opens
our eyes to the various roles we play and the perspectives through which we impact
the hearts and minds of young men and women during their highly formative teen

years. Dudley Chancey and Ron Bruner have compiled the key ingredients for a youth ministry revolution!"

—**Greg Anderson,** Connections Minister, A&M Church of Christ, College Station, TX, Doctoral Student in Organizational Leadership, Pepperdine University

"A cornucopia is a symbol of abundance and nourishment. As such, there's no better metaphor for this book. *Owning Faith* is packed full of an abundance of nourishing challenges, encouragement and instruction, rooted in the best and most current research about creating a context for lasting faith to develop in teenagers."

—**Mark Oestreicher,** Partner, The Youth Cartel

Brilliant! A wonderful, practical book of sound advice for parents and youth ministers working together to guide teens into a loving life-long commitment to Jesus."

—**Joe Beam, PhD,** Author of *Seeing the Unseen,* Chair, Marriagehelper.com

"With a blend of stories, research, and practical strategies, *Owning Faith* is a catalyst for refocusing youth ministry on engaging families and the whole community in promoting Christian maturity in today's young people. In the words of one of the authors, we are challenged to see youth and family ministry as 'the Spirit-led, discipleship process by which Christian adults lead teens and families into relationship with God and Christ-like maturity, in the context of the church.' *Owning Faith* provides the inspiration and tools to help us realize that vision."

—**John Roberto,** LifelongFaith Associates, Author of *Families at the Center of Faith Formation and Reimagining Faith Formation for the 21st Century*

"Christian parents want our children (and grandchildren) to know, love, follow, and model Jesus. But who can best help them along that path? Do we give them over to youth ministers? Do we let their teachers—Christians in public schools, teachers in Christian schools, Sunday School teachers—mentor our offspring? Do we refuse to trust them and take the task to ourselves alone? Or might we find a way to partner these and other Christ-loving, youth-serving, and faith-building persons for the sake of our young people? Dudley Chancey, Ron Bruner, and some of their friends in Christian service have produced a volume that will help replace skepticism and fear among the key players with intergenerational cooperation and evocative hope. All of us who care about the faith of the young can benefit from this well-written volume.

—**Rubel Shelly,** Distinguished Professor of Philosophy and Bible, Lipscomb University

"Dudley Chancey and Ron Bruner have assembled a strong crew of researchers and practitioners to navigate the stormy seas of young people coming to faith. Using deep wisdom, biblical theology, and concrete practices, this book serves as a reliable compass to guide parents, church leaders, ministry students, and youth ministers as they set the sails and head out of the harbor. Families and churches are longing for what this book offers . . . and this book delivers!"

—**Carson E. Reed, PhD,** Vice President, Church Relations, Executive Director, Siburt Institute for Church Ministry, O. L. and Irene Frazer Chair for Church Enrichment, Abilene Christian University

"*Owning Faith* puts you in the room with a panel of youth ministry experts and veterans who provide you with practical insight and ideas to help you build a growing faith in your child."

—**Jonathan McKee,** Author of over 20 books including, *If I Had a Parenting Do Over*

"When many church youth ministries are focused on what we do for our teens— programs, trips, events —the authors of *Owning Faith* challenge us to instead think about who we are called to be before and with them. How do families and faith communities walk with this way of faith with our kids? Where does youth ministry actually reside? In the pages of this book, parents and church leaders will find ways to reconsider how we nurture our teens toward spiritual maturity—a critical conversation for these complex times."

—**Dana Kennamer Pemberton, PhD,** Professor and Chair of Teacher Education, Abilene Christian University

"We often ask if our children will have faith. We should also ask if our faith will have children. What can our homes and churches do to own the next generation as they seek to own their faith? The authors in *Owning Faith* have given their lives to this challenge. They have spent time in the trenches and have wisdom to impart. Listen, reflect, and then engage."

—**Rick Atchley,** Senior Teaching Minister, The Hills, Richland Hills, TX

"The primary arena for Christian nurture is the home. But somehow, some way, our youth ministry world has morphed over time into philosophies and practices where youth ministry is primary and parenting is secondary. What's needed is a reboot to put things back into their proper Biblical order so that we are cooperating with God's will and way for the spiritual nurture of children and teens. *Owning Faith* issues not only a call to that task, but loads of practical and hope-filled how-to's to move us ahead on the journey to come-alongside and support parents as they fulfill their God-given calling. *Owning Faith* will launch you on a journey that will bear great fruit in the life of your church, its families, and its kids!"

—**Dr. Walt Mueller,** Center for Parent/Youth Understanding

"Nothing is more important, yet seemingly more neglected, than the intentional passing of our faith to our child. As *Owning Faith* points out, the most effect methods always involve a village-wide, life-long process. As a lifelong professor of communication, I've noticed that while our students claim to (and likely do) have an active spiritual life, they often lack the ability to articulate their beliefs in any systematic fashion. This book is a good start in bridging the gap between faith that is merely 'taught' and faith that is also 'caught' by our children."

—**Philip Patterson, PhD,** Author of *Stay Tuned: What Every Parent Should Know About Media,* Professor of Communications, Oklahoma Christian University, President of the National Christian School Association

"*Owning Faith* is a must read for parents and church leaders who are looking for ways to deepen the faith of their teens and maintain their commitment to Jesus and connection with the church. Learn from the experts and look deeply into the role of families in faith formation. The editors have collected the wisdom and experience of those who have worked with teens and understand them."

—**Lynn McMillon, PhD,** Distinguished Professor of Bible, Dean Emeritus, Elder, Memorial Road Church of Christ, President, *The Christian Chronicle*

"If we only do one thing for the next generation it must be to help them *own* their faith. That's exactly what Dudley Chancey and Ron Bruner do in this new book. Drawing on a lifetime of youth ministry experience and a raft of gifted youth ministers, they bring together a helpful and inspiring tool for any youth worker or parent. Whether your kids are 6 or 16, this book will give you courage and confidence in passing the baton of faith to the next generation. As a parent, I wish I had this book 20 years ago!"

—**Jeff Walling,** Director—Youth Leadership Initiative, Pepperdine University

"Youth workers who don't pay attention to families are like farmers who don't pay attention to the soil. Every teenager in every student ministry is rooted in some kind of family context, and what we know about those roots—be they healthy, tangled, or just downright toxic—is that they have a profound impact on the what grows in and out of that student. With an impressive roster of contributors, a welcome attention to practical questions, and a broad range of topics, two veteran youth ministry thinker-practitioners have given us in this a book a welcome tool for those wise youth workers who realize that nurturing and enriching the soil of families is one of the surest ways to impact the fruit of real life youth ministry."

—**Dr. Duffy Robbins,** professor of Youth Ministry, Eastern University

FOREWORD BY **DAVID KINNAMAN**

OWNING
FAITH

Reimagining the Role of Church & Family

in the Faith Journey of Teenagers

EDITED BY

DUDLEY CHANCEY & RON BRUNER

LEAFWOOD
PUBLISHERS
an imprint of Abilene Christian University Press

OWNING FAITH

Reimagining the Role of Church and Family in the Faith Journey of Teenagers

L E A F W O O D
P U B L I S H E R S
an imprint of Abilene Christian University Press

LIBRARY OF CONGRESS CATALOGING-IN-PUBLICATION DATA
Names: Chancey, Dudley, 1953- editor. | Bruner, Ron, 1954- editor.
Title: Owning faith : reimagining the role of church and family in the faith
    journey of teenagers / Dudley Chancey and Ron Bruner, editors.
Description: Abilene, Texas : Leafwood Publishers, [2017] | Includes
    bibliographical references.
Identifiers: LCCN 2016037232 | ISBN 9780891124764 (pbk. : alk. paper)
Subjects: LCSH: Church work with teenagers. | Church work with youth. |
    Parenting—Religious aspects—Christianity. | Child rearing—Religious
    aspects—Christianity. | Teenagers—Religious life.
Classification: LCC BV4447 .O96 2017 | DDC 248.8/3--dc23
LC record available at https://lccn.loc.gov/ 2016037232

Cover design by ThinkPen Design, LLC
Interior text design by Sandy Armstrong, Strong Design

Leafwood Publishers is an imprint of Abilene Christian University Press
ACU Box 29138
Abilene, Texas 79699

1-877-816-4455
www.leafwoodpublishers.com

17 18 19 20 21 22 / 7 6 5 4 3 2 1

*This book is dedicated to those who broke ground in youth
and family ministries, who discipled us to own our own
faith, and who called us to share our faith with others, especially adolescents and their families. With gratitude to God
in our hearts for these extraordinary servants, we honor:*

John Paul Blankenship

Jim Burns

Les Christie

Dolores Curran

David Lewis

Roland Martinson

Jim Moss

Mike Myers

Wayne Rice

Barbara Varenhorst

Dan Warden

Wally Wilkerson

Big Don Williams

Mike Yaconelli

Contents

Section Four—Preparing for Launch

Foreword

David Kinnaman

O f the many pressing challenges facing today's Christian community, I know of none more urgent than the transfer of faith from one generation to the next. In our research at Barna, we consistently hear from pastors and parents that they have equal parts worry and wonder about passing on the faith to today's younger cohort.

There are several reasons why so many of us are feeling the pressure.

First, we forget that passing on faith from generation to generation is an age-old task. It seems that even the earliest human civilizations were concerned about the morals, values, and priorities of their youth. We should not overlook the timelessness of the questions raised in *Owning Faith*. We are in good company, surrounded by a great cloud of witnesses, who cheer on our efforts to keep our eyes on Jesus and trust him to initiate and perfect our children's faith (see Heb. 12:1–2).

Second, we assume that, because these are long-standing questions within the faith community, the matter and method of faith transference are somehow settled. Deep and lasting faith that children and teens take with them into adulthood does not happen by accident anymore (if it ever did). The cultural default is no longer Christian, and that reality demands new thinking about how faith is passed on. Today's society eats faith and faithfulness for breakfast: two-thirds of practicing Christian Millennials tell us they feel "misunderstood" as a person of faith (65%) and nearly half feel "afraid to speak up" (47%).

Third, the institutions that for centuries have enabled effective faith transference—church and parish, marriage and family, community and neighborhood, and so on—seem to be deflating faster than we can pump air back into them.

That's why I am grateful for *Owning Faith* from my friends Ron Bruner and Dudley Chancey. We need clear-headed thinking about how to make Christianity real in the lives of our kids and grandkids, and in our own lives in these skeptical days.

I've known Ron and Dudley for years and have admired their commitment to serve God's people by being honest—truth in love, as the Scriptures would call it. Few people I know like Dudley cut through the clutter and get to the heart of an issue. I've been learning from him since he first asked me to speak at a youth conference about a decade ago. He was flying around the conference center, dealing with technical setups and speakers running over their allotted time. He had a million things to do, but he immediately focused in on serving me—and as a young Christian leader, it meant the world to me.

As I got to know Dudley better, I also got to see his heart for orphans, for college students, for youth workers, for Churches of Christ—and most clearly his love for his sons, Drew and Matt, and his wife, Vicki.

I can tell you, knowing Dudley and Ron as I do, that *Owning Faith* is a product of their love for God's people and for their own families.

As you read this book, think about it as a warm conversation, hosted by Ron and Dudley, with people who have real wisdom and insights to offer about the most urgent challenge we face today. Their wisdom can help us understand and translate following Jesus into the language and experience of the next generation.

David Kinnaman
President of Barna Group
Author of *unChristian, You Lost Me* and *Good Faith*
November 2016

YOU'RE NOT SUPPOSED TO DO THIS BY YOURSELF

Dudley Chancey

Bud and Temp, two country boys from Frederick, Oklahoma, did what many would consider unthinkable. Without parents along, at ages nine and five, they set out on horseback on a solo, one-thousand-mile round trip. This interstate journey was organized by their father, who felt that his boys needed a test. How would they do on their own? His thinking was that if they did well, they might set out on an even greater adventure.

Bud and Temp did win their father's approval, so he organized a longer trip for them, this time from Oklahoma to New York. The prize: the opportunity to meet Theodore Roosevelt. In later years, Bud and Temp traveled to New Mexico, New York City, and San Francisco. Eventually, Bud became a lawyer, and Temp worked in the oil and gas industry.

Times have really, really changed. I do not know of a parent who would intentionally let one of their children at five years of age ride a horse by themselves for one thousand miles, (unless of course, his or her nine-year-old brother would be tagging along). Is the world today more dangerous? I doubt it; we just know of danger instantly now, almost every minute of the day from everywhere around the world. Instant access to news has caused many of us to live in an almost constant state of fear and anxiety.

Out of concern, or perhaps reacting to this pervasive fear, some parents have adopted a hovering, helicopter style of parenting (please read the sidebar). They monitor their kids and remain in constant contact with them.

However, as practitioners and researchers with over two hundred combined years of ministry experience and teaching, the contributors to this book find it intriguing that helicopter parent-

Helicopter parenting refers to "a style of parents who are over-focused on their children," says Carolyn Daitch, PhD, author of *Anxiety Disorders: The Go-To Guide*. "They typically take too much responsibility for their children's experiences and, specifically, their successes or failures," Daitch says. Ann Dunnewold., author of *Even June Cleaver Would Forget the Juice Box*, calls it "overparenting." "It means being involved in a child's life in a way that is overcontrolling, overprotecting, and overperfecting, in a way that is in excess of responsible parenting," Dunnewold explains.

Why do parents hover?
- Fear of dire consequences for their children
- Feelings of anxiety about the world surrounding us
- Overcompensation for their own past experiences
- Peer pressure from other parents

ing often doesn't cross over into the spiritual lives of children and adolescents. How and why do parents seemingly turn off this excessive concern when they assess the spiritual lives of their children? Why are they not outwardly concerned about the spiritual destiny of their progeny?

Many well-meaning parents who know it is their responsibility to bring up their children to know God simply seem to lack an understanding of how to pass on their faith. These parents attend church on Sundays fairly regularly, and they bring their kids to plenty of faith-based events. But on the whole, they leave the work up to "the professionals," and they have unusual ideas about what "the work" of youth ministry actually involves.[1] In fact, I have had parents walk up to me right after I had baptized their teen and hug me and say, "It's over," as in, "We did it . . . we got him/her into the club. We're done."

A good question to ask here is, "How did we get this way?"

I must confess that, while I was working as a youth minister for years, instead of serving in a facilitating role, I often took the main-teacher role away from parents. Many of us who did youth ministry in the '70s, '80s, and '90s, realize now that this was not a good thing.[2] While all of us would also agree that we did do some good, perhaps much more could have been done if we had helped parents facilitate a more biblical model of ongoing, transformative, spiritual journeys for their children.

Today many of us who serve as youth ministers or who train youth ministers are trying hard to give the spiritual formation of children and adolescents back to parents.[3] While this is good, throwing the role completely back into the laps of parents does not necessarily result in a more biblical model. Jesus said, Go and make disciples of all nations, baptizing them . . . and teaching them . . ." The process of making disciples requires more than one person (but it certainly must begin with parents). The concept of being the church requires more than one person. God made us relational. We need others. It does take a village—a church, a family—to accomplish effective spiritual formation in our children and adolescents.

Discipling is not a one-time thing—it is a lifetime venture. Our research, both past and present, indicates that children and adolescents who had several adults involved in their lives to disciple them during their spiritual journey tend to remain faithful to the church and strong in their relationship with Christ in their college years.[4]

Perhaps the most important research completed to date on churched adolescents and their parents in North America found that these teens were a little less "religious" than their parents.[5] This is good news if their parents were spiritual giants—not good news if the parents were only passively involved in church. Parents are the models. Another finding of the first wave of this massive study was that "churched teens cannot articulate their faith." In the second wave of the study, the researchers found that the parents of these teens also could not articulate their faith. The apple does not fall far from the tree.

So, how should we respond to this reality? We can beat ourselves up and wring our hands in despair. I think this is what the evil one would have us do: to feel helpless and hopeless about being the spiritual leaders God made us to be. Perhaps there is another way to think about what to do.

We can blame society, culture, modernity, and post-modernity. While these certainly provide context, we still have to own up to our lives. I use a small paperback book in one of my graduate classes at Oklahoma Christian University. It is actually a class about evangelism. [6] The book's author, Walter Brueggemann, may be on to something when, in chapter three of that book, he compares Christians today to Israel of the Old Testament. Israel seems to have amnesia. They have forgotten from whom all blessings flow.

They have forgotten who they are. They have forgotten why they exist. They have forgotten that they are the light to the nations. They have forgotten that they were given the responsibility to pass the story on to every generation. They have forgotten.

Walter Brueggemann makes a case that the purpose of evangelism is to bring *outsiders* in. A close second purpose of evangelism is to get *insiders* (the forgetters) to remember. Israel forgot its core memory. This forgetting put the entire nation in jeopardy. The very existence of Israel was doomed because they forgot the story, the memory. These *insiders* (who made the covenant with God) became hollow and uncaring, following idols of their time. Thereby they were completely cutting themselves off from the blessings, demands, and joys they once had in their relationship with God.

Could it be that we as the *insiders* today (the church) have a similar case of amnesia? Have we lost the memory of "so great a salvation"—so much so that we cannot pass it on to our children? Have our tremendous wealth and blessings and our self-sufficient individualism distanced us from our greatest duty? Brueggemann compares what we need to do to with what happened in early Bible times when the nation of Israel, God's chosen people, forgot God:

- Today, we need a modern "back to the scroll" movement which is not scholastic in its intent, but which entertains the wild images and awesome possibilities of the Scriptures as life-defining.
- We need a disciplined, intentional relearning of the specific, detailed substance of the memory, with an awareness that these specifics touch every aspect of our life, both for joy and for obedience.
- We need a bodily act of vulnerability, so that the claim of this memory touches our marrow in unmistakable ways.[7]

Why Now?

I have plenty of things to do in life. I'm sure I am too busy. My coeditor Ron is very busy too. We have day jobs, and we do ministry with children and teens all over this country in other venues of our lives. We love what we do. Do you remember the *Jaws* movie? "Just when you thought it was safe to go back into the water . . ." Well, just when we thought we were finished with children, along came two granddaughters for me. Ron now has four.

Maybe it was the grandkid thing that kicked us into thinking more about the spiritual development of children and teens. You ask yourself, "Did I do a good enough job with my boys in their faith development that they can pass it on to their children?" Both Ron and I know that this is not the case with many of our church people. Why? What causes so many of us to drop the ball in this area? How can we be so concerned about what college our child gets into but not seem to be aware of whether or not he/she gets into heaven? Can we blame it all on North American culture? Can we blame the church? The sad thing is that there really isn't even much blaming going on. In comparison to all the other issues in our lives, sustaining spirituality in future generations doesn't even appear on the radar.

Both Ron and I have done research on teens, children, inter-generational ministry, parenting, and other areas related to families. Both of us have been paid youth ministers. We also have done youth ministry unpaid (paid and unpaid are almost identical). We love teens and their families. Years ago we realized that to get a teen to own their own faith would take more than us. Ron and I now know the importance of parents being the number one influence in their children's lives. From our own parenting experiences, we also know this is a tough job. Along with the other writers in this book, we realized way back and may be even more aware today that we must surround ourselves and our children with Christlike peers and adults to assist our kids in their faith journeys. While I love the hiking quote—You don't know if you don't go!—I also know that you don't go alone.

Somewhere during our travels to conferences last year, Ron and I began thinking about how we could help get the word out that it truly does take a whole village (intentional, intergenerational—parents, family, community, church) to move children along in their faith journeys. As we sat up at night and talked about this, we decided it would be wise to get other people involved in such a project. We began asking insightful folks who loved children and teens and their families to think about contributing a chapter to a book like this. What you hold here is the fruit of those seeds.

The writers in this book have been or still are youth ministers, professors, parents, grandparents, lovers of young people. We want all children to *know Christ*—to love God and to love others. We do not want to forget—and we do not want them to forget—what the Lord has done for us.

One would think that, given all the miracles the Israelites witnessed and the miracles people saw Jesus do, no one would forget. But they did, and we still do. So the Bible reinforces the concept of telling the stories to every generation. We cannot afford to skip even one generation. We have to keep telling the Bible stories. We have to tell our stories. We have to tell The Story. This book is filled with stories of faith and practical information. The contributors to this book have given their lives to pass on The Story. In the pages that follow you will be challenged and encouraged to begin or keep on sharing your story along with The Story. Our prayers are that parents and youth ministers and youth workers will be encouraged and challenged to do this. We must do this!

In the endnotes you can find many links to extra reading. We have also set up a website (www.teendisciples.org) with articles and links to other resources to use in classes or at home to help parents in this daunting task. God bless you as you grow in your faith and walk by your children's sides while pointing them to Jesus.

Whose Job Is Youth Ministry Anyway?

2

TO BE A PARENT IS
TO BE A YOUTH MINISTER

Robert Oglesby

I had dreaded this night for eighteen years. It wasn't a surprise, so I couldn't claim I didn't see it coming. Sociologists call it a "family developmental transition." It was one of those marker moments as a parent: our first child was about to leave for college. We all went to dinner. We shared some laughs, a little last-minute advice, and then drove back to the house to pack a few items for her dorm room. My wife started to get weepy the moment we pulled into our driveway; she quickly gathered the items for my daughter and put them into Lauren's car. She hugged our daughter quickly because she was struggling not be reduced to a puddle of tears, then she ran inside the house to cry. Tonight would mean for us the closing of a chapter of life.

I told Lauren that I was proud of her and hoped she would enjoy the journey ahead. She gave me a quick hug, and I watched her taillights disappear as she pulled out of our cul-de-sac and headed to her new home in a college dorm. I stayed downstairs for a few minutes wondering how she would adjust to life in a dorm. What friends would she choose? Would she thrive in the academic environment? I fondly dreamed about the journey she started that night.

My custom each night had been to leave the porch light on and the door unlocked for a senior in high school who stayed up much later than her parents. I never could sleep well until I heard the deadbolt latch and the porch light go off when she came in, but tonight was different. I locked the deadbolt and flipped the light off, because she was not coming home that night. She would be sleeping in another bed besides the one in our home.

In that moment, tears came from a place I do not frequently visit. I knew the transition was good and healthy, but it was difficult for me as I was faced with the biggest questions of the night: Have I taught her everything that she needs to be a faithful disciple of Jesus? Will she remember that the Lord loves her in spite of her mistakes when I am not there tomorrow morning to remind her? Had I shown her that prayer was powerful as I tucked her in bed at night? Did she see Jesus in my daily steps as I interacted with the people in my life? Did we give her a foundation that was solid?

The embarrassing part of the story is that Lauren was attending college exactly twelve minutes from our home. She was enrolled at Abilene Christian University, where I teach in the department of Bible, Missions, and Ministry. She would be sitting at the feet of some of the finest Christian professors I know. I still would be allowed to have moments of involvement in her world, yet I struggled with the questions. The Lord entrusted to us a wonderful daughter, but had my wife and I shaped her into a disciple of Christ?

When Christians are unsure, we often look through the Bible searching for models of "How to have a healthy marriage" or "How to parent our kids." As we look through the pages of Scripture, frankly it is hard to find examples of a family that any of us would want to pattern our lives after.

- The first family of the Bible had a rough start in family life with one brother killing another because of jealousy, even though that killer/brother received a personal warning from God.
- Abraham and Sarah devised a plan for starting a family—a plan that showed a lack of trust in God.
- Noah seemed to be a faithful leader during a world crisis. He saved his family at that moment, but during the second half of his life he struggled with drunkenness, which led to an immoral event with his sons.
- Joseph's family was filled with jealousy, violence, and deceit. His brothers devised a wild story that would make sure they did not have to watch the overt favorite of their father. They had no problem living with a lie as their father grieved at the dinner table every night for years.
- What about the man who chased after God's own heart, David? Surely he will show us what a godly family looks like! David stopped pursuing God for a brief moment in his life and pursued an illicit affair with Bathsheba. The impact of his indiscretion on his family was unmistakable.
- David had a son Amnon who raped his half-sister Tamar. One of his other sons, Absalom, waits for two years to get revenge. He got Amnon and his men drunk, but hired others to actually kill Amnon, maybe to feel a little less guilty.
- David's son Absalom eventually rebelled and started a civil war to take over his father's kingdom.

The wonderful thing about the Bible is the brutal honesty it reveals about humanity. The characters aren't airbrushed so that we see a sanitized version of faith or family. After looking at these families in the Bible, one might feel that one's own family is not that bad in comparison. The Bible helps us understand that most families dealt with some dysfunction, yet God was able to work through these flawed families to accomplish holy purposes. Perhaps you have heard the famous challenge of Moses to the people of Israel as they stood at the edge of the Promised Land:

> Hear, Israel, and be careful to obey so that it may go well with you and that you may increase greatly in a land flowing with milk and honey, just as the LORD, the God of your ancestors, promised you. Hear, O Israel: The LORD our God, the LORD is one. Love the LORD your God with all your heart and with all your soul and with all your strength. These commandments that I give you today are to be on your hearts. Impress them on your children. Talk about them when you sit at home and when you walk along the road, when you lie down and when you get up. Tie them as symbols on your hands and bind them on your foreheads. Write them on the doorframes of your houses and your gates. (Deut. 6:3–9 NIV)

FLASH! No youth ministers were present. As you read this text, I'm sure you would nod your head, agreeing that this is a good thing for our families to do. The simplicity of the words is powerful, but notice what is not talked about in this text: there is no mention of how to deal with conflict in a family. Not a word about guiding our kids to be responsible in their career paths. No mention of how to discipline a rebellious spirit. As parents, we have been charged to teach our kids to be obedient and faithful to the Lord.

Our primary job is not about creating perfection in our family dynamics. Our job is to develop children who love the Lord and are willing to follow God no matter where the Spirit leads, as they develop *owned faith*.

Churches have paid youth ministers for years to do this critical work. No wonder we haven't had positive results. It was not the youth minister's job in the first place. This assignment definitely belongs to the parents. So how do we as parents become our teen's youth minister?

In Mark 3:33–35, Jesus's mother and brothers came to visit him. They did not come to listen to his teachings. They came to take him back home. What he said in response tells us how his mission trumped family every time. When he heard his family was outside calling for him, he asked a strange question: "Who are my mother, or my brothers?" He gazed at this band of followers who listened intently to his teachings. He announced with great pride, "Here are my mother and my brothers [*you guys*]! For whoever does the will of God, he is my brother and sister and mother" (ESV).

Can you imagine how Mary felt when she heard his words? Crushed, hurt, confused. Mary had been a good mother. She had devoted her life to raising this young man and now this is the thanks she gets. Jesus, though, makes it clear that he is seeking disciples, not looking to spend time at the lake for family reunions. He makes some similar claims in Luke 14:25–27. Jesus turns and tells his listeners, "If anyone comes to me and does not hate father and mother, wife and children, brothers and sister—yes, even their own life—such a person cannot be my disciple. And whoever who does not carry their cross and follow me cannot be my disciple" (NIV). The message is not actually hate. Instead, his words show the priority Jesus places on the mission of making disciples.

The hard sayings of Jesus challenge parents. He calls all parents to something much higher than getting along or having great holiday memories. Jesus will disrupt the serenity of peaceful conversations and the enjoyment of being with our kids at sporting events in the name of being a good family. Jesus will ask a terrifying question of each parent: "Are you making your kids into disciples, or are you raising teens who will do all the right things to get into an upper-tier university? Are you more interested in launching them into successful business careers or in sending them out as dedicated disciples of Jesus who will turn the world upside down as they live out the radical call of Christ?

So we have the Old Testament instruction of Moses about passing on our faith and knowledge of God to our children. Then Jesus comes along in the New Testament and says we have to give up everything to be his disciples. If we put these two together, do we become the ultimate parent/youth minister?

The chapters in this book are meant to be an encouragement to parents and an affirmation to keep on keeping on with your teen. It is a tough job, with many blessings and, hopefully, not much heartache. We want to come out of this with our teen loving God and loving others. We want our teen to be a faithful disciple of Jesus. Is something from the Old Testament and something from the New Testament good enough and new enough to help me as a parent be a good youth minister?

Fighting our culture is an uphill battle today. Much current research connects teens leaving the church after high school with parents not doing their spiritual task, but this is not new. Consider this letter written by a minister to the parents at his church: "It is a complaint, and I fear made with too much justice, that many parents are too negligent respecting the religious education and instruction of their children; . . . I am grieved to add that I apprehend this declension is much to be attributed to the spiritual weakness and indulgence of parents."[1]

While it may seem pointed at parents today, this letter actually was written to a church in 1805. Solomon was right when he said there is nothing new under the sun. People are people. Even God's people are people. Think about Israel in the Old Testament. The whole book of Deuteronomy consists of three sermons by Moses. He reminds the people over and over and over again: "Don't forget!"

But we do forget. We modern Christians certainly aren't turning the world upside down as they did in the book of Acts. It appears that many parents have chosen to give material blessings to their children and point them toward great universities, sports, careers, and other distractions that have caused more teens than ever to give up on church when they leave high school,[2] and many well-off teens to have more problems than their peers.[3]

Much of this has led to disagreements about the roles and responsibilities of parents and youth ministers in the spiritual lives of teens. Ultimately, the buck stops with the parents. They are responsible for the spiritual welfare of their teens. Youth ministers have been and can be a significant influence on youth. With hindsight and hope for the future, youth ministry's greatest legacy could be that of equipping parents to be confident disciplers of their teens. We must remember that adolescents are in a life stage that requires them to think independently and establish their personal identity in order to construct an *owned faith*. In youth ministry, we assist teens in this development by providing marker-type events (make no mistake, any parent can provide these) that assist teens in their journey to own their faith. We were warned in the 1980s that these markers were vanishing.[4] As parents, we need all the help we can get from our church communities in setting these markers.

As a youth minister, I was blessed to offer teenagers a spiritual buffet of these marker-type experiences—experiences that I wanted each of my children to have. During those times, we focused on developing deeper relationships with God and building a beautiful sense of community within our youth group. Students took off their masks and confessed their sins to one another. We were able to live out James 5:16 fully, as teenagers huddled in prayer over those who had shared their sins. We encouraged students to go on mission trips where they found what Jesus called "the least of these" in Matthew 25. They discovered what true poverty looks like at City of Children, an orphanage in Ensenada, Mexico.

Each summer for a week the teens in our youth ministry painted houses in the poorest neighborhoods in Houston. After painting, we visited another level of poverty by meeting the homeless under the bridges of Houston. Students had a chance to see people who were so poor that they did not have a house to paint. They saw some wonderful families in poverty who stored all their belongings in the I-beams under the freeway system of inner-city Houston. Our teens fed homeless teenagers on the streets of downtown Denver through a ministry called Dry Bones. Our youth not only fed them, but they got to know them as real people who had been tossed aside by society. They looked into the eyes of people their own age who had been discarded. Our students saw kids Jesus wanted, and it broke their hearts. We saw a tunnel where kids had thrown down their syringes after shooting up. Letters were painted on the wall that looked like "Freedom" at first glance, but on closer inspection you saw the letters were actually "Freedoom." Our students saw the darkness of evil miles away from their upper-middle-class existence, and they were changed by what they experienced.

While parents appreciated this immersion in ministry each summer, they noticed that their kids came back seeing the world differently, and sometimes this caused tension in their homes. Our teens were challenged to give the best things in their closets to kids in the orphanage. The problem is that the parents don't always get to have the same intense spiritual experience of seeing the children of poverty up close, or perhaps the parents never had this type of marker events in their lives. Youth ministers sometimes forget to take the parents along for the ride. In fact, we purposefully used to keep the parents at a distance. After all, raising teenagers requires an expert (so churches hire twenty-two-year-olds just out of college to be the experts in adolescent development).

This is changing for the good. The trend for youth ministries to be more family friendly is on the rise.[5] Remember, parents individually, or a group of parents can provide events like these for their teens, with or without a youth minister. It takes time and commitment as we pursue the heart of God and the hearts of our teens.

Another important way that parents can be the youth minister to their teens—in fact, better spiritual guides than youth ministers—is to intentionally connect their teens with other like-minded people. For their book, *Faithful Parents, Faithful Kids,* Christian Smith and Melinda L. Denton interviewed hundreds of parents whose children were living faithful Christian lives.[7] The authors discovered that one of the most important factors in kids having a lasting faith was whether they had at least six spiritual mentors in their life. The first generation of youth ministry students that I taught at my university learned about how many adult volunteers you should have to successfully manage a youth group. We taught adult/student ratios like one adult for every six middle-school students, or one adult for every eight high-school students. (If any of my older students are reading this book, I would like for you to forget that lecture.) Instead, we would like you to think of a new paradigm in which we reverse the ratios. The Fuller Youth Institute's Sticky Faith research found that a student's faith was profoundly influenced if five or more adults committed to mentoring the student, even after they left for college.[6]

I'm sure some parents reading this may be thinking that this would be a great youth ministry program. Again, let me emphasize, connecting our teens (and ourselves) to other members of our church family is Basic Discipling 101. We intentionally choose folks who have things in common with, or seem connected to, our children. We invite those folks to encourage, confront, or just walk beside our teens through their adolescent years. Imagine five trusted adults loving, befriending, and advising your teen. This may be the second greatest thing you can do for your teen as they journey toward an *owned faith*.

My own children have all been blessed with this kind of relationships—beautiful people who literally helped me shape my children into disciples. These adults have been a part of birthdays, graduations, and wedding celebrations. They've also been there for my children at the tough moments in life. They have written our children encouraging notes, taken them to lunch once a month, and invited them to bake cookies late at night. Even though my children are grown and gone, these people still ask about my children's faith.

These folks were there for the positive moments and the not-so-positive moments. They were lifesavers during rough parenting times. I still remember one of those not-so-good parenting nights when a discussion turned into a disagreement that quickly degenerated into an ugly fight in our driveway. Things went from bad to worse. We had a complete breakdown in communication, and our child left our house with gravel flying off the back tires. I called my child's number. No response. The hour was late, and our worry turned to panic. At one A.M. we received a phone call from one of our best friends and one of our child's community of five. It was at that point that we realized that our child had run away from us to someone who loved the child and loved us. We have been so thankful that our children were able to experience the reverse-ratio principle of intentionally chosen adult believers.

A Biblical Model for Ministry to Students and Parents

One scripture that remains a measure of good ministry is from Paul's letter to the church at Ephesus. The Christians at Ephesus had nuclear families, but they had become a part of the larger family of God. They were all about making and maturing disciples. As you read this passage about ministry, think about the goals you have for your children:

> So Christ himself gave the apostles, the prophets, the evangelists, the pastors and teachers, to equip his people for works of service, so that the body of Christ may be built up until we all reach unity in the faith and in the knowledge of the Son of God and become mature, attaining to the whole measure of the fullness of Christ.
>
> Then we will no longer be infants, tossed back and forth by the waves, and blown here and there by every wind of teaching and by the cunning and craftiness of people in their deceitful scheming. Instead, speaking the truth in love, we will grow to become in every respect the mature body of him who is the head, that is, Christ. From him the whole body, joined and held together by every supporting ligament, grows and builds itself up in love, as each part does its work. (Eph. 4:11–16 NIV)

Do you remember teaching your children how to ride a bike? Do you remember running beside them while holding on to the back? Eventually it was time to let go. They got up enough speed, achieved balance, and gained expertise at going without help. I bet you can remember the joy on their faces when they knew they were riding on their own.

This is how it is supposed to work spiritually as well. We run beside them in those awkward first attempts, but eventually we must let go—they have to own their own faith. On college campuses, we often joke about helicopter parents who continue to hang around because they want to hold on to the back of the bike. Don't be that parent.

Several principles leap off the page as we read back through this section of Ephesians. Once again, remember this was written before we had youth ministers. God doesn't set us up to fail. Parents, you can do this with your teen. It is amazing how similar the goals of a good parent and a good youth minister are. Both ministers and parents start this process with the end in mind. We intentionally equip children/teens for independence, not dependence. A youth minister who doesn't guide his students to maturity is misguided. Parents who do not guide their children to spiritual maturity are misguided. We can do this. It is much easier as a team, but when the rubber meets the road, it is the parents' responsibility.

Jesus lived out this independence principle with his own disciples. He had three years to equip and mature his team. I am sure he was not certain at times that they would ever mature into the men he knew they needed to be. After all, even at the Last Supper they still were fighting for position, Peter was cussing, and one of his disciples was plotting to kill him. Still, Jesus knew that he had to prepare them to carry on in his absence. As a parent, our goal—despite the challenging, wobbly moments—is to launch our teens into their own faith as they leave our homes.

Notice Paul's expectation of growth throughout the Ephesian passage. When the people of God teach the faith and knowledge of God, Paul expects the outcome to be maturity and discernment. Parents have the same expectation when a child has been blessed with teaching and experience. The result is stable maturity and spiritual discernment that is not easily fooled.

The ultimate goal should be obvious. We will all grow up to be the incarnational presence of Christ in this world. We will become a vital part of a body of believers who will help shape and mold us more into the likeness of Christ. You may have received a piece of mail that was stamped "Time Sensitive." Moving teens toward spiritual maturity is time-sensitive. Jesus had three years. We as parents have triple that time through the teen years with our children. We can do this! Those teen years, with many joys and some heartache, will disappear so quickly. Take advantage of every minute.

It appears sometimes that parents don't want to push their children toward the spiritual maturity Paul speaks about in the passage from Ephesians. Think about it this way: When I tell my son to mow the lawn, I expect it to be done. I expect him to move into action. I don't want him to go to his room and think about what I meant when I said to mow the lawn. I don't want him to call a group of his friends over to contemplate why I think it would be a good idea to mow or all the possible ways that one could mow. I want the yard *mowed*!

Maturity means we implement the teachings of Christ in our life—right now! Don't be afraid to start now. Surround yourself with folks in your faith community who have "been there, done that." You may even need to apologize to your teen for not being their spiritual leader until now. Suck up that pride and apologize. Beg for forgiveness if needed. Take it slow so you don't scare them. Remember if you haven't been the leader, they may be suspicious. *Warning:* you must be pursuing God yourself and working on your relationship with God before you can lead others, including your own children. Make sure you and God are on the same side.

A great youth and family ministry assists in transforming adolescents into the image of Christ through two God-ordained institutions: the family unit and the community of faith. God will use the parents. God will use the group of five significant adults. God will use a youth and family minister who will create opportunities for students and their families to mature. It is clear though the history of the Bible that God has desired that parents be the primary means of teaching and equipping the next generation. We are blessed in many of our churches to have significant adult volunteers and paid ministry staff that can be resources as we move our teen toward his/her *owned faith*. Use every tool available to help your children see the value of living their lives for the glory of God.

Youth and the Mission of the Church

The children of the church should be at the heart of the church's mission. Children should be the focus of every believer's family. Our children should intuitively sense that their parents and their church see them as the *first* mission of the church. If the church isn't making its students feel like they are a vital part of the church, the parents need to visit with the leaders to encourage changes, or move to another church. We don't need to hear more adults saying things like, "These kids are the future of the church." They are not the future; they are the church now. They should not be cute decorations in our assemblies. We cannot put them on the sideline, hoping that someday they will take over. If we do not give them a place at the table now, they will not be prepared when we finally decide to hand the reins over to them.

I get to watch high school students come onto our college campus each year as beginning freshmen. One of the things I notice is that many do not plug into a church. Perhaps one of the bad side effects of youth-ministry-in-a-silo is the fact that students do not know how to engage in "adult" church. They outgrow their youth group, and it appears they outgrow the church. This shouldn't be!

Some churches, including mine, are doing something about this. We have found a variety of ways to involve teens in the important activities and proceedings of our church. Teens are involved in the missions committee, the preacher-search committees, and the service committees. We have ten-year-olds who sing on the praise team, teenagers who do incredible communion meditations, students who help organize massive community outreach events, and teens who are heavily involved in our summer musical.

In carrying out the aforementioned Ephesians passage, our church equips parents through the various stages of the family life-cycle. Our ministers have identified some milestone events (marker events) in the typical family lifecycle. We encourage families to make a "faith memory" with their children when those milestones come around. Here are some examples of milestone moments:

- **Baby blessing**—Each young couple is asked to pick a mentoring couple that will pray for them and watch over them. It has been one of the highlights for our young couples.
- **Bible class prompts**—Our Bible class teachers send home a brief description of the lesson and possibly an idea of how to reinforce the lesson at home.
- **First grade**—The church provides the first easy-to-read Bible for these students who have just started learning to read.
- **Late elementary**—The church holds a "Preparing for Adolescence" class for parents and late-elementary students. Prayer groups of parents are formed. This is a good time for parents to intentionally choose some "sticky faith" adults to come alongside their children.
- **Junior high**—The congregation forms parent support groups, helps parents know how to talk about sex with their children and understand how to help their teens discern wise use of technology and media. The youth ministry holds a "True Love Waits" class for the students.

- **Senior high**—The church prepares parents for launching their teens. There is teaching on how to share a blessing with your teens. Parents and teens share their spiritual pilgrimage with each other. Finally, there is the celebration-of-graduation event.

If you are reading this chapter and feeling inadequate at this point, that was not the intention. Sometimes when I read a book, I feel worse after I finish. I have noticed that some sports only allow you to finish feeling like a loser. Consider the pole-vaulter. He or she may win the gold medal, but their final jump always knocks the bar off the standard. The 100-meter-dash winner feels great at the end of the race—pole-vaulters, not as glorious at the finish. Here is my encouragement for you parents or youth ministers who don't feel like you measure up at times. Despite the missteps and distortions in the reading below, do you still get the intended message? Read through it quickly and I will tell you why this gives me hope as a parent.

> Fnillay, bleeovd, wahteevr is ture, wahteevr is hnorobale, wahtever is jsut, wahteevr is peur, wthaever is palesing, wathever is commndebale, if theer is any ecxelenlce and if theer is anithyng wothry of pirase, tinhk aubot teshe things. Kepe on doing the tihngs taht you hvae leraned and recveied and herad nad sene in me, nad the God of pceae wlil be wiht you. (Phil. 4:8–9 NRSV)

We are never going to be perfect in training our kids to be disciples in this world. We are earthen vessels that are weak and inconsistent in our teaching and our lives. Take heart, though; our children are not reading every "letter" or situation. They are looking for those consistent spiritual anchor points in our lives. Do we believe prayer makes a difference? Are we willing to do the difficult things because

40

Jesus called us to do them? Are we willing to serve others, rather than be served? Are we truly followers of Christ or just fans who admire him but are not willing to change for him?

If you were blessed to have a youth minister in your life growing up, I pray that he or she was a blessing to you. If you are blessed to have one now working with your teen, I pray that he or she is a blessing to you, and to your teen. The challenge of this chapter is for you as a parent to serve as youth minister to your teen. You are responsible for launching children who are well on their way to owning their own faith.

You can do this. God did not set you up to fail. I am almost positive that I would choose you to be one of the five significant adults in the life of my child. Don't let me down. We need you.

Questions and Exercises

1. Robert reminds us that there are no perfect families described in the Bible, yet some of these messed-up people ended up as heroes of the faith. How does this encourage you? What do these stories mean to you as a parent?

2. Robert says "our job is to develop children who love the Lord and are willing to follow God no matter where the Spirit leads, as they develop *owned faith*." What does it mean for a person to own their faith?

3. Have you launched one of your children off to college, career, military, missions, or trade school? What thoughts would you share with other parents who are getting ready to do this? If you could do it again, what would you change, especially spiritually?

4. How do you understand Robert's challenge for parents to see themselves as youth ministers to their own children? What

would this look like in your family? What keeps you from being your own child's youth minister?

5. Are there ways we, as youth ministers, can bring the spiritual into everyday life?

6. Jesus points out that God will give us other "mothers, fathers, brothers, sisters." Who are these others in your family's life? Who are the people that pour into your life spiritually?

7. Who are the people who you would like to be the five adults in the lives of your children? How could you invite them into this relationship?

8. If you could ask your church for anything to help you with the spiritual formation of your children, what would you ask for?

9. What suggestions would you have for youth ministers in planning a balanced program that allows parents leadership in the spiritual development of their children and others in the youth program?

10. Read Ephesians 4:11–13. Since we each have different gifts and need each other, what gifts do you bring to the table? How can you help your children learn how they are gifted?

11. Evaluate your church. How many times in the last month have you seen children or teens involved in "big" church? The more they are involved, the more likely they will not leave church. As a youth minister to your kids, what can you ask church leadership to do that will involve more children?

12. What are some of the milestone markers, or rites of passage in your church that mark growth and maturity for your children? What markers should be there?

3

DISCIPLES LEARN FROM DISCIPLES

Dave Pocta

L et me begin with an introduction so that you know a bit about the Pocta family. I met my wonderful wife, Beth, in Minneapolis in a campus ministry, and we were married March 21, 1992. We have served together in full-time ministry our entire married lives. After being in Minneapolis for a few years, we spent fifteen years in Chicago. When our daughters were twelve and fourteen, we moved to Johannesburg, South Africa, to serve as missionaries in a twelve-hundred-member congregation that needed help developing family life. After our oldest daughter graduated from high school in Johannesburg, we moved to San Antonio, Texas, in 2014 to help the girls prepare for college life.

After we got married, Beth and I waited four years to have children. We wanted to build a strong foundation in our marriage before raising kids. Our oldest daughter, Hannah, was born in 1995, and we adopted Maddy from India in 1998. She was thirteen months old when we brought her home. As I write this, my girls are twenty and eighteen.

We have had an amazing life, filled with trials as well as many adventures. Being a dad is by far the toughest and yet most rewarding part of my life. It has challenged me to my core, exposed the deepest parts of my sinful nature, and helped develop the most genuine aspects of God in my character.

We have worked in small churches and large ones. We have ministered in the inner city and in the suburbs. We have worked with campus students, singles, and adults, and in 1999 we were unexpectedly asked to start working with teenagers. At the time, Hannah and Maddy were four and two years old. We had never parented teens, and we certainly didn't know much about them. We were intimidated about working with teenagers because we were old enough to feel the generation gap with them but young enough that our own kids weren't close to that age. We really didn't know what we were doing.

To my shame, I must say that I was critical of some of the parents of teenagers in our church. I couldn't understand why raising a teen could be so challenging. What was the big deal? I distinctly remember visiting the home of a well-respected family in our church to spend time with their teenage son. I opened the door to his room, and it was an absolute mess. How could that be? These were solid Christians, both parents and son. I thought to myself, "A Christian teen should not have a messy room like this." If all of the cylinders were firing in this family, they certainly should have set the tone for their son to have a room that would be a good example.

After raising two daughters who are now both in college, it's crazy how differently I see things. After seventeen years of working with teens and their families and navigating through the teen years as a parent, I realize that there are bigger battles than clean rooms. Certainly nothing is wrong with a clean room, but that is much lower on the priority list than so many other critical battles that need to be fought.

God and the Word have changed me over the years. My own discipleship has proven invaluable to my parenting. I have been very fortunate. When I became a Christian on June 6, 1990, I was taught about discipling and its vital role in my own development. I had a great family, but spiritual development wasn't part of my life. We went to church every Sunday, but we never talked about faith at home.

So, as a young disciple of Jesus, I needed to be trained in biblical discipling. Experienced Christians taught me about relationships like those of Moses and Joshua, David and Jonathan, Elijah and Elisha. I learned about Jesus's relationship with his disciples. So much of those early years required learning how to imitate these relationships. There were men in my life training, equipping, and maturing me. They were *discipling* me.

I love the word "discipling." It communicates the active art of bequeathing the disciple's lifestyle to another person. It is what Jesus commanded in Matthew 28:19, "Therefore go and make disciples of all nations . . ." (NIV). "Make disciples" uses the Greek word that means not only to learn, but also to become attached to one's teacher and to become their follower in doctrine and conduct of life.[1] It is exactly what Jesus modeled with his disciples. Jesus was intimately involved in their personal development and spent three years walking with and training them. He then told them at the Last Supper in John 13:34–35, "A new command I give you: Love one another. As I have loved you, so you must love one another. By this everyone will know that you are my disciples, if you love one another" (NIV). Jesus called them to imitate what he had developed with them. After three years with them, he revealed the endgame. "As I have loved you, so you must love one another." The same standard. The same expectation. Determined followers of Jesus build the kind of relationships that Jesus modeled with his disciples.

This demonstrates what "discipling" really means: relationships that follow the pattern Jesus set with his disciples. These relationships have been compared to the mentor/mentee or the coach/player dynamic. There are great similarities, but discipling relationships are all that and more. Coaches are generally concerned about one area of life: a sport, a job, or our finances. Discipling is more holistic. It really concerns every aspect of our lives because, as followers of Jesus, we want our whole lives to be a light. We want to be the best Christians, employees, neighbors, spouses, and parents we can be.

I spent a lot of time with the men who were training me. I had a lot to learn. One of the most important lessons I learned was the need for the discipling relationship itself. Discipleship requires being discipled. That was the beginning of a lifelong pursuit. If I was going to become the man God intended, having men in my life training me should be the norm. In my twenty-five years as a Christian, I have always had multiple men training, encouraging, and helping me in all areas of my life. I have given them permission to ask anything and say anything they needed to. I also have given my wife and my kids the freedom to share anything without repercussions.

One day when I stand before Jesus, my life will be an open book, so I have determined to make it an open book now. If my family doesn't feel they can talk to me about something, they are free to get help from the men who disciple me. Over the years I have been encouraged, trained, corrected, and occasionally rebuked in these discipling relationships. And I thank God for all of it. Sure, there are times when someone has been harsh or insensitive. That is true of teachers and coaches as well. It doesn't negate, though, the need for being taught or coached. I've had to work through conflicts and misunderstandings, but I can say genuinely that being discipled by other disciples is one of the greatest blessings of my Christian life. What worthwhile relationship does not have conflict? As Proverbs 27:17 says, "As iron sharpens iron, so one person sharpens another" (NIV). I have needed a lot of sharpening in my life, and I appreciate the people who have been willing to do it. When iron sharpens iron, sparks fly. I love that. For the most part, healthy discipling relationships are so encouraging. I appreciate the input, perspective, training, and reminders of the hope I have as a son of God. I need friends in my corner if I am to continue to fight the good fight.

Being discipled has also helped me understand how to help and train others. And, of course, the most important place to put this learned spiritual discipline into practice for me has been in raising my own children, because disciples learn from disciples. I need to be a healthy disciple to pass discipleship on to my children. I lead them by modeling for them and training them to be what I am: a disciple of Christ. As Paul says in 1 Corinthians 11:1, "Follow my example, as I follow the example of Christ" (NIV).

Becoming a parent is such an amazing experience. Friends and family get involved. There are baby showers, gifts, nursery preparations, and so much anticipation. Certainly, there are some sleepless nights and messy diapers, but it's a wonderful time of bonding with your newborn and building a family. You live in a world of firsts. The first word. The first step. The first day of school. The first piano recital. There is so much joy. Being a parent is fun. Yes, it is physically exhausting, but definitely fun.

Most parents emotionally connect with their children during the early years. They pay close attention to developmental markers and want to know about feelings and thoughts as their child becomes a toddler and transitions to the school years. Unfortunately, many parents do not consider the spiritual aspect of parenting at this stage. They may not see the need for it. They may not understand how to do it. But most likely they never had it modeled for them when they were children. And then adolescence arrives.

It is eye-opening for most. Yes, they've heard stories from their friends, but they never believed that their sweet child would ever behave like this! All of sudden we have a new set of firsts. The first curse word. The first eye-rolling. The first time caught lying. The first time they say no just because you say yes. These firsts are not met with the same celebration. They are not written down, dated, and phoned home to the grandparents. What happened to the sweet little child?

Darkness. The spiritual battle has now begun. What does that mean? Sometimes an internal battle starts raging in a teenager's life when they enter puberty and start coming of age. It's the beginning of their struggle with light and darkness. It's when they start encountering Satan and his demons. We are all thankful that kids don't start off that way. We see in the Scriptures that Jesus clearly recognizes children as part of the kingdom. They are innocent. They are saved. Jesus says in Mark 10:14b, "Let the little children come to me, and do not hinder them, for the kingdom of God belongs to such as these" (NIV). But at some point this can change. Their own sinful nature starts developing. They start wrestling with sin and choice. They struggle with an internal rebellion against God and authority. And we can see the same effect in their lives that happened with Adam and Eve in the garden when they sinned: shame, guilt, and wanting to cover things up.

This shouldn't surprise us. The Scriptures are filled with passages describing this spiritual battle. Ephesians 6:12 tells us, "Our struggle is not against flesh and blood, but against the rulers, against the authorities, against the powers of this dark world and against the spiritual forces of evil in the heavenly realms" (NIV). Our children are not exempt. Satan is on the prowl.[2] We are called by Peter to be sober and alert. He warns, "Your enemy the devil prowls around like a roaring lion looking for someone to devour" (1 Pet. 5:8 NIV).

Intellectually, most parents are aware that free will and rebellion will eventually rear their heads, but still they are often surprised. They have a hard time navigating a spiritual reality when they haven't been preparing for it. They may not have developed the spiritual disciplines to fight the spiritual battles. Parents of young teenagers are often found reeling in disbelief and eager to invite the church to step in. "Thank goodness for the youth ministry!" They quickly shell out cash for camps and retreats. They are quite relieved that there is help, and they appreciate the break at home when the teenager has somewhere to go where parents don't have to worry about them.

I am not criticizing youth ministries. I have worked in youth ministry for seventeen years. I deeply believe in the value that can be added to a teenager's development by the church. (The role of youth ministry is addressed in Chapter Four). What I am saying is that youth ministry shouldn't be a crutch or an escape for parents. How do I know that it often becomes just that? When parents accuse the church of not doing enough. When they have a "drop-off-and-dash" mentality about teen events and functions. When parents leave spiritual development up to the church instead of owning it themselves.

I get it. Parenting is scary. I remember feeling scared the day we left the hospital with Hannah. No more doctors and nurses surrounding us. I had never been responsible for the life of a helpless little baby before. But when you look across the kitchen at your twelve-year-old daughter who just rolled her eyes at you because you asked her to help with the dishes, there is a new level of fear that enters your heart. Wait, can she do that? How do I discipline that? How come I can't control her anymore? And so, yes, we are desperate for help.

I believe that is good. It can force us to our knees to pray and pursue help from those who have been through this before us. It can make us stronger and better as parents. It can force our discipleship to new heights as we continue to grow and learn. Or, it can be the place where we start stepping back and allowing the church or teen ministry to fix our problems. Again, I am not saying that the youth ministry cannot play a vital role in helping us through these years. Beth and I are immensely grateful for every teen leader, parent, and friend who has spent time with our girls. I think the teen ministry and church play an even larger role in the lives of single or spiritually single parents (parents married to a nonbeliever). The church should be there to help. That is why God created it. But God has always placed the responsibility of child-rearing and spiritual formation on parents.

Consider again Deuteronomy 6:4–9 that Robert Oglesby quoted earlier,

> Hear, O Israel: The LORD our God, the LORD is one.
> Love the LORD your God with all your heart and with all
> your soul and with all your strength. These commandments that I give you today are to be on your hearts.
> Impress them on your children. Talk about them when
> you sit at home and when you walk along the road,
> when you lie down and when you get up. Tie them as
> symbols on your hands and bind them on your foreheads. Write them on the doorframes of your houses
> and on your gates. (NIV).

This text is awe-inspiring, gut-wrenchingly convicting, and life consuming. As we grapple with this passage, we will be stunned, sobered, and humbled at the task. It is daunting. It is supposed to be. It should cause us to pursue help, seek input, and grow personally.

This Deuteronomy passage is called the Shema by the Jews. Shema means "hear" in Hebrew. If there is a passage of Scripture considered to be a core creed of the Jewish faith, this would be it. Jewish parents would make this the first passage they taught to their children. They repeated it every morning ("when you get up") and every night before bed ("when you lie down"). They wrote this passage on small pieces of paper, rolled up and placed them in Mezuzahs (small rectangular boxes), and nailed them to the doorframes of their homes. Even today we can witness Jews praying in public places with their Tefillin around their forehead or wrapped around their arm, close to their heart when they pray. This too has a copy of the Shema rolled up inside of it. Why all of this? Because they take this passage seriously.

Let's summarize the heart of what God is saying. It can easily be broken into two simple commands.

1.   Love God with your entire being.
2.   Train your children to love God with their entire being.

Isn't that what God is telling us in this passage? If you are skeptical, read it again.

In other words, impressing our love for God on our children is an all-in, all-consuming life's work. It starts the moment we begin to influence them. It continues throughout every stage of their lives. We are to talk about God and his word at home, in the car, on the sidewalk, at dinner, and when we get ice cream. God is everywhere. A disciple of Jesus should see God in everything and view the world through spiritual eyes. Spiritual parents will spend their lives training their children to understand the world the way spiritual people see it. The Bible presents stark contrasts. Darkness and light. Angels and demons. Sin and righteousness.

Jesus and Satan. Saved or lost. Devout parents will work to help their children choose the right way. They will work at helping their children develop spiritual disciplines from their genesis (we prayed and sang with ours while she was still in the womb).

Worship. Singing. Prayer. Learning to apply God's Word. Loving people. Self-denial. Taking responsibility. Learning to forgive. Openness. Contentment. Gratitude. Serving people. Loving the lost. Showing hospitality. We are to produce spiritual offspring as we partner with the Holy Spirit to instill Christ in our children. God is showing us the time and effort that it will take by telling us how to "impress them on [our] children."

Modern culture is influencing our teens (and churches) and downplaying God's expectation for parents. Our society has divvied up the responsibility of child-rearing so much that parents often do not consider the primary task of spiritual development to be their own. Our education system has evolved from teaching reading and arithmetic to somehow now being held responsible for moral and character development. The church now offers religious education from cradle to campus. As a matter of fact, youth ministry over the last hundred years in the United States has systematically if unintentionally removed this God-given expectation for parents to form Christ in their children. Parents should be providing the main meal and the church the supplement. The meat and potatoes should be happening at home as we have seen in Deuteronomy 6. The church and the youth ministry should be a multivitamin. I fear that in many families this is unfortunately reversed. The church is often the main meal and in many cases, the family just a supplement. Without the church, many children would not receive the vital life-giving sustenance needed to develop a relationship with God. Of course, this is not true in every situation. Many families do an incredible job of raising godly children.

We are called by our Creator to replicate our life, pass on our passion for God, train our children to walk with God. We have about eighteen years with our children to partner with the Holy Spirit to help form Christ in them. This is active work, not passive. This is not osmosis. It is not just bringing our kids to church. It is not just opening the Bible for fifteen minutes once a week. This is "all-in" participatory partnership with God in raising spiritual offspring.

Being a spiritual father is by far the toughest and most demanding aspect of my spiritual life. God takes these innocent children, created in the divine image, and puts them in our custody. They are sponges. They quickly learn to imitate us, their parents. They learn to talk like we talk and walk like we walk. From their earliest days on this earth they are absorbing the world around them and learning how to process it.

We need to raise them to know God. It is our life's work. It is our legacy. But it is also God's legacy. We have to ensure that our vision and purpose in raising our kids reflects God's vision and purpose. So how do we do this? Let's talk about emotional connection and intentionality.

Staying emotionally connected to our teenagers is vital to influencing them. We begin when our children are young. We delight in them. We celebrate them. We mark things down and share their milestones with friends and family. We read to them and spend quality time with them. But, as they get older, they start pushing us away. Their guilt and shame or our parenting mistakes can make them want to put up walls and stay in their rooms. Or they may want to avoid being home at all. Many parents take a wrong turn when this happens. They accept it. The growing expectations parents have for their teens during this life stage complicates matters.

Parents are concerned about homework and grades, chores, relationships, jobs, sports, and behavior. Expectations increase and relationship connection often decreases. This leads to exasperation. It is the very thing Paul warned about in Ephesians 6:4: "Fathers, do not exasperate your children; instead, bring them up in the training and instruction of the Lord" (NIV). Exasperation happens when expectations exceed the emotional capacity of the relationship. This is true of all of us. When we feel loved, we can handle a lot. If we don't feel respected and our viewpoints considered, we often reject other people's demands on us. Our real influence on our teenagers is only as strong as the respect and love they feel from us.[3]

I have learned this lesson over and over with my girls. I remember one time in particular when we lived in South Africa that I really blew it. Maddy was fourteen and didn't do the dishes as we had expected. The consequence of not doing the dishes was losing the use of her mobile phone. I marched into her room ready to dole out the punishment. She was sitting on her bed. I stood over her and sternly corrected her. I told her to give me her phone. She said no and put it behind her back. I about blew a gasket. I was *so* mad! I can't remember exactly what I said but it was not godly. I went into my room and felt horrible. I knew I had blown it. After praying and talking with my wife, I went back and sat down next to her on her bed and apologized. I explained that I was wrong and asked for forgiveness. She forgave me, and we had a good talk about her not doing her chores and losing her phone privileges. That day made an indelible mark in my parenting. I had to stop coming *after* my girls. Instead, I needed to come *alongside* them. If the boundaries and discipline were in place, there was no need to get emotional or take it personally when they didn't comply. I could lovingly come into their room, sit down next to them, maintain the relationship, and still reinforce the discipline while saying something like, "I'm sorry that you won't be able to use your phone today." I could even be empathetic.

In order to really fight for emotional connection with our kids, we have to learn to come alongside of them and stop coming at them. Yes, we are still the parent, but we can't take their behavior so personally. Most teenagers struggle with chores, responsibilities, and homework. I know that I sure did. And it wasn't because I had bad parents; it was because I was a teenager.

The other important element to staying connected relationally is both quality and quantity of time together. When my girls are home, I try to connect with them multiple times in a day. We try every day to have a meal together as a family. We talk about music, movies, relationships, school, jobs, and boys. We talk a lot about boys. We have to. It is a huge and consuming part of their lives. By being involved and connected, I can continue to disciple them or, as Paul puts it in Ephesians 6:4, to "bring them up in the training and instruction of the Lord."

When parents have been engaged emotionally and spiritually from the beginning, they are much more prepared for adolescence. They have been developing spiritual disciplines, and the emotional connection with their children will blossom as their children grow. The bank account is full. When the relationships with our children are strong, withdrawals can be made without bankrupting the relationship. Unfortunately, when parents and children are not spiritually prepared, their relationships often come under attack. They start feeling distant from their teenager and lose real influence.

The good news is that there is always hope. If you haven't done a great job maintaining that connection, start now. Prioritize your relationship. At times we have actively held back from correcting and training our girls because of where our relationship with them was at that time. We had to regroup and really focus on putting some relational deposits back in the bank to increase the account balance. I guess that couple I mentioned in the beginning—the ones who didn't expect their son's room to be clean—knew this long before I did. Relationship over expectation is the key to not exasperating our teenagers. The answer is not to back off entirely on our expectations. The answer is to build a relationship with our kids that can support the discipling relationship God wants us to have with them.

Before we conclude, let's talk about intentionality. We should know where we are heading when we are training our children. When I meet with teens and their parents, I often ask the parents to write down the answer to the question, "What are the top three things you are trying to instill in your teen?" I ask the teen to write down, "What are the top three things your parents are trying to instill in you?" We then compare notes. Some parents are very encouraged to see that their message is getting through. Others really seem to not be on the same wavelength at home.

When Hannah and Maddy were about ten and twelve, it hit me that I only had six to eight years left with them at home. We have always had Monday nights set aside for our family night. We have dinner, a devotional, and then do something fun together. I decided that it was time for all of us to be on the same page about what we were trying to accomplish before they left home. I shared the seven things I wanted to see in their lives before they moved out. I wanted them to know what we would be working on during our remaining years under the same roof.

Here is my list of our seven goals. There is nothing sacred here. It just has helped me to stay focused over the years and helped them know what it would take to be ready to leave home.

1. **Spiritual**—to be a faithful disciple of Jesus and self-motivated in their relationship with God.
2. **Family**—to understand the importance of family and to prioritize these relationships.

3. **Financial**—to understand how to live within their means, how to budget and handle money well.
4. **Social**—to build healthy relationships that are secure and godly. To understand boys and how to build pure and godly relationships with them.
5. **Character**—to be responsible, have integrity, and have a strong work ethic.
6. **Physical**—to have a healthy self-image and know how to eat well and take care of themselves.
7. **Vocational**—to develop good study and work habits and choose a career that would be spiritually rewarding and wise.

You may have a different list for your kids. This is ours, and it has really helped. We have revisited it on occasion and talked about how each one is doing in the various areas. Hannah actually approached me a little while ago, asking me to talk through them with her as she was thinking about whether she was ready to get out there on her own. Obviously they will not have all of these seven things perfected when they leave home. I am still striving to master them myself. But it has given us a great platform to talk very intentionally about what we are discipling in their lives and characters.

I know discipling our children can be scary or intimidating. I feel it every day. My wife and I wrestle through it constantly. It consumes our prayer lives and conversations with close friends. We need to have strong Christians in our lives all of the time. We need help, insight, and wisdom from outside. We need friends who know everything—our strengths and weaknesses, faults and flaws, and our sin. This is a spiritual battle we are fighting. We all need help. This is one of my favorite aspects of being a disciple of Jesus. God gave us the church to help us be who we need to be. Yes, the responsibility of raising godly offspring falls on me, but God surrounds me with help. Help for me, help for my parenting, and yes, help for my children. Even though I believe that the burden is mine to bear, I cannot express enough gratitude for the decades of help I have received from the church—spiritual aunties and uncles, big brothers and sisters, youth ministers, teen mentors, and spiritual peers. My girls have been blessed by all of it. And yet, I direct, involve others, and drive the process. I can't sit idly by, waiting for someone else to come and save the day. It is my responsibility. No other mothers and fathers are waiting in line to raise my children.

We can do this, though. Being a disciple of Jesus always gives me hope. Beth and I remind each other that we can't be perfect parents, but we can be great disciples. When we make mistakes, we repent and trust in the grace of God. God is always there, filling in the gaps of our mistakes and helping us to grow. And we can boldly claim as Paul did in Philippians 4:13, "I can do all things through him who strengthens me" (ESV).

Questions and Exercises

1. If you have older teens and have been there and done it, what advice would you give younger parents about fighting battles versus waging and winning the war when it comes to your teens?
2. What does it mean to be a disciple? Beyond the baptistery, in what ways might the church become more effective in "making disciples"?
3. Is "making disciples" a priority at your church? If not, how can you work on this?

4. Dave mentions the value of being discipled. Who do you have in your life that disciples you in the everyday challenges of being a Christian in our world? If you don't currently have someone pouring into your life, make a list of potential people from which you could choose—then ask them.

5. What sort of attitudes would you want to be present in those who are seeking to disciple you?

6. Dave mentions the early thoughts and concerns that we have as parents about the development of our children. He mentions that it is rare that parents think of young children's spiritual development. Why is this?

7. We wake up one day and find our children struggling with sin. The evil one is attacking our children. The spiritual warfare our children are in is what we have experienced ourselves for years. What can you do to prepare your children for this battle?

8. Much of parenting is modeling; how are parenting and discipling alike? How are they different?

9. What are some spiritual disciplines of yours that you want your children to replicate?

10. What spiritual legacy do you want to leave with your children?

11. How is youth ministry at your church helping with the parental responsibility of spiritually training your children?

12. As our children get older, Dave observes that we raise our expectations about grades, chores, relationships, jobs, sports, and behavior. Expectations increase and relationship connections tend to decrease. Dave says that "exasperation happens when expectations exceed the emotional capacity of the relationship." How is this true for your children? How is it true for you?

13. What are some ways you can you keep the lines of communication open as your children get older?
14. Think back on a time when you needed to apologize to your children. Why is difficult for us to ask for forgiveness from our children?
15. What does it mean to "be engaged emotionally"?
16. What are the top three things you are trying to instill in your teens? What goals do you have for them? What do you want them to know when they leave your home?

WHAT IS A YOUTH MINISTER'S JOB, THEN?

Houston Heflin

When one of my children was eight years old, she asked a piercing question. Even though I had been a youth minister for several years of her childhood, I had written a book on youth ministry, I was teaching college students to do youth ministry, and my wife and I were co-teaching as youth volunteers at our church, my daughter asked this question: "What's a youth minister?" It was a fair question, but it caught me off guard because I assumed she already knew.

The brief conversation I had with my daughter explaining the important responsibilities of youth ministers seemed to help her understand what these people do. And it struck me that putting into words our answer to the question, "What is a youth minister?" would be an excellent exercise for parents, church leaders, and anyone remotely connected to youth ministry programs in churches, especially since this question has been answered in so many ways by Christians over the past half century. If you had to answer the question right now, what would you say? What is a youth minister?

Celebrating the Past

Before I answer this question, I want to take a moment to celebrate the impact of youth and family ministry in churches and then to highlight why it's an important time to reevaluate what we expect of a youth minister. We need to celebrate the fact that the introduction of the specialized role of youth ministers within churches has resulted in countless conversions. Young people have learned spiritual practices in youth and family ministry like worship, Bible study, and prayer—disciplines that are essential to Christian life. They have been exposed to loving Christian community and the truth of the gospel.

It would be impossible to chronicle all the ways youth ministers have saved young people's lives physically because they were available to talk in a time of need, or the ways youth ministers have helped save people's souls with a prophetic message from the gospel. There have been families reconciled when youth ministers stepped in to keep families from ripping apart during domestic strife between youth and parents. Youth ministers have led youth into foreign mission fields and inspired them to become not only professional missionaries, but also medical missionaries, and missionaries in the context of whatever profession they chose.

The work and impact of youth ministers must be acknowledged. They have accomplished many things that are good for families and for the kingdom of God.

Assessing the Present

At the same time, an honest assessment of youth ministers must acknowledge that their presence in churches has had some unanticipated consequences. For example, when churches hire a youth minister, it becomes easier for parents to slip into a perspective that assumes the hired professional has the job covered. Too often this creates a dangerous environment: parents have been tempted to back off of intentional discipleship, the adult church family assumes young people are being mentored sufficiently, and the youth are not engaging with the people and opportunities they most need if they are to mature. This isn't always the case, but it's been happening more often than it should and marks a stark change from how faith communities operated in the past. For millions of people over thousands of years, it was clear that the members of a faith community *all* bore responsibility for teaching their young. Today, some faith communities aren't sure whose job it is. This is especially true for churches who have hired a youth minister.

> Youth ministries have been good at getting adolescents to like Jesus and Christianity . . . but not good at helping people grow out of an adolescent faith into a spiritually mature one.
>
> —**Thomas Bergler**
> *From Here to Maturity,* xii

When youth ministers are present in churches, there is a temptation for some to categorize them as they would other professionals who offer services in the community. The mechanic fixes the car when it is broken, the orthodontist fixes teeth when they aren't straight, and the youth minister teaches adolescents about God. The problem with this perspective is that it is an outsourcing of spiritual formation to someone

> Multiple studies indicate that 40–50 percent of young people who graduate from a church or a youth group will leave their faith and the church after they head to college.
>
> —**Kara Powell**
> *Sticky Faith,* 18

else, when parents actually bear the primary responsibility for teaching faith to their children. The church community should be an active partner supplementing the parents' work.

In addition, churches must address the unpleasant reality of the vast number of youth who grow up in churches but reject Christian faith once they graduate from high school. There are simply too many youth who were active in youth and family ministries but cease to be active in church once they leave home. It's possible that we are perpetuating this problem by allowing youth ministries to function divorced from the larger church. In essence, we've created an organization separate from the larger church body. The members of these organizations (the youth) feel loyal to the organization (the youth group), but not to the church. These youth ministry "organizations" have become surrogate caretakers of youth when the adult members of the faith community should be filling this role. For too many young people, participation in youth ministries insulates them from significant adult relationships. Youth ministries should be doing the exact opposite of this by facilitating mentoring relationships between adults and youth.

> The church too often gives over its responsibility for youth to youth ministries that are "initiatives disconnected from the life of the church."
>
> —Andrew Root
> *Bonhoeffer as Youth Worker,* 56

In light of this, it may be time to redefine the roles and responsibilities of youth ministers to ensure that the results we're getting are the ones we want. Maybe the best way to identify the roles a youth minister should play is to begin with the mission of God through the church. Understanding this mission will allow us to clarify the purposes of youth and family ministry. This, in turn, allows us to highlight what a youth minister should do.

The Mission of God in the Church

The mission of the church is to glorify God through loving God, loving other people, and making disciples. These are the greatest commandments (Mark 12:29–30) and the Great Commission (Matt. 28:19–20). Everything the church does should align with one of these ultimate purposes for its existence. In fact, when we consider what the first Christians were doing in Acts 2:42–47, we can see that they were involved in worship, fellowship, teaching, prayer, service, and evangelism. These are ways the church lives its purpose and accomplishes the mission of glorifying God by loving God, loving others, and making disciples.

Because youth ministry is one expression of the church's many ministries, and because it flows out of the church, it should be aligned with the mission of the church. Therefore, youth and family ministry should also exist to glorify God by helping people participate in loving God, loving others, and making disciples.

The Purpose of Youth and Family Ministry

The relationship between professional youth ministers and families within churches must be—if nothing else—a collaboration, as these two groups partner for the education and spiritual formation of youth and families. *Youth and family ministry is the Spirit-led discipleship process by which Christian adults lead teens and families into relationship with God and Christlike maturity, in the context of the church.* This can happen in churches without a paid, professional youth minister, or in churches that have the resources to employ more than one youth minister. This can happen in small rural churches or urban megachurches. But in churches where a youth minister is present, there are certain responsibilities and roles that she or he fills for the purposes of the ministry's mission.

As with any job, some tasks and responsibilities that occupy a youth minister's time are not exactly the most important part of the job. For example, youth ministers serve as janitors by cleaning up classrooms after messy Wednesday night object lessons, and they serve as chauffeurs who not only drive but also clean up church vans after trips. These and many other responsibilities are part of the job, but they're not the primary roles that should define who and what the youth minister is. Recalling the mission of the church and the extension of that mission in youth and family ministry offers clarity about what we should expect from a youth and family minister.

The Responsibilities of a Youth Minister

Looking at the examples of God's people in the Bible and considering the ultimate objectives of youth ministry within the church, youth ministers need to keep in mind some roles as primary responsibilities of their profession. From examples in the Bible, ten roles emerge that help ministers accomplish the purposes of the ministry.[1]

Youth ministers can be **evangelistic missionaries** to non-Christian youth by sharing the gospel with those who don't know Jesus. In this role they enter into the foreign culture of youth and learn the language of young people to speak truth and shine light into darkness. Like ambassadors in a foreign land, they reach out to adolescents and their families with a gospel message of reconciliation so that people will be brought near to God. They are taking the gospel to the world (Acts 1:8) and fulfilling the Great Commission to "go make disciples" (Matt. 28:19–20).

They are **discipling teachers** of Christian youth—teachers who help young people mature as they grow up in the church. Rather than leaving youth just as they are, these educators challenge and stretch young people in their faith as they move toward adulthood, responsibility, and maturity. In this role, youth ministers model what it means to be a disciple of Jesus and invite others along on that journey of learning to live with the wisdom and passions of Jesus.

They are **bold prophets** of God who spend time listening to God in solitude, silence, Bible study, and prayer, so that they can confidently speak messages of truth rather than repeating trite messages of cultural wisdom. As prophets, they are willing to confront sin in order to point people back to God.

They are **compassionate priests** who help others approach God in worship. These priests help youth and families make sacrifices of praise, offer sacrifices of time, and they even invite others to make sacrifices of their possessions. In this priestly role they also offer a shoulder to cry on and pray prayers of intercession to God for the sins of the people.

They are **pastoral shepherds** who know that when left alone, sheep are defenseless against the attacks of the enemy. They spend time among youth just as shepherds spend time living among the sheep while leading, serving, and protecting them. They know who is in their flock, and the sheep recognize their voice. If any of the sheep wander away, they are willing to chase after them to bring them back and heal their wounds.

They are **organized administrators** who have counted the sheep to know when one is missing. They manage schedules, budgets, receipts, and files in the most efficient way possible to ensure that the ministry functions. This entails time spent in an office with the resources and technology that facilitate organization.

They are **spiritual friends** to youth who invest in relationships with young people to walk beside them and provide mentoring. In this role they offer love and affection to young people who need healthy relationships with mature Christian adults.

They are **equipping recruiters** of other adults who not only model engagement in ministry, but also recruit others to join them. This role requires identifying mature Christian adults who are available and willing to serve. These volunteers are then equipped with training, resources, and encouragement to serve in ministry.

They are **faithful teammates** on a church staff who are often asked to fill in for others on the team when they're away. This might mean preaching, visiting hospitals, conducting funerals, performing baptisms, and doing any number of responsibilities the ministry staff covers through their roles.

They are **visionary leaders** of youth ministry, specialists who know important information about adolescent development, youth culture, and the unique challenges of adolescence. They strategically lead the programming of this specialized ministry by maintaining a healthy, balanced diet of activities, classes, and experiences to help youth grow.

A Little-Known Secret about Youth Ministry

While any job will entail multiple responsibilities, I have yet to meet a youth and family minister who did every one of the ten roles well. In fact, Jesus is the only person who has skillfully excelled in each of these roles. Most of us have tendencies and areas of less inclination. I am convinced a youth minister cannot be all of these roles all of the time in the lives of youth. This leads us to the solution: professional youth ministers need to surround themselves with a community of parents and other adult volunteers who fill these roles in the lives of students.

> Because youth ministry, like every ministry, is life-on-life, we reproduce who we are.
>
> —Mark DeVries
> *Sustainable Youth Ministry,* 111

Ephesians 4:12 says that one job of ministers is "to equip [God's] people for works of service, so that the body of Christ may be built up until we all reach unity in the faith and . . . become mature, attaining to the whole measure of the fullness of Christ" (NIV).

It's possible that after maintaining their own spiritual health, the most essential professional task of a youth minister is to recruit and equip mature Christian adults to join them in ministry.

The Most Important (and Neglected) Role

Over the past decade I've asked groups of youth ministers at conferences and students studying youth ministry to consider this list of ten roles and identify which of the roles they feel like they do well and which is most difficult for them. Overwhelmingly, the "spiritual friend" to youth is the one role that most students of ministry and current youth ministers describe as their dominant role. This makes sense, because people going into youth and family ministry usually love youth and want to be around them. But what if a strength of those serving in youth ministry has concealed a weakness that has gone undetected? And what if this weakness is the one thing that churches need to recognize in order to have a successful youth and family ministry? I believe that is happening in many churches today.

The one role that youth ministers and students of ministry say is the least natural for them is the "equipping recruiter" role of building relationships with adults, inviting them to ministry, training them for service, and continuing to support them with ongoing resources and affirmation. Ironically, the one role that is most challenging for youth ministers may be the most important role in the entire list.

The success of youth ministry in churches will largely depend on the ability of youth and family ministers to function as equipping recruiters of volunteers in ministry. They may have been hired with a charge to "grow the number of teens in the ministry" or to "create a physical space where youth want to hang out" or even to "take us to the next level of effectiveness." These are not bad goals, but they do not acknowledge this one vital component

> A youth minister's primary work is ensuring that each student in the ministry has multiple godly adults pouring into his or her life . . . The youth minister is primarily an architect of a constellation of relationships.
>
> —Mark DeVries
> *Sustainable Youth Ministry*, 144

of successful ministry: building a team of mature Christian adults who invest in relationships with youth—joining their world and inviting youth into the adult world—for the purpose of discipleship within the church.

Churches must ask themselves when they plan to hire a youth minister what they truly want. If it's to assign one person the job of teaching youth and planning activities for them, that will only accomplish a few things: some of the youth will have a relationship with a Christian adult, and the teens will have plenty of activities to attend. But this is not accomplishing the mission of the church. This pattern of structuring youth ministry is insufficient and will continue to produce the kind of results we've been getting, where too many youth are disconnected from the church and mature Christian adults. If, however, a church has the courage and willingness to say, "We want to hire someone to help us all fulfill the mission of the church, to lead us into growth and maturity as we all serve in ministry," then that church has a chance of turning the massive youth-ministry ship that has too often been off course.

What I'm advocating is deliberate communication from church leaders that this one role—the equipping recruiter—be the primary responsibility on any job description for youth and family ministers. Of course, this must be matched with a willingness on the part of mature Christian adults (including elders and parents) to volunteer in the ministry. These adults could be mature college students to senior saints in the congregation, but there must be multiple mature Christian adults invested in youth and family ministry in order for that ministry to succeed.

An Equipping Recruiter Youth Minister

As an equipping recruiter, youth ministers should consistently be asking two questions: "Can you help me disciple young people?" and "How can I help you disciple young people?" The first is a question of recruiting. The second is a question of equipping. The first will require youth ministers to overcome self-reliance and a fear of rejection by asking others to help them. The second will require awareness of family dynamics, and the sensitivity to offer resources to parents with humility.

It's the ineffective execution of this equipping recruiter role (and sometimes, the absence of it) that is perpetuating some of our greatest challenges. When youth ministers function effectively as equipping recruiters, several problems that have arisen in youth ministry will be overcome. I believe a youth minister who is an effective equipping recruiter will do several things well:

- Build relationships with mature Christian adults who can serve as teachers, mentors, and friends to students. One youth minister can only have so many close relationships with youth. When the youth minister enlists other to join, more youth can encounter mature Christian adults. These adults will bring their own faith, experiences, and talents to the relationship, and these will all bless the teens they are mentoring.
- Equip parents with resources for their roles as spiritual leaders in their homes. Youth ministers can offer resources to parents and inspire them to set an example of growing as disciples who lead their children in growth. This may mean writing curriculum or purchasing

devotional material and Bible studies to encourage conversations between youth and parents at home.

- Equip the church with information about youth culture. A youth minister must consistently be looking for resources and researching material that might be helpful to adults as they make disciples of youth. This material might include resources explaining youth culture, news stories about trends at middle schools and high schools, or common terms used by adolescents.

- Equip volunteers with training on teaching and mentoring youth. Young people today reject repetitive lecturing as an educational format and prefer more interactive experiences of learning. Youth ministry equippers can coach others on creative teaching methods and how to build relationships with young people.

- Serve as an advocate for youth and families among the ministry staff and the elders so youth and families are considered in the discussions of the leadership and incorporated into public assemblies.

- Recruit youth for service in ministry, teaching and training them so they are equipped to serve in the church. When young people discover their ability to make significant contributions in the mission of the church, they might continue serving God and the church into adulthood.

> The variable most correlated with mature faith in high school and college (students) is involvement in intergenerational worship and relationships.
>
> —Kara Powell
> *Sticky Faith,* 96

What Can Parents Do?

As an adult member of a Christian community (and especially as a parent with children in the youth ministry), there are two things you can reasonably expect. There is something you should expect of your involvement, and there is something you should expect of the youth and family minister.

First, you should expect to contribute something to the youth and family ministry. The church was designed with your talents in mind. It functions best when "each part does its work" (Eph. 4:16 NIV). You may not be a bold prophet, but you can be a compassionate priest to a teen, by listening to their struggles and praying for them. Maybe you haven't had experience sharing the gospel as an evangelist to a non-Christian, but you can be a discipling teacher by leading a small group of Christian teens who want to

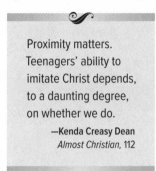

Proximity matters. Teenagers' ability to imitate Christ depends, to a daunting degree, on whether we do.

—Kenda Creasy Dean
Almost Christian, 112

grow spiritually. Maybe you're not inclined as a pastoral shepherd to lost youth, but you're good with Excel and PowerPoint or know how to manage registration at an event as an administrator. As Paul said in Romans 12:6–8, we all have different gifts that we've received from God. Whatever your gift is, use it. Use it to join in the ministry and the mission of the church that is fulfilled through youth and family ministry. This may mean you need to reflect on your own gifts and how you've served in the past. What do you have to offer? Take a look at the ten roles discussed in this chapter and evaluate your own strengths for ministry. Then offer these to God in service to adolescents and other families.

Second, you should expect that youth and family ministers will use the time, resources, and talents they've been given to do their jobs well. This involves equipping adult volunteers, but it also means communicating effectively to churches who have not always viewed youth ministry with the highest regard. One of the greatest challenges youth and family ministry will face in coming years will be to ensure that churches confront their former schema or paradigm of youth ministry. Churches must adapt to a model of youth and family ministry that permits the youth and family minister to rise to an administrative role of organization, recruiting, and equipping for ministry. Rather than viewing the youth minister as a classroom teacher, churches need to view this role more like a school principal. The similarities between the two roles are striking: youth and family ministers are responsible for students in multiple years of their education, they have responsibilities in recruiting, training, program organization, curriculum, facilities oversight, budgets, etc. It's obvious to us that a principal cannot be in every class engaging every student. The best principals are effective when they are leading others to serve well within their areas of giftedness. The same should be true of youth ministers. In this role, ministers can multiply their effectiveness and inspire the church to refuse to neglect the priceless treasure it has in its children and youth.

I am convinced that when youth ministers and churches (including parents, elders, and youth) collaborate to fulfill the mission of the church, those churches are more likely to get the results they are seeking. When youth ministers serve as equipping recruiters of adults, and those adults are using their talents to invest in ministry with youth, it creates the fertile soil where good fruit can grow. People will be growing spiritually, and just maybe, in a few years, we'll see more and more youth faithful to God throughout adulthood.

Questions and Exercises

1. If your congregation has a youth minister, what does their job description say that their job is? What are the responsibilities of youth ministry with which you might be able to help your youth minister?

2. If your congregation doesn't have a youth minister, what are the responsibilities of youth ministry in which God might calling you to use your giftedness for the sake of the congregation?

3. What are ways you have seen churches (or parents) expect youth ministers to be the sole provider of spiritual experiences for teens?

4. In what ways do you find yourself sometimes behaving as if "it's the youth minister's job"? What do you do when you recognize this?

5. Houston mentions ten roles of a youth minister. What would you add to this list? Does your church require more from this position? If yes, what other tasks are there?

6. If you are helping with the youth ministry at your church, list ways that you have been equipped to work with teens. What gifts/talents do you have to bring to the ministry to teens?

7. Houston says that the "equipping recruiter" role is usually the hardest and most neglected—but most important—role for youth ministers; make a list of ways that parents in your congregation can empower or encourage the youth minister with this issue.

8. Ephesians 4:16 requires that "each part does its work." In what ways might you bring resources, relationships, and momentum to youth ministry at your church?

Becoming Whole Persons

BUILDING FAITH AT HOME

Johnny Markham

It was only a few decades ago that churches began offering youth and children's ministries. Parents welcomed the additional help and were pleased with the opportunity to afford their kids more Christian education, positive friendships, service opportunities, and good, clean fun.

Some churches have slowly begun to realize that it is easy for parents to fall into the mode of using these good programs as the sole provider of faith training. What was meant to be a supplement to the efforts of mom and dad at home morphed into being the only faith training children receive. Intended or not, we moved away from home being the primary place where faith is nurtured.

In his book *FaithLaunch,* John Trent describes the time when he asked three questions to a large crowd of parents:

1. "Do you think it's important to pass down your faith to your children? As you might expect, 90 percent said, "Yes! It's very important!"
2. "Do you think your child will have a strong faith when he or she gets out of college?" Again, 90 percent of those responding said, "You bet."
3. "Outside of going to church, what are you doing intentionally to introduce and build a growing faith in your child?" Fewer than 30 percent were doing anything purposefully to meet that goal during the 166 hours a week their children weren't at 'church.'

Trent notes, "Those wonderful, godly, well-intentioned parents strongly believed they should be involved in the children's faith development. They were also confident that their children would embrace the faith by the time they were on their own. But when it came to actually preparing their kids, they were just dressing them up for church—and setting themselves up for a failure to launch."[1]

Search Institute conducted a nationwide survey of more than eleven thousand church-going teenagers and found that only

12 percent have a regular dialogue with their mother on faith/life issues

5 percent have a regular dialogue with their father on faith/life issues

9 percent have experienced regular reading from the Bible in their home

12 percent have experienced a servanthood event with a parent as an action of faith[2]

George Barna's research confirms these results: "We discovered that in a typical week, fewer than 10 percent of parents who regularly attend church with their kids read the Bible together, pray together (other than at meal times) or participate in an act of service as a family unit."[3] It is easy to come to the conclusion that religious life in the home is almost nonexistent.

We live in a service-based economy. We outsource many of our responsibilities like laundry, lawn care, and window washing. Increasingly, many parents treat the faith development of their children like a trip to the dry cleaner. They deliver their children through the drive-thru window to get them cleaned, pressed, and made presentable. They return later to pick them up, believing the job is done. This works well for cleaning clothes but not for nurturing faith in kids. This drop-off approach might keep kids busy in church for a few years, but it doesn't necessarily lead to any kind of lasting faith in their adult years.

We can't outsource spiritual formation for our children. Parents are more influential than anyone else in a child's life. Studies show that mom and dad are two to three times more influential than any church program. Kids must be hearing about faith at home.

Peter Benson notes,

> Teaching values through programs is useful, but it is secondary in impact to how cultures have always passed on the best of human wisdom—through wisdom modeled, articulated, practiced, and discussed by adults with children around them. It is learning through engagement with responsible adults that nurtures value development and requires intergenerational community. Programs are an important reinforcement, but they are not the primary process.[4]

In *The Family as Forming Center*, Marjorie Thompson writes, "For all their specialized training, church professionals realize that if a child is not receiving basic Christian nurture in the home, even the best teachers and curriculum will have minimal impact. Once a week exposure simply cannot compete with daily experience where personal formation is concerned."[5]

After thirty-plus years of leading youth programs for teens, I can tell you that no matter how good a program is, if children don't see godly living modeled and hear issues of values and faith discussed in the home, any faith they gain outside the home is much less likely to stick.

> When God called Abraham and Sarah to be our ancestors in the faith, the definitive act was to make the parents.
>
> —Eugene Peterson, @PetersonDaily, July 21, 2016

There are 168 hours in a week. Let's assume that a child is at church two hours each week. It is unreasonable to think that in only two hours a week, a child can receive all the training necessary to develop a vibrant, genuine, informed, tested faith in God. Something has to happen in the other 166 hours for that faith development to have a chance of succeeding. The good news is that you can do this. You can make the choice.

What Do We Do Now?

I'll never forget the day when my wife and I brought our brand-new, firstborn daughter home from the hospital. I'd never felt such joy, excitement, pride, and fear, all at the same time.

On the trip home, I drove the car more defensively than ever before. We arrived safely at our house, where we carefully got our newborn out of the car, walked down the sidewalk, greeted the neighbors, crossed the threshold into our condominium, shut the door, and sat down on the stairs.

There were three of us in the house now: mom, dad, and child. My wife held our precious child in her arms. We stared at our new baby, then we looked at each other. There was awkward silence for a few moments. Then, it hit us like a rolling boulder: what are we going to do with this child? We've never done this before! She didn't come with an instruction manual. Can I do this? Will she sleep? Will she cry all night? Who will be her friends? Will she be healthy? Will she be happy? Will she become a faithful disciple of Jesus? What do we do now? There were so many questions, doubts, and fears.

I suspect that most parents have felt the same way. God addresses these questions, doubts, and fears in the book of Deuteronomy. As a new generation of Israelites stood on the banks of the Jordan River, God gave the answer to the question, "What do we do now?"

God said, "What I'm about to tell you is the way to live . . . how you can have a strong faith in me, and how you can pass that faith on to your children and grandchildren." What follows there in Deuteronomy 6 is the famous Shema passage we've already looked at in two previous chapters. We do well in this Christian age to follow the instructions God gave the people of Israel as they entered the Promised Land. Their future and survival—and ours— depended on how effective the parents were in transmitting their faith to generations to come. That day beside the Jordan River Moses described how to live as followers of God and how to pass faith along to our children and grandchildren. Moses told moms and dads to impress the godly way of life on their children by living it out at home.

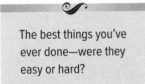

The best things you've ever done—were they easy or hard?

Where and When Parents Share Faith

When should a parent do these? Deuteronomy 6 specifically gives us four settings.

1. When you sit at home. When you are at home, what do you talk about with your children? Meal times are a great opportunity to share about what is going on in each of our lives. These meal times can even be at a restaurant—if you can hear each other. Talk and listen in the kitchen, in the family room, in the yard. Maybe we are too busy watching television, surfing the web, going to sports events, or looking at our phones to spend significant time listening to or talking to our children. When you are at home, what do you talk about with your children?

2. When you walk along the road. Most of us don't walk along the road much anymore. Instead, we travel in cars and trucks and SUVs and minivans! Are you in the minivan stage of your life? Embrace it. Take advantage of that crucial time to communicate with your children. Talk. Listen. Often parents listen to music or some radio show that distracts from possible conversation. Many of us even wear earbuds that serve to separate and segregate us from one another. They inhibit conversation. We need to talk and ask about things. Do you ask your kids about their day? Do you like to talk to them? They really need to talk to you. As Moses instructed, utilize the precious time while you're "on the way" in a positive and productive way.

3. When you lie down. In the "old days," houses were smaller. Sometimes all the males would sleep in one room while the women and girls slept in another. This provided a lot of opportunities to talk. I remember some of my good conversations with my dad happened while we were camping together. Just before falling asleep, we would tell stories. Today many children have their own bedrooms, with enough electronics to distract them from connecting with their parents. This makes it even more challenging, yet critical, for parents to talk with each child each night before they go to sleep. This is one of the most important moments of the day. It is the last interaction of the day. It's the final input into their hearts and minds as they go to sleep. All the activities and emotions of the day vie for prominence in their subconscious spirit. Review the day with them. Pray. Read God's word. Give them a hug and kiss. End well.

4. When you get up. My wife was really good at this. Before our children went to school each day, she would say something in the kitchen or in the minivan that would help set the tone and pace and attitude for the day. We need positive focus for each day. A morning reminder is helpful in establishing the right direction.

Choose the Path Carefully

On this journey, we find ourselves at a dangerous place. Much like the man and his young daughter who were hiking in the desert mountains. They came to a place where the hiking got difficult, even dangerous. The father stopped to think about which way he should go. Then he heard his little girl say, "Pick the good path, Dad; I'm coming right behind you!"

Whether our kids articulate it that way or not, that's what's at stake here. Your kids, grandkids, and the future of our faith are all saying to you, "Choose the good path, Dad, Mom, Grandma, Grandpa . . . I'm coming right behind you!"

God blessed my wife and me with three tremendous children. We've experienced two additional trips home from the hospital with newborn babies like the experience described earlier. Our three children are now grown. They left our nest and moved on to college, career, and marriage. My heart is full of family memories I'll cherish forever—rich memories of meal times, playing in the back yard, vacations, holidays, camps, worship times, and ball games.

Among the most indelibly etched memories are the days each of my bundles of joy was born. Witnessing God's miracle of birth humbled, terrified, and excited me all at the same time.

The day that each of our newborn children came home from the hospital, my wife dressed them up in the same outfit that her mother dressed her in when she made her first trip out into the real world. The dress was a family heirloom, carefully saved and preserved for the occasion. It was a day gown made of fine white cotton decorated with simple smocking and tiny buttons that were incredibly difficult to fasten, especially when my nervous fingers were shaking!

We had agreed that it would be a special symbolic measure for our kids to wear home from the hospital the same clothing that their mother had worn when she made that journey. We decided that we wanted our children to have that link to their past. We wanted in some small way to indicate that the children belonged to and were connected to a family that loved and cared for them deeply.

A similar but much more important decision was also made. We made the commitment to train our children in the nurture and admonition of the Lord. That one decision has made all the difference.

That decision must be made for effective Christian parenting to occur. Each parent must make that simple choice. Each mom and dad must decide that they will make it a priority to raise their child to know, love, and follow Jesus Christ. It is the same commitment Joshua made to all the people of Israel when he affirmed, "As for me and my house, we will serve the LORD" (Josh. 24:15 ESV). That is the same resolve needed in our homes today: the firm, resolute commitment that says, "As for me and my family, we have decided that we will serve the Lord."

This is the decision to follow the prescription of Deuteronomy 6 to impress the godly way of life on our children by living it out at home. Making that decision will mean that as a parent:

1. I will seek first the kingdom of God.
2. I will consistently model faith.
3. I will talk about faith with my children.

1. I will seek first the kingdom of God. A living and active personal faith in Jesus Christ is a must if you want to pass faith along to anyone else. It is impossible to hand off something you don't possess. If you don't have a faith in God that informs and guides you in all the decisions of your life, you won't be able to fool your kids for long. They can quickly sniff out an imposter. Teenagers, especially, have little respect for fake people. One of the mantras of today's teen is to "Be real." Integrity and genuine faith are required of parents if they expect to impart real faith to their children.

It might seem to be a given that the faith of the parent must be real, but through the years I've had countless Christian teens tell me that the parent we see at church is not the same as the parent they see at home. Teens hate hypocrisy in their authority figures. One of the surest ways to turn off your child to God and the church is for you to be lukewarm about your own commitment.

Making personal faith a priority means that you submit your will to the will of God. Your desires become secondary to what God wants. No parent has ever been or ever will be perfect, but our children deserve to see us give our best effort to allow the Spirit of God to live in us and through us.

If you have a desire for your kids to know God and have a real and meaningful relationship with him, you must first look deep inside your soul and ask the question; "Do I have that kind of faith? Am I living my life in a way that reflects Jesus?" Partial commitment won't get it done. We must be all in. Your kids will recognize early on if you are not serious about making God's kingdom your top priority.

So the first question is not so much about the faith of your children as it is about your own faith. Jesus must be the center, the foundation, and the highest priority of your life.

2. I will consistently model faith. Maybe you remember seeing the old Academy Award-winning blockbuster *Jaws*. Steven Spielberg's shark scenes created lasting and terrifying mental images, but they weren't the only scenes that made a powerful impression. There was a poignant moment between the Police Chief Martin Brody (Roy Scheider) and his little boy at the dinner table. As his wife cleared the dishes from the table, the chief sat staring off into the distance, clearly in deep thought about all the problems caused by the shark. He didn't notice his young son sitting nearby, watching his every move. When Brody took a drink, his son took a drink. When he folded his hands, his son folded his hands. Finally, he noticed his son mirroring him. He began to playfully make movements and faces for his son to copy. The scene ended with a kiss. The moment was a vivid reminder that parents are an incredibly powerful role model for children.[6]

The research of George Barna indicates that behavioral modeling "is the most powerful component in a parent's efforts to influence a child."[7] Barna also verified that even if parents are not particularly effective at verbally articulating the values, attitudes, beliefs, and lifestyle they want their children to embrace, but their own behavior consistently displays those elements, their kids will naturally follow suit. In these situations, our actions do speak louder than any words we offer.[8]

In many ways our children's faith will mirror our own faith. Parents pass things along to children every day. They're watching us, learning from us, and imitating us. The question is not *are* we passing things on to our children? The question is *what* are we passing on to our children? Do my children see me reading the

Bible? Do my children see me being faithful in worship? Do my children see me treating all others with respect? Do my children hear me speak with kindness and gentleness? Do my children see me being generous with my time, talents, and money?

In more than thirty years of youth ministry it has been clear to me that moms and dads are the primary influencers in the lives of Christian teens. Other influences like peers and media are profound, but nothing else rivals the power and importance of a parent's influence.

This observation was validated by the excellent research of Christian Smith and Melinda Denton in their National Study of Youth and Religion. The goal of their extensive project, the largest and most detailed study of its kind ever undertaken, was to better understand the religious and spiritual lives of American adolescents. Their study found parents and other adults to be the number one influencers of teenage religious faith and practice.[9] This is true, even in the adolescent years, when teens sometime feel embarrassed by their parents or avoid being seen with their parents.

God makes it clear in his word that parents are responsible for passing faith along to their children. A quick look at Bible passages like Deuteronomy 6:4–9, Psalm 78:1–7, 2 Timothy 1:5, and Ephesians 6:1–4 clearly reveal that God has given parents the crucial role of passing on a legacy of faith to their children. When moms and dads take seriously their responsibility to teach their children, they create an ideal setting for their children to grow and mature in their own relationships with God.

Martin Luther put it this way: "Most certainly, father and mother are apostles, bishops, and priests to their children, for it is they who make them acquainted with the gospel."[10]

3. I will talk about faith with my children. While participating in a youth ministry conference, I heard Jon Acuff speak. Acuff shared something profound and important. He told the story of when he used to work for Bose, the high-end stereo company. Their goal at Bose was to get college students to buy a Bose stereo with their first paycheck after college. It was not a bad business plan. The problem for Bose, though, was that those college grads most often would choose Sony instead of Bose. Those young adults were making that choice because Sony started talking to those twenty-three-year-olds when they were six. Sony sold them a pink stereo in the first grade. Sony sold them a PlayStation at age thirteen. Sony sold them headphones at age fifteen. So by the time Bose showed up at twenty-three to sell them a stereo, there was a sense of "Who are you? I've never met you before." Sony essentially had a seventeen-year head start in building a consumer-business relationship. Bose got into the conversation far too late to be effective.

Top 10 List of Traits to Model for Your Kids:

Love
Holiness
Prayer
Humility
Bible Study
Worship
Grace
Generosity
Kindness
Service

Are there other traits you would add?

Acuff used this superb example to illustrate what is also happening in our families in regard to all the "tough" conversations parents and their kids need to be having—conversations about faith, church, sexuality, alcohol, social media, entertainment media, marijuana, relationships, tolerance, and boundaries. We need to be having these conversations with our kids, because our culture already has been having those conversations with them for years. And they do a terrific job of selling their message! Has the culture been communicating its message so effectively that our conversations as Christian parents, like the sales pitch of Bose, will be too little and too late to be effective?

We tend to be reactive, not proactive. Typically, we are missing out on sharing the truth with our kids. If we aren't having a steady, consistent dose of communication about topics that we Christians most likely hold a highly different view on as compared to our popular culture, we will not be able to lead our teens in "the way they should go."

Unless we parents are having real, intentional conversations about what our kids are doing with phones, computers, televisions, social media, music, movies, and pornography, we are missing the boat. If we aren't having these conversations early and often, our teens will become loyal customers of what our culture says is all right. Culture will make the sale and our young people will buy the product this world is selling. Don't get into the conversation too late to be effective.

Acuff says it this way,

> We let the world start the conversation, let celebrities
> drive their dreams, and let society define their values.
> Then at age 15 we show up in their life and wonder why
> they're lost. It's not whether your kids will have a con-
> versation about the world they live in, it's whether you'll
> have a voice in it. It's time to start talking with our kids.
> Earlier than we want. More often than we like. Don't
> give the world a head start with your kids.[11]

These conversations require intentionality. We have to do it with thought and on purpose. It must be our mission to make a real, an active, a vibrant, a living faith in God a reality in our homes. To do that, we have to talk about it. When was the last time you talked about God in your home? When was the last time you talked *to* God in your home? When we talk about it—out loud—something special happens.

Parents who've "been there and done that" in regard to talking to their children about faith matters offer the following advice:

- Limit lecturing.
- Ask questions.
- Share personal experiences.
- Tell stories.
- Be vulnerable.
- Provide discipline.
- Show boundaries.
- Identify expectations.
- Serve together.
- Read positive materials.
- Be consistent.
- Share the load with your spouse, other parents, grandparents, and the church.
- Earn the right.
- Pray.
- Depend on God.
- Seek advice from those who've already done it.

Thomas G. Long said, "We don't just say things we already believe. To the contrary, saying things out loud is part of how we come to believe. We talk our way toward belief, talk our way from tentative belief through doubt to firmer belief, talk our way toward believing more fully, more clearly, and more deeply. Putting things into words is one of the ways we acquire knowledge, passion, and conviction."[12]

In Hebrew tradition, uttering God's name is the same as invoking God's power. Proclaiming the name of God, therefore, is a formative act. It changes things. It changes us. It's a powerful occasion. You don't have to have the ability of a famous preacher or the theological depth of a university professor. Just be yourself. Start where you are. Children appreciate it when they see a parent "being real." You can do it!

Parents can choose to use a planned, structured lesson time or to wait for those more naturally occurring teachable moments to make a point or illustrate a biblical truth. Some combination of both methods is most helpful.

Ten Tips for Having Meaningful Conversation with Your Child

1. Kids must know and feel that you truly love them and care about them. (Show them by your consistent actions that your love is unconditional.)
2. Find the right time and place to talk. (Affirm in public, rebuke in private.)
3. Be patient, calm, and self-controlled. (Someone has to be the adult.)
4. Practice active listening. ("So, what I'm hearing you say is . . .")
5. Be available and approachable. (Your body language and the tone of your voice are a huge part of your communication.)
6. Don't nag or manipulate. (Don't provoke your children to anger.)
7. Find opportunities to encourage and affirm. ("I really appreciate the way you talked kindly to your little sister.")
8. Value and respect their opinions. (Do your best to remember the feelings you had when you were that age.)

One family used the Christmas holidays as a strategic moment for bringing faith into family conversations. Every year, they lit candles and read Advent scriptures as they counted the days to Christmas. It took only a few minutes, but it made a lasting spiritual impact.

—**John Grant,**
College Hills Church
Connections Minister
Lebanon TN

9. Learn how to ask the right questions in the right manner. (Ask questions that start with words like who, what, when, how, or why.)

10. Pray. (Let them hear you pray at times other than at meals.)

11. Use this tool, create one of your own, or find another, but be sure to find a tool to go along with the Bible that will help guide you as you teach your child.[13]

The Role of the Church

None of this is to say that the role of the church is irrelevant. It's quite the opposite. The church maintains a critically important place in developing and nurturing faith in people of all ages. The church is there to inform, encourage, support, and supplement what is taught and practiced at home. A healthy church will provide encouragement, teaching, and support. Children's and youth ministries remain important and have a definite role in the faith development of our children.

Unfortunately, not every child will have the opportunity to be nurtured in faith at home. This reality makes it even more important for the church to have people and programs in place to stand in the gap for every child as much as possible. Loving, caring Christians can come alongside these young people, teach them, mentor them, support them, and encourage them in their faith journey.

While God's primary place for faith development is the home, the church, as a community, is called to support and supplement you as you

> A huge thing for me was knowing that the people at church really cared about me. My decisions were based on what the people I felt like cared about me the most expected from me.
>
> —Jeremy B.
> *Twenty-six years old*

nurture faith in your children. The church should do all it can to equip you to be the parent God called you to be. Experience the blessing of an extended spiritual family that will provide roots and real relationships, community and accountability, purpose and mission. Allow your kids the benefit of knowing other Christians who are also on the journey of faith, disciples of all ages who can influence and encourage them in their walk.

There is great blessing and wisdom in the church. Foster in your family the habit of regular, weekly participation in a church community. Don't allow things of this world to crowd out the crucial time with your church.

Depend on God

Keep in mind that we can do our very best and we still will make mistakes. Our children will make poor choices too. Things won't always turn out like we hope. Proverbs 16:9 says, "In their hearts humans plan their course, but the LORD establishes their steps" (NIV). It's in God's hands. Ultimately, God determines success. But if we are willing to depend on God, God will work through us to accomplish the Lord's will in our families.

It *is* possible, even in the fast-paced, hectic, busy world we live in, to nurture your family's faith in God. You *can* do it. It begins with a simple decision—a decision to do all you can to leave a legacy of faith to your children and to their children.

Questions and Exercises

1. Describe your family's morning or evening rituals. You have rituals whether you realize it or not. How might these rituals shape faith in the life of an adolescent.

2. In what ways do you see your teens imitating your spiritual life?

3. What are the challenges as parents in being "the number one influencers" of teenage religious faith? Beyond going to church, what are some things you could do to intentionally build a growing faith in your child?

4. In this chapter, Johnny lists four settings described by Deuteronomy 6:4–9. What can you do in each of those settings to pass your faith on to your children?

5. Johnny lists ten traits for parents to model for their kids. Which ones are your strengths? Which ones need some work?

6. How can we bring conversations about faith into the time that we already have with our teens?

7. Thomas Long says, "Saying things out loud is part of how we come to believe." How could this work in your conversations with your adolescents?

8. What intentional conversations (and conversations of opportunity) are you having with your children about phones, computers, television, social media, music, movies, pornography, and other cultural issues?

9. Johnny lists ten tips for conversation with youth; which ones of these are especially important with your teens?

10. How does your congregation support you as a parent seeking to be the primary source of spiritual training for your children? What other resources do you need?

DISCERNMENT: Core Spiritual Practice of the Disciple

Ron Bruner

lashes of lightning shatter the early morning darkness and reveal a meadow surrounded by trees. A tent stands near the tree line and just beneath a higher ridge. Rain falls hard on the tent, runs down and around it, draining harmlessly down the slope. Fabric ripples in the wind, but stakes hold, poles flex, and the tent weathers the storm. Inside, the lightning illuminates the rain fly and the tent wall to reveal a hopeful reality: it's bone dry in here.

More than once I've slept in a tent during a thunderstorm or a snowstorm. Knowing that the storm has tested your choices of tent and location and revealed your good decisions allows you to sleep the sleep of the innocent, the kind of sleep that is a gift from God.

Not all rainy nights in a tent are like that. One vivid example was a trek through God's outdoors in my youth as the senior patrol leader of a Scout troop. At sunset we finished our hike and prepared to set up camp. After studying the sky and the lay of the land, I pointed out where to pitch tents. One of the boys laughed and argued, "Nope. My tent goes in this nice, soft sand." When I walked over to see, he smoothed the sand with his hands and taunted, "Guess who's going to have the softest bed tonight?"

A native to this part of Oklahoma, I took another look at the evening sky and saw thunderheads building in the distant southwest. I asked him, "What if it rains?"

"Rainwater will drain away in this sand," he reasoned. We argued the pros and cons, but when I realized I was hardening his heart more than changing his mind, I left to pitch my own tent.

A little after midnight, the sky fell. Rain poured off my tent, but I stayed dry and warm. I listened for sounds of trouble among the troop, but everyone appeared to be weathering the storm well. About an hour later, though, I started hearing whooping and hollering from the direction of the tent pitched in the sand. Putting on my poncho, I went out into the storm to investigate.

The Spanish have a lovely word for the phenomenon: *arroyo*. An *arroyo* is a small watercourse with a nearly flat, sandy floor that is usually dry—except after a thunderstorm. In the evening, my friend's tent was comfortably pitched in soft, dry sand. After the storm his *arroyo* became a swift creek, washing out tent stakes and soaking every bag inside. There was much unhappiness.

Whenever I remember this excursion, I recall a story Jesus told.

Everyone then who hears these words of mine and acts on them will be like a wise man who built his house on rock. The rain fell, the floods came, and the winds blew and beat on that house, but it did not fall, because it had been founded on rock. And everyone who hears these words of mine and does not act on them will be like a foolish man who built his house on sand. The rain

fell, and the floods came, and the winds blew and beat against that house, and it fell—and great was its fall!
(Matt. 7:24–27 NRSV)

Jesus reminds us that decisions have consequences. The nature of creation is such that it tests all decisions, some sooner than others, some more dramatically than others. These challenges test more than our discernment; they test our commitment to the decision that discernment produces. Challenges may go unnoticed because we survive them, and yet they remain real regardless of our awareness of them.

Adolescence is a time when humans face a ceaseless barrage of life-changing decisions, many of which are considerably more significant than choosing where to pitch a tent. Do-overs are possible for some choices, but others remain irreversible. Reversible or not, all decisions face a test—some immediately, some over time. Thank God, none of our choices as young people are beyond the reconciling grace of God. Thank God for the coaches, mentors, and parents who walk beside adolescents as they learn how the discipline of spiritual discernment can empower godly choices.

What Is Discernment?

Discernment is a contemplative practice, but it is neither just meditation nor just decision making. We can define it more clearly by describing the spiritual practices it involves. Discernment is an overarching contemplative practice weaving together attentiveness to our surroundings, meditation on interpretive possibilities, prayers of self-examination (*examen*), and dwelling in the biblical story so as to create a narrative describing God's work on our world and to imagine our God-preferred place in that story. We can also explain it by describing how it works. Discernment empowers disciples

- to read and interpret their environment;
- to imagine responses to the opportunities or problems their environment presents;
- to select an ethical choice coherent with the work of the Holy One among God's people;
- to enact that solution; and
- to evaluate the fruit of that action to gauge the value of the discerned response.

Adele Ahlberg Calhoun believes that "discernment opens us up to listen to and recognize the voice and patterns of God's direction in our lives."[1] God creates each of us in the image of God as spiritual beings capable of making free choices, equipped with spiritual perception, skilled at moral thinking, gifted with creative ability.[2] God created us with the necessary equipment and freedom to receive discernment as a gift and then to grow in that gift. Spiritual discernment may change our direction, but inevitably it transforms our being as well.

How do we learn spiritual discernment? Mark Powell asserts that we can grow our spiritual ability to discern through a number of practices:

1. Meditation on Scripture
2. Practicing prayer and other spiritual disciplines
3. Living life deeply imbedded in a community
4. Obedience to what God has already revealed[3]

Meditation on Scripture prepares us to better understand the story of God and the character of God. Prayer—alongside other spiritual disciplines—can clarify God's ongoing work in our world. Together, meditation, prayer, and spiritual practices empower us to discern ways our story can better connect with the ongoing story of God at work among us. It seems obvious, too, that discernment can't be godly unless it agrees with what God has already done and said. Let's consider more carefully the need to learn spiritual discernment in community.

Learning and engaging in spiritual discernment can be challenging for any disciple, but especially so for youth because of the complicated cultural forces in their world and their often inadequate connections to healthy role models. David White observes that cultural pressures "reach into the very heart of adolescent life—destabilizing identity formation, manipulating desires, suppressing curiosity and comprehension of the world, determining status in peer groups, fragmenting family relationships, normalizing passivity, and inhibiting imagination of an alternate reign of God or a greater common good."[4] The result? Youth often feel alone in the face of weighty situations. Sally Gary describes this feeling from the perspective of youth: "It's hard to discern the truth all alone. It's hard to figure which path to follow when you feel as if you have to keep everything to yourself."[5] Discernment with others, though, helps defuse negative cultural forces by providing: (1) identity, (2) a world view, (3) a mission that requires us to better understand our surroundings, (4) stronger relationships, and (5) a call into the work of God in this world.

Robert Audi mourns the lack of positive role models for youth who are learning ethical decision-making. Beyond that—in politics, entertainment, and sports—heroes are too inclined to "violence and exploitation, power and ostentation."[6] Discernment alongside caring adults gives youth better role models and affirmation to follow their better motives.

So, the solution is simple, but not easy. As parents and friends of adolescents, we must invite them into relationships—into a learning community—where we discover the practice of spiritual discernment together. The purpose of this chapter is to equip friends of youth with the necessary tools to do that very thing. We'll explain discernment more deeply in the following pages. We will consider some basic habits of discernment, talk about a framework for a discernment process, and describe some spiritual practices, which, if developed into habits, can invite God into our practice of discernment. What we learn can improve all of our lives.

Habits of Discernment

Discernment is a habit—sometimes intuitive, sometimes intentional. Like prayer and study of Scripture, it is a core part of our everyday existence as disciples of Christ.[7] Instead of cracking the book on decision-making when each new choice arises, we need to build solid and godly discernment habits into our daily practice of our faith. What are some of those habits?

Habit 1

We become better at discernment by practicing the hard work of discerning alongside God and with other disciples.

Making decisions for youth undermines their development of discernment. Instead, becoming transparent about choices we share with our young companions and working through these problems alongside them develops discernment skill and experience in both generations.[8] If we make this a habit, students will more likely come to us for counsel. When they do, we must avoid quick answers and, instead, ask questions that empower them to explore the habits of discernment in their own lives. Importantly, this practice also develops our ability (young and old) to engage in communal discernment.

Habit 2

Our discernment will become godlier as we habitually seek to work alongside God in this world.

Can you imagine trying to work *against* the Almighty? How did that work for Jonah (Jon. 1:1–17) or Balaam (Num. 22:22–35)? Instead, we should ask, "Where is God acting in my world?" Remember Jonathan's faithful words as a young man: "Come, let us go . . . It may be that the LORD will act for us; for nothing can hinder the LORD from saving by many or by few" (1 Sam. 14:6–7 NRSV). Where do we feel called to make a difference? Remember the words of Isaiah that Jesus obediently understood to be his call to ministry? "The Spirit of the Lord is upon me, because he has anointed me to bring good news to the poor" (Luke 4:18 NRSV). To read God's current activity in this world well, we'll have to read Scripture well, as did Jonathan and Jesus. If we work where God works, we're more likely to do what God will bless. To see that blessing, though, we'll have to be content to accept success on God's terms.

> Christian discernment means living in such a way that the basic fact that we are daughters and sons of God shapes and colors our decisions, both small and great.
>
> **—Elizabeth Liebert**
> *The Art of Discernment*, 9

There are some traps, though, in attempting discernments that we hope will draw us alongside the work of God. The first and obvious trap is believing we can predict the thinking of God. Even though we are creatures made in the image of God, the mind and the ways of God are not ours (Isa. 55:8–9). We need to remain humble in imagining how God might be acting in our world. The second trap, especially challenging for teens, is to believe that only one pathway has been mapped out by God for their life, and if they miss it, they're ruined. Some people, attempting to describe God as complete sovereign of the universe, imagine God to have mapped out our every decision and event in infinite detail. I believe that this makes God too small. God truly is sovereign over the universe, yet so completely so that the Holy One can give humanity freedom of will and still remain supreme. Our freedom-giving Creator can cope with the reality that we humans do not always make the best choices or make them at the best time and yet still gracefully work toward the future desired in the mind of God. This means that we can freely choose from multiple possible futures and remain within the will, providence, and grace of God. It also means, unfortunately, that we can choose paths that are less blessed than others (2 Kings 13:16–19).

Habit 3

We need to make a habit of understanding how our decisions affect others.

Every decision we make affects everyone else in some way. Over my years in youth ministry, I have found that this has been the idea students struggle most to believe. "What if," they hypothesize, "I go out and spend the day in the woods alone? Who does that affect but me?" When I point out that this choice deprives family or friends of time they could have enjoyed together or that, for example, they might have spent that time earning money to share with a child in poverty, they begin to understand.

In affluent societies, adults too often shelter youth from the consequences of their choices. While grace may empower second chances or softened consequences, action and reaction must remain connected or adults become enabling, not empowering. God gives humans the privilege of free will; responsibility for the consequences of our choices is the burden of that privilege. Our task is to be and become the best possible disciples of Christ while blessing as many others as possible.

Habit 4

We should consistently invest more time in decisions that are important, deeply affect others, or are difficult to undo.

Conversely, if it's easy to get a do-over, why waste hours deciding? If I decide that my experiment with a new item on the menu fails, I can afford to try again. As we walk with adolescents, though, it's critical that we help them see that seemingly harmless decisions can turn out to be more important than might be thought. Often the discernments youth find most time-consuming require them to choose, not between good and evil, but the best from among the good. Such choices include select-ing a college or career, for example. After years of preparation, changing a career isn't impossible, but it is much more difficult and painful. So, the time we are willing to invest gath-ering information, comparing differ-ent pathways, and talking things over with friends and family should be significantly more for important decisions affecting a large life span.

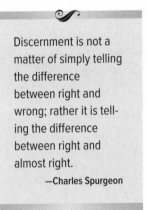

> Discernment is not a matter of simply telling the difference between right and wrong; rather it is tell-ing the difference between right and almost right.
> —Charles Spurgeon

Habit 5

Imagine the future a decision empowers.

It's hard to believe that either young Jacob or Esau understood the complications that one bowl of stew would bring to their life stories (Gen. 25:29–34). Discernment, though, requires us to engage our imaginations in foreseeing those plot twists. If a decision empow-ers a future that God would desire, then there is wisdom in it (see Habit 2); if not, then it's time to re-engage our imagination. When we adults discern alongside teens, it's important to remember that, although our experience allows us to see potential train wrecks more clearly, we may miss seeing the positive in some possibil-ities that they will see. They will almost certainly see the future differently than we will.

Habit 6

Make your decisions at just the right time.

Timing is important. Deciding too quickly may find you making decisions without complete information or with an incomplete awareness of how God is acting in this situation. When we read about Saul in the 1 Samuel stories, we find him constantly hurrying God and the prophet, and this bad habit led to several regrettable decisions. Waiting too long, though, may mean finding that someone else has acted or that circumstances have changed. In any situation there is an optimum time frame for a decision, and deciding how long it lasts becomes a part of the discernment process.

Habit 7

We should practice discernment with a habitual awareness that human beings are complexly motivated.

We don't even understand all of the reasons that we act or that we do not. How can we expect to know the motives of others? Even our most careful readings of their motives often turn out to be wrong. For disciples of Christ, godly discernment is rooted in attributing the best of motives to others while keeping a keen eye on our own motivation. When it turns out that others are poorly motivated, then we need to be "wise as serpents and innocent as doves," as Jesus told us (Matt. 10:16 NRSV). Working on discernment alongside others, especially those of another generation, can help keep us honest.

Habit 8

We have to see ourselves clearly and accept our own humanity.

It's nearly impossible to discern wisely if we misperceive our abilities, resources, or relationships. Even more deeply, we have to be honest about our thoughts and feelings and about how these connect with our actions.[9] Deep self-examination can cause us to obsess over our imperfections, but God loves us despite our imperfections. We should imitate God by accepting ourselves and our humanity. That doesn't mean that God isn't interested in transformation or that we should exempt ourselves from change. We should engage in transformation, though, believing that God has found us worthy of divine attention.

The Moves of Discernment

Discernment is both a way of being and a way of acting—a process. Once learned, the habits of discernment empower us to deal with some decisions without a long, drawn-out process. For beginners, a structured process helps keep the necessary pieces together on the way to acquiring healthy habits. Some difficult decisions, though, require deliberate practice, even for the experienced. There are several ways to approach discernment,[10] but in the pages that follow, we will focus on one. The phases of this process are interpretation, imagination, selection, action, and evaluation. Let's take a closer look at each of these.

Interpretation

It is essential to begin the discernment process with *holy indifference*.[11] That term doesn't mean we don't care about the outcome of the process. Instead, we care enough about living in the will of God that we are willing to lay our personal prejudices, thoughts, and feelings at the feet of God. "I am indifferent," Ruth Haley Barton says, "to anything but God's will."[12] We then attempt to figure out where we are and what best brings the future that God desires. We shouldn't settle for interpreting our world in a way that makes us comfortable; we should seek to see our situation as God sees it. A disciple looking at the world from a godly perspective will

> If we do not reach the point of indifference, or if we are not at least honest about the fact that we are not indifferent, the discernment process becomes little more than a rigged election.
>
> **—Ruth Haley Barton**
> *Pursuing God's Will Together*, 191

more likely find a godly solution. So, we begin with a prayer for indifference to allow us to remain open to God's vision and will.[13]

The world is what we see—or is it? Does God see it the way we do? It's best to be humble about what we think we know about our universe.[14] Remember God's warning: "My thoughts are not your thoughts, nor are your ways my ways" (Isa. 55:8 NRSV). We must seek the divine perspective because the foundation of solid discernment is truthfully understanding our situation. More than separating relevant facts from the mass of available information, discernment requires testing the many interpretive choices we use to construct our daily reality. One of the hardest truths for many adolescents to understand is that humans live in an interpreted universe. Our senses constantly feed us data and our mind continuously interprets data into narrative.

How does this work? Let's say you're playing tennis with your best friend. You volley back and forth for a while and then your friend drives a hard shot to the far side of the court. You turn, run hard for the baseline, get past the ball, and return it over your shoulder with an amazing shot. After a few steps, you manage to stop and look back to track the ball. You see it bounce inside the line right at your friend's feet. You start celebrating the point, but your friend simply says, "Out."

This is a common but classic problem: two people watch the same event and yet different viewpoints result in opposite interpretations. The ball bounced somewhere—in or out—but only God knows the truth. Unless God tells us, though, we have to choose an interpretation of the event to be the "truth" for us. Absolute truth exists; unfortunately, it's not always humanly accessible. The challenge of interpretation doesn't relieve us of responsibility to understand our world as best we can. If you trust your friend, you'll consider the possibility that, from your perspective, the ball only *appeared* to land in bounds. The best interpretations of an event take different perspectives into account. Interpretations ought also to consider the truthfulness of voices in the conversation. John's warning to "test the spirits" is appropriate here (1 John 4:1). We are wisest in our discernment when we interpret life together.

Moving back and forth between the big picture and the details can also be helpful.[15] If our interpretation of the events of one day of a life doesn't match up well with a longer narrative, then we need to reconsider our interpretation. For example, if someone we've known well suddenly appears to do something totally out of character, then a piece of the story is probably missing. We need to find the missing narrative. This is a time when we need to be particularly careful about guessing the motives of others (see Habit 7).

Imagination

Carson Reed tells us, "Our imagination envisions the future in order that we may live more fully in the present."[16] We can live with greater purpose today knowing who we want to become tomorrow. Where is our life going (Deut. 32:29)? In the imaginative move of discernment, young people get to play into one of their greatest strengths: visualizing where they are, where they believe God would have them to be, and ways to bridge that gap (see Habit 5). Since the Spirit indwells Christians, it is more probable than possible that inspiration will multiply the power of their imaginations. Trusting their imaginations, teens are less likely than adults to screen out possibilities because "we've never done that before" or "we tried that once and it didn't work." Since adolescents are adept at using their critical capabilities, they are likely to disallow the excuses and "Get Out of Jail Free" cards adults might play.

Adolescents are in the identity formation stage of their lives.[17] They consider and experiment with different roles in search for a personal identity that fits, and *this is healthy*. A teen adept at imagining who they might want to become may not clearly understand who they are now. Adults who walk alongside these students can help by giving them safe space and robust experiences to experiment with alternatives, refraining from choosing for them, and serving as a "mirror" to help them see what a particular choice of role or behavior might look like for them. In the process we gain insight into our own identity formation.

Selection

Having been through the moves of interpretation and imagination, it is important to remember that we started this process with an attitude of holy indifference. We should maintain an attitude of seeking God's will and glory, not ours. Often selection doesn't require separating good and bad solutions but choosing the best answer from an array of choices with positive possibilities. Wise selection also requires waiting on God; we should restrain our need for closure by waiting for God to have time to make divine moves and choices evident (see Habits 4 and 6). Whether deciding individually or communally, if the best answer isn't readily apparent, perhaps revisiting interpretation and imagination might help.

We sometimes fool ourselves by assuming that our choices are always logical. They neither are, nor should they be. Humans use a number of God-given tools to make decisions: logic, emotion, habit, identity, Scripture, and communal discernment. Most adults are comfortable with all of these except emotions. Emotions are good, though. God made them. We should pay attention to emotions because they access the life experiences in our unconscious mind. Through emotions our unconscious speaks: "Thinking about choosing this option makes me nervous. Last time I tried it and failed." Or, "I'm happier about deciding on this plan because, even though it takes more time, it plays into my strengths."

On the positive side of emotion, adolescents are sometimes provoked to do the most amazing things by compassion or by righteous indignation. We can help them become more deeply aware of the connection between their spirituality and emotions. Instead of denying their emotions, we can coach them to slow down and read their emotions and situation: "What's happening here?"[18] "Why does this bother me?" "How can I cope with feelings that hold me back from the right course?"

Sometimes choosing the right thing to do is frightful. If you think through your favorite Bible stories, you quickly remember that almost every heroic character, young or old, male or female, faced life-and-death decisions for themselves and for their people. Each of those heroic lives stand as a testimony to the words of Martin Luther King, Jr.: "The time is always right to do right."[19]

Standing tall over all these courageous choices is the night of discernment and decision Jesus faced in Gethsemane. For Jesus, the way forward to the future desired by God was difficult but clear. "Not my will but yours be done" (Luke 22:42 NRSV).

Action

All of the wisdom and intelligence in the world are meaningless in the face of inaction. Truly enacting a solution, though, means thoroughly and energetically doing what we decided. Anything less may cause the right answer to fail. Sometimes youths struggle to understand that trying a solution once and failing doesn't mean that a solution doesn't work. Trying at different times, in differing ways, and persistently, may be necessary, especially when the issue involves relationships with others; reconciliation can be a tedious and trying process.

Evaluation

Perhaps the most courageous question we can ask in our discernment process is: "Did the action we chose in our discernment process work?" We must ask it. We should never assume that our discernment answers a question once and for all. Our hope is not to always be right. To expect that would be arrogant or unrealistic. Instead, we would hope to be right more often than not.[20] If our answer worked, how might we do even better next time? If it didn't work well, might it work better by making a few adjustments here and there? Did we execute the solution with as much thoroughness as we did the decision process? Did it work at first and then begin to fail again? We may find that our answer was so inadequate that we have to go back and work our way through the entire discernment process again, this time armed with better information and a more critical view of assumptions.

With many decisions, a work/fail standard of success is inadequate. The true test of discernment is the fruit that it brings.[21] Does our discernment bring the fruit of "love, joy, peace, patience, kindness, goodness, faithfulness, gentleness, self-control" (Gal. 5:22–23 NRSV) or other godly fruit (James 3:17)? A prayer of thanksgiving is in order. Or is the fruit more toxic—"hatred, discord, jealousy, fits of rage, selfish ambition, dissensions, factions and envy" (Gal. 5:20–21 NIV)? If our work is yielding mixed fruit, can we find a way to stop whatever is causing the bad fruit? Remember, success is a matter of perspective (Matt. 11:4, 18–19). In some cases, our discernment apparently fails us, but even so, we have learned by eliminating one possibility. Often we can learn from our "nearly right" solutions and, step by step, move toward a better answer.[22]

Moving Back and Forth

The phases of this process don't have hard-and-fixed boundaries. Sometimes, for example, it will be necessary to back up from the imagination phase and think through our interpretive work again; it may be that imagining a route to the future causes us to consider new interpretive possibilities. Even in the process of enacting our decisions, the early results may cause us to finesse our plan. Remaining flexible is wise.

Spiritual Practices Empowering Discernment

One positive way to vitalize our efforts at discernment is through prayers of *examen. Examen* is a practice rooted in centuries of practice and in the work of Ignatius.[23] Normally a prayer that comes later in the day, *examen* is a spiritual review of the day *alongside God*. We thank God for the day and its blessings; then in our continuing talk with God we consider a number of paired *examen* questions:[24]

- What in my day made me most grateful? For what am I least grateful?
- What time was most life-giving? What seemed to take the life out of me?
- When did I feel closest to God? When did God seem most remote?
- How did I feel connected with God's work? What felt disconnected?

The positives in our answers give cause for thankfulness. The negatives are not meant to overwhelm us but to help us ask for God's aid in moving through those challenging situations. Prayers of *examen* can help us more clearly see ourselves, understand our emotions, and find clues as to paths that would give us joy.

Journaling can also add focus to discernment. Journaling is a practice concerned with writing truthfully, not with writing well.[25] It provides the opportunity for praise and lament, hopes and concerns. When written over a length of time, journaling gives those who practice it the opportunity to see their life story unfolding and to imagine where it might go next. Journaling can also be a written method to practice *examen*.

Moving from Theory to Practice

"The spiritual life is first a *life*," says Thomas Merton. "It is not merely something to be known and studied, it is to be lived."[26] In this chapter we've studied the habits of the spiritually discerning. We've also considered in some detail a spiritual discernment process that can help us make godly decisions. You've been given some helpful resources if you want to study these ideas more carefully, but, if we are to take Merton's advice about the spiritual life seriously, we have to put these things into practice. In my experience, practicing discernment requires a constant cycling between theory and practice. Some theoretical discussions only make sense once we've tried to enact them. Some experiences are so demanding that we go back to the books, seeking wisdom to help us grow wiser in our practice.

As you set out to practice the spiritual discipline of discernment in your lives with youth, my charge to you mimics that of Paul to the Romans:

> I appeal to you therefore, brothers and sisters, by the
> mercies of God, to present your bodies as a living sacri-
> fice, holy and acceptable to God, which is your spiritual
> worship. Do not be conformed to this world, but be
> transformed by the renewing of your minds, so that you

may discern what is the will of God—what is good and
acceptable and perfect. (Rom. 12:1–2 NRSV)

May God give you the courage to pursue the "good and acceptable
and perfect" in the will of God, so that God may transform you as
you walk alongside young people all the days of your life.

Making a Discernment Process Work

Move	Definition	Student work	Adult work	Helpful Habits
Interpretation	How do we read the events that surround us? Is there more than one way to understand them?	Determine what is happening and why we see it this way	Help the youth consider all perspectives, even those of potential opponents	**Habit 1**, practice discernment alongside others; **Habit 4**, invest more time in important choices; **Habit 7**, remember humans are complexly motivated
Imagination	Visualize where we are, where God would have us be, and how to get there.	Imagine future possibilities and the different persons we become if we choose them	Become a mirror that shows youth what they or their future might look like with a specific choice; create safe space for experimentation, experience, and brainstorming	**Habit 3**, how will our decision affect others? **Habit 5**, imagine the future a decision empowers; **Habit 8**, see ourselves clearly
Selection	Choosing from an array of possibilities one that moves alongside God	Seek the path that glorifies God, remains righteous, and fits our strengths	Help youth understand the decision-making tools they're using: logic, emotion, habit, identity, Scripture, or communal discernment	**Habit 2**, work alongside God; **Habit 6**, make your decisions at just the right time
Action	Enact the selected possibility	Thoroughly and prayerfully enact the right answer	Help youth with resources and encourage them to persistently pursue their solution	**Habit 2**, work alongside God
Evaluation	Did our choice work? Can we incrementally improve our decision?	Gather information to show pass/fail success, or find the fruit of the decision	Make certain they consider the fruit as seen from varied perspectives; help them see that even failure is learning	**Habit 8**, see ourselves clearly

Questions and Exercises

1. Did anyone intentionally try to teach you about discernment growing up? In what ways might your life have been better if more time had been spent on this?

2. Ron tells us that we learn discernment by meditation on Scripture; by practicing prayer and other spiritual disciplines; by living life deeply imbedded in a community; and by obedience to what God has already revealed. If learning discernment through these practices is true, how could you improve your discernment in each of those areas?

3. As we discern our path through life with adolescents, Ron calls us to "seek to work alongside God in this world." How can we do this? Where do you see God at work in your part of the world?

4. When we are making decisions that affect others, what are our responsibilities to them? What are the biblical principles that apply here?

5. How are your children learning to make decisions? What can they learn from good and bad decisions?

6. Ron discusses eight habits that will help us with discernment. How can each of these help you teach your children about making good choices?

7. What kinds of decisions would you encourage a teen to take the most time in discerning?

8. How might the adolescent perspective of time cause them to view discernment differently than most adults?

9. How can serving as a "mirror"—a way for a teen to see what they might look like if they make certain choices—help them make godlier decisions? What are some other ways that you have helped your children learn to make better decisions?

10. Perhaps the most important part of the discernment process is evaluation. As you think back on your life, when and how did you make the best possible decisions? How would this discernment process help you to make better decisions?

11. Can you describe a time in your life where you made a poor decision because you misinterpreted the situation? How might sharing this story with a teen help them improve their discernment abilities?

12. How can the discernment process help you rearing teenagers?

7

COMFORT WITH THE COMFORT WE RECEIVE FROM GOD

Beth Robinson

Tears rolled down Emily's face as she sat in the back seat, gazing out at a landscape she looked right through. Her seat belt held her securely in the car while her thoughts wandered far away.

She was thinking about her boyfriend, Joshua. Emily was still stunned. Joshua's parents separated four weeks ago because his dad was having an affair. Now Joshua had moved with his mom more than five hours away to be closer to his mom's family.

As Emily thought about how Joshua had left so suddenly, she felt her chest tighten and more tears rolled down her face. She felt completely alone and had no desire to do anything except text Joshua and cry. Her pain seemed intolerable. She didn't know if she would ever feel anything again except sadness and pain.

In the front seat, Emily's mom and dad exchanged worried glances. They were driving Emily to an interview for a scholarship. She had worked for months to get admitted to this college, but now she seemed completely uninterested. When Joshua moved, Emily's parents expected her to be sad, but they didn't expect her to be completely overwhelmed, to withdraw from everything she enjoyed.

Last night, Emily's parents talked about how much more intensely Emily grieved Joshua's moving away than she had grieved when her grandmother died. Emily loved her grandmother and had spent many hours with her. Since Emily was a toddler, she had a special bond with the elderly woman. She sat with her grandmother at church and studied the Bible with her. The two worked on projects to help raise money to buy homeless people coats. Church—and their love of God—were the foundation of a special, loving relationship.

Tragically, Emily's grandmother fell ill and didn't respond to treatment after she was diagnosed with cancer. Within six months she was dead. Though her grandmother's final illness went quickly, Emily had been able to prepare for the death and to say goodbye to her grandmother. She was in the room as the family surrounded her grandmother's bed and sang her favorite worship songs as she took her last breath. Emily grieved her loss and cried off and on for several months; unlike the situation with Josh, though, she didn't lose interest in all of her activities and cry constantly.

Now, as they drove Emily to the scholarship interview, her parents felt helpless. They were bewildered by Emily's reaction and didn't know how to help Emily deal with such overwhelming grief. After all, Joshua was

> The way our children feel about situations might not have any connection whatsoever to the facts. . . . Because of this disconnect between the facts and the feelings, our children can feel extremely vulnerable as they move through their childhood.
>
> — Tim Kimmel,
> *Grace-Based Parenting*, 171

just five hours away—he didn't die. And Emily was constantly texting and talking to him on Snapchat. They couldn't understand why Joshua's move was so devastating to their daughter. Even before Joshua left, the two friends had planned to attend different colleges next year anyway, and to date other people.

Searching for answers, Emily's parents took her to see a doctor. The doctor didn't prescribe any medications; instead he encouraged them to be patient and to let her grieve Joshua's loss. Emily's parents also set up an appointment with a minister at their church. He encouraged them to pray for Emily and to listen to her.

No one explained to Emily's parents, however, that the teenager's intense grief was actually developmentally appropriate. While adults grieve the loss of a family member more intensely than a friend moving away, for a teen, the loss of a peer can be the most significant loss she may experience. Because teens define themselves and explore their identity in peer groups, they may experience the loss of a peer more intensely than the loss of a grandparent or even a sibling.

Different Types of Losses: Places, Lifestyle, and Relationships

Unexpectedly, Joe found himself in a new town. He had been forced to leave his home and school, and he didn't know anyone in town. His mother, recently diagnosed with cancer, needed to move closer to her parents. Joe knew his mom needed her parents' help since she was a single mom. He just couldn't understand why his grandparents didn't move where he and his mom lived. Having to move and live with his grandparents didn't make sense. Now he had to share a room with his brother, and his grandparents treated him as if he was a kid like his brother. He missed having his own space. He kept his headphones on all the time and cranked up the music to block out what was going on around him.

His grandparents always wanted Joe to eat dinner with them. They didn't cook anything he wanted. Their food had the flavor completely cooked out of it. Even when he ate with them, they weren't satisfied but would pressure him to join them in the living room and watch lame shows on TV. When he tried to be nice and watch TV with his grandparents, they kept arguing about stupid stuff in the shows.

He missed his mom; she cooked the foods he liked, talked about what she'd done at work, and asked questions that showed she cared about his friends and his life. Now his mom was constantly tired because of the chemo. His mom and his grandparents kept telling him that cancer wasn't going to kill her and that chemo would make her better. He didn't understand how chemo could make anything better. His mom was throwing up and losing her hair. She didn't even get out of bed some days.

Looking back, Joe realized that he'd taken for granted the comfort of his home, his school, and his friends. Nothing in his new surroundings felt like home. He felt completely alone living with his grandparents. He missed his old life and his routine. He couldn't shake off the immense grief he was feeling.

What Joe experienced—making a sudden move that disrupted his routine and removed him from familiar settings—represents another kind of loss. While adults think of grief being primarily associated with death, different types of losses can trigger grief. Teens may intensely grieve losses that aren't related to a death; teens often grieve the ending of a relationship, whether a friendship or a romance.

Moving to another city or school as Joe did can profoundly impact teens. They lose friendships, teachers, and familiar surroundings. Moving to a new house can cause grief because it may feel as if someone is forcing them to sacrifice familiar spaces connected to childhood memories. Losing an election for a student leadership role or not making a sports team may be experienced as the loss of a dream; that loss may be compounded by the perceived loss of status among their peers. Not being included by peers may be experienced as a loss. Losing a competitive event can provoke grief. Teens feel intense emotions when disappointed. Even the death of a pet may be a first experience of grief.

How to Respond: Adults don't always recognize when teens are grieving. Because we have experienced the ending of relationships many times and survived, the intense emotions that adolescents feel about such an ending may seem dramatic to us. We've moved to new cities and new jobs, so many of us think that making those adjustments is routine and can even make our situation better. We may have difficulty recognizing how it feels to move to a new town or a new school as a teen. It almost never seems better.

To help children who are experiencing losses that don't seem significant to us, we must see the experience through their eyes. We will be much more empathetic when we view the loss as our children view it. When we minimize the impact of a loss, we create distance between ourselves and our children.

However, it's unrealistic to think we can fully understand the deepness of a teen's grieving. Proverbs 14:10 says, "Each heart knows its own bitterness, and no one else can share its joy" (NIV). Part of responding in a godly way is recognizing that their grieving is real and accepting how they feel about a loss. We can encourage our teens by listening and validating their thoughts, feelings, and observations—without pretending to know exactly how they feel.

Intense Emotions

Marissa played soccer ever since she was four years old. She loved running full speed and striking the ball. She could adeptly weave in and out of players on the field with grace and speed. By the time she was a junior in high school, major colleges began to recruit her. That year her club team won the state tournament and qualified for the national tournament. Marissa spent the summer between her junior and senior years attending soccer camps and preparing for the big year ahead of her. Her parents even agreed that she didn't have to get a summer job. She could use those months to prepare for her senior season of soccer.

During the third game of her senior year, Marissa became tangled in group of players and tumbled to the ground. As she fell, she felt the sickening twist of her knee. The doctor delivered bad news: she had torn her ACL. Her season was over, and he warned that even with surgery and good rehabilitation, her knee might not ever take the pressure of playing competitive soccer again. Marissa underwent surgery the next week.

Afterward, the normally well-groomed Marissa refused to take care of herself. She wouldn't shower or fix her hair. When Marissa's friends came to visit, she refused to talk to them. When the doctors released Marissa to go to school, she avoided going as much as she could. She exerted little effort on her schoolwork or her physical therapy. Most of the time she stayed in her room with the lights turned off. When Marissa's parents checked on her, they would find her in bed crying. Sometimes, her parents would hear her crying in her sleep.

When the doctor told Marissa that she might never play competitive soccer again, she thought her life was over. Soccer was the focus of her life, and she didn't want to do anything if she couldn't play soccer. The intense sadness and despair Marissa felt was heavily influenced by the limbic system in her brain.

The limbic system is important.

- It's the part of the brain that helps regulate the formation of memories and emotions. During the teenage years, the limbic system undergoes major changes that can make a teen feel—and struggle with—intense emotions.

- The amygdala, a part of the limbic system, connects sensory information to emotional reactions. Add the normal hormonal changes of this stage of life to the development of the amygdala and the result can be sadness, rage, fear, aggression, excitement, and intensified sexual urges.
- But, good news: over the course of adolescence, the limbic system comes under greater control of the prefrontal cortex which helps modulate strong emotions.

However, until the prefrontal cortex kicks in, teens may be confused by their emotional reactions. Because adolescents have limited experience with loss, they may not understand that grief is a natural reaction to death and loss. No adolescent will feel that grieving is natural or comfortable. Instead, teens are likely to experience grief as being out of control. Movies about dying teenagers may cause unrealistic expectations of how they should feel or behave while grieving.

Adults aren't able to fully control the emotions, thoughts, or physical feelings associated with a significant loss either, but experience has taught us that eventually these feelings will subside. Life will resume, with a new normal. But when teens first experience grief, their thoughts and feelings seem completely overpowering. They fear their emotions may never be under their control again. This terrifying prospect may make them resist grieving and shut down emotionally. When teens try to avoid grieving, it's important for adults to help them understand what they're experiencing.

"This is normal," a parent might say. Even a great prophet like Elijah became depressed when it seemed his life dreams had been crushed. In 1 Kings 19, Elijah experienced great success on Mt. Carmel, and yet he crashed and burned emotionally just days later when he found out the queen wanted to kill him. Elijah didn't want to drink or eat; he wanted to die. But God could see past this crisis to a time when Elijah would be able to function and even bless others. The same God, you can assure your teen, can see past their crisis to a time when, eventually, things will be better. Meanwhile, God is there, in all the grief and pain.

How to Respond: We adults may want to minimize losses rather than acknowledge the intense sadness and drama our children experience. This can be self-protection, because it's painful to see them hurt and be powerless to stop it. We can't afford, though, to ignore the emotional reactions of our children and allow them to adopt unhealthy methods of coping. Teens frequently turn to drugs and alcohol to numb emotions when they feel overwhelmed. They may also turn to unhealthy relationships to help them cope.

By focusing on how teens feel about the loss, we can more effectively be present and walk with them through the journey of grief. Despite our resolve to be present, the reality of a teen in an emotionally-escalated state is very difficult for most parents to handle. When teens cry for extended periods of time or isolate themselves because they are emotionally overwhelmed, we parents want to be able to stop their pain and ours as well.

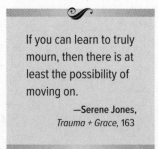

If you can learn to truly mourn, then there is at least the possibility of moving on.

—Serene Jones,
Trauma + Grace, 163

If we want to protect our teens from extended pain, the healthiest way to cope with sadness and anger is to express it *now*. Ideally, our teens will talk with us or another trusted adult, but they may be more comfortable expressing their emotions through writing, drawing, or music. They may find other creative ways to process their intense emotion, and parents must actively look for anything that would help them express it rather than holding it inside.

Wanting to Be Like Everyone Else

One afternoon after school, Carolyn asked her mom if they could move to another city. Carolyn's mom was stunned because they had lived in the same community all of Carolyn's life. The community and church had supported the family in tremendous ways when Carolyn's dad had struggled with Lou Gehrig's disease. People had provided money and food. Friends sat with them as Carolyn's dad died. Community events raised thousands of dollars to pay medical costs that insurance hadn't covered.

Even though Carolyn's dad had died six months ago, the support continued. Men from the church mowed the lawn and changed the oil in their car. People left encouraging notes attached to casseroles on their front porch.

Carolyn's mom couldn't imagine moving somewhere else where people wouldn't know them and wouldn't provide the support of their current community and church. She became more and more upset with her daughter as she talked.

Carolyn wanted to move because she was tired of being the daughter of "that man who had Lou Gehrig's disease." She wanted to "be a normal kid," not the girl with no dad. Carolyn believed that if she moved, she would be like other kids because people would just think her parents were divorced.

Carolyn's mother was deeply hurt that Carolyn wanted to move where people wouldn't know her dad. For her part, Carolyn's mom felt that the community and church were honoring her husband. Moving away would betray all that. What Carolyn's mother didn't understand was what was going on inside her very-normal daughter's body. Hormone changes in puberty spur the production of more receptors in the brain for oxytocin, a hormone that modulates social behavior. These receptors, almost like a skinned knee, become highly sensitive to the stimulation of oxytocin. Those levels go up, and what is going on in the brain is translated into a teenager's feelings of self-consciousness: teens feel like everyone is watching them.

Perceiving themselves to be the focus of attention, teens yearn to be like everyone else. They want to be "normal" and fit in with their peers. Teens will try to keep grief at a distance because they don't want to be seen as "the kid whose father died." Carolyn was trying to keep her grief distant by moving away from the community that knew her story.

How to Respond: It is important to remember when your children are wanting to be "normal" that they are not trying to hurt you. They are not being selfish. Because of changes in their limbic system, their desire to be "normal" is linked to physical growth and change. As they get older, their limbic system will regulate sensitivity to oxytocin better and they will not feel like they are on center stage with everyone watching them.

Meanwhile, it will help if you can be gentle when your children are feeling pressure to be like everyone else. When your children are learning to walk, you encourage them to take just one step, and you celebrate that step. You exhibit lots of patience with your toddlers. Teens need that same kind of encouragement and patience. Lecturing them about selfishness won't change their behavior.

One of the best ways to help teens feel like their peers is to find an environment where they can interact with other teens who have lost their parents. Peer support groups or teen grief camps can be safe places for grieving teens to feel "normal" with other teens who have had similar experiences. A number of terrific grief camps exist, and many local hospices have their own peer support groups and grief camps.

When adolescents experience a loss, they may go online for support and for additional information about their loss. While teens may find accurate information and healthy support online, they may also encounter inaccurate information or support from unhealthy or dangerous people. They may expose themselves to bullying, and cruel comments, or receive the attention of online predators. It is important that we monitor what our teens are doing online and guide them to healthy forums for interaction. We can help our children find safe places to share their grief in sources such as hellogrief.org, a website monitored for safety by Comfort Zone Camps.

Perception of Time

Jake and his granddad spent lots of time together. They loved sports and always watched ball games together. His granddad also taught him car repair, and some of their favorite times together were underneath the hood of the family's old minivan. When Jake wasn't at school, he could almost always be found at his granddad's house. The family laughed about how they would scheme up trips to watch a game, or attend a hot-rod show. Jake's granddad always encouraged him and helped him figure out solutions to problems, whether a radiator leak or an umpire's call. They worked on things together.

One evening the phone rang at Jake's house. He heard only one end of the conversation, but he knew something terrible had happened. Jake's mom started crying. When she hung up, Jake asked what happened. In a trembling voice, his mom told him that his grandma had found his granddad lying on the bathroom floor. She had tried to help him, but when the paramedics arrived, they told her that he was dead.

In the next twenty-four hours, Jake alternated between crying and raging with anger. He felt it was so unfair that his granddad had been taken from him. He wanted him back. But when he realized that he couldn't change what had happened, he just wanted everything to go back to being normal, as normal as they could be without his granddad. He wanted all his relatives to go home, and he wanted people to quit stopping by his house to talk to his mom.

He began pressuring his mom about when the funeral was going to be, when relatives would arrive, and when everyone would go to sleep. He was overwhelmed by the emotional reactions of other people. After the funeral was scheduled for two days later, Jake began to obsess about how long it was taking for that day to arrive. His mom became frustrated with Jake and couldn't understand why he was whining about how long it was until the funeral.

Jake's mom didn't realize that Jake's perception of time and her perception of time were different. When a child is one, a year is literally forever. As we get older, time moves more quickly because it becomes a smaller and smaller percentage of our experience. We perceive time based on our lifespan, inversely proportional to how long we have lived. When we are five, a year is one fifth of our lived experience. It feels like forever. When we are fifty, a year is one fiftieth of our lives, a much less significant amount.

We see this in the way children experience the month before Christmas. To a child that month feels like a fifty-four-year-old's year. Time was moving more slowly for seventeen-year-old Jake than it was for his mom. For teens who are experiencing loss, even hours of grieving feel like an eternity, because time moves more slowly for them. Teens may actually express that they don't think it is ever going to get better because the weeks and months it will take for them to cope with the loss literally seem like forever to them.

How to Respond: When time seems to stretch on forever, it can be helpful to break the total amount of time into segments. In Jake's case, instead of perceiving the funeral to be two whole days away, it might help to break the time into morning, afternoon, evening, and night, and let Jake cross those off the calendar.

While we want to assure our children that they will get through their current experience, it doesn't help to tell them that it will get better as time passes. Time passes so slowly for them that this is not a comforting statement. The Bible acknowledges this: "Hope deferred makes the heart sick" (Prov. 13:12 NIV). For a grieving teen, it seems that relief is being put off again and again while they just stand still.

Strategies that engage teens in activities distracting them from their grief for short periods and marking the progression of chunks of time will help them cope with the sense that their grief won't end. Exercise, listening to calming music, writing, journaling, or talking to a family member are all strategies that can help teens cope with their sense that time is moving too slowly.

Death of a Family Member

Juan's dad left the house like he did every morning, calling out to everyone, "Have a good day. See you tonight." Juan barely heard his dad, because he said the same annoying thing every morning. Juan rode the bus to school and went to his classes just as he did every day, but halfway through the third hour, the principal called his classroom and asked the teacher to send Juan to the office.

Juan gathered up his books and shrugged. He was pretty sure he wasn't in trouble, but he had no idea why he needed to go to the office. When he saw his youth minister, Juan knew something was wrong. Juan's mom had called, the youth minister explained, and asked him to bring Juan home because his father had been in a car wreck. All the way home, Juan bombarded the youth minister with questions about his dad, but learned that he didn't have more information.

Juan's worst fears were confirmed by the sound of his mother crying in their living room. She gestured for him to sit next to her and through her tears explained that the accident had been serious—Juan's dad had not survived. Juan could hardly believe his ears. At first he felt numb. Then slowly he began to realize that everything in his life was different without his dad.

When a family member or someone close to your teen dies, it is important to be as honest as you can be. Communicate information about the death to your teen in an age-appropriate way, but don't hide information from them. For instance, if a family member's drinking led to a car wreck, you need to be honest about how drinking contributed to the death. Invariably, teens will discover the information we try to conceal, and then lose their ability to trust us. We need to be honest and upfront about the circumstances surrounding a death.

> Grief is hard, actually the hardest of all emotions and perhaps the most intolerable because its demands are so excruciating. It requires a willingness to bear the unbearable. As mourning, it requires turning private agony into public, shared loss.
>
> —Serene Jones, *Trauma + Grace*, 163

Losing someone to death can be more complicated for teens if they weren't on good terms with the deceased, or if they had a negative interaction with them prior to the death. We need to relieve teens of any magical thinking that their actions may have contributed to the death or that the deceased died angry with them. We can remind teens that all relationships are based on more than one interaction. Conflicts between teens and adults are a normal part of life, and those clashes don't define relationships, especially in the minds of adults. As teens seek their own identity, they may feel alienated from parents, siblings, and other family members. If a family member dies during this emotionally turbulent time, teens can be left feeling guilty.

I've frequently heard adults say that someone was so special or good that God needed them in heaven. While we may believe that this statement will comfort family members of the deceased, it may actually create more problems for teens. First, teens could become furious at God for taking their family member, and experience serious barriers to their spiritual development. Second, teens may begin to fear that if they are really good, God will choose them next. Teens could begin acting badly to make sure God doesn't want them. Third, teens may want to join the loved one that God has chosen. We don't want to inadvertently encourage teens to kill themselves while they are grieving.

How to Respond: When teens lose a family member, they need to be a part of the process of deciding how to grieve the loss and how the funeral or celebration of life will be handled. They need to have a voice in their role in the funeral or celebration of life. They need to be allowed to speak at the graveside if other family members are speaking. Because of their tech savvy, teens may take on a special role in preparing video reviews of the life of the deceased. However, they don't need to be pressured to take on a role or to speak if they don't want to be involved.

We frequently have ideas about how family members "should" handle a loss. We may think that adults must be strong and not show emotion, but we need to allow our children to see us upset and crying. When they see us express our emotions about a loss, it gives them permission to cry and grieve too. Teenagers will cope only as well as the adults around them.

Sometimes we put pressure on our children to "be strong" for other family members. Teens need to be able to mourn without

OWNING FAITH

feeling pressure to be strong. We don't want our teens to cut off their feelings. While teens need permission to grieve, they also need permission not to be grieving all the time. Part of coping with loss is being able to stop grieving and participate in fun activities. It's not disloyal for teens to vacillate between grieving and engaging in fun activities, and we can model that for our teens.

Grief is Different for Everyone

Lana and Dena had helped their parents care for Grandpa Joe ever since he had a stroke three years ago. Before the stroke, Lana had spent hours reading books with him. They had talked about different characters and plots in books. Grandpa Joe had instilled a love of books in her. Dena had loved Grandpa Joe, but she hadn't spent nearly as much time with him as Lana did before his stroke. When Grandpa Joe had his stroke, Lana was devastated because his personality and his communication skills changed so drastically. The Grandpa Joe she had known was gone. Dena noticed the personality changes in him, but she still felt like he was her grandpa.

After three years of being bedridden and unable to care for himself, Grandpa Joe died. Lana felt relieved that his suffering was over, but Dena felt a sense of loss. She was sad and grieved the loss of experiences she shared with her grandpa. Because Lana felt like she lost Grandpa Joe years before when he had the stroke, she didn't experience the sense of loss that Dena felt when he died.

Dena and the family couldn't understand why Lana wasn't grieving Grandpa Joe's death. They were confused and frustrated by Lana's reaction. Lana had been the grandchild closest to Grandpa Joe, yet she didn't seem to be sad about his death. What other family members didn't recognize is that Lana had grieved the loss of Grandpa Joe's personality three years before when he ceased to be the person she knew.

134

Each person within a family may mourn differently at different times. One may be talkative, another may tend to cry often, and a third might withdraw. This can generate tension and misunderstanding within the already-stressed family. Each person's response to death should be honored as his or her way of coping in that moment. Remember that responses may change from day to day or even from hour to hour. Teens who want us to hold and comfort them one day may be slamming doors the next.

Because everyone experiences grief differently, it's difficult to anticipate whether teens will cry and express sadness directly, or use humor and laughter. Grieving can also express itself through physical symptoms, including crying, sighing, headaches, loss of appetite, difficulty sleeping, weakness, fatigue, feelings of heaviness, aches, and pains.

> The gift of mourning is that fully awakening to the depth of loss enables you to at least learn, perhaps for the first time, that you can hold the loss: you can bear terrors of heart and body and still see your way forward with eyes open.
>
> —Serene Jones,
> *Trauma + Grace,* 163

How to Respond: Each of us believes that the way we process information and react to it is normal, but the behavior we see in our teens may mean something different than we think. The most important strategy for helping grieving teens is to accept them where they are. They may not express their grief in the same ways we do, or on the same timetable that we do, but they are processing their grief. Statements about expected behavior or questions about their behavior will just create distance or barriers. We want kids to talk to us and let us know how they are processing loss rather than turning to other coping mechanisms.

While we may be coping well with some changes, changes in lifestyle and circumstances may be difficult for our children. To a teen, a change might symbolize leaving behind the person they lost. We need to be sensitive to how we approach change and try to limit the number of changes we make immediately after a loss. In some cases, changes are unavoidable, and when we involve our teenagers in the decision-making process, they are assured of their importance in the family and in the success of the process. We should share as much information as we can without making them feel like they have to take on adult responsibilities.

Holidays, birthdays, and other significant occasions may be difficult for our children, depending on who they lost. Some children will adapt, but others may struggle for years. Occasions like weddings and childbirth may also be difficult for children who have lost a family member, because these occasions can evoke an imagined scenario of what it would be like if the family member were still alive. Allowing children to process loss in their own time and own way is the best way to help them.

Accepting the Loss

Resolving grief in a healthy way can help our teens accept the loss and move forward. Grief is actually the mechanism by which teens' emotions, thoughts, and behaviors try to make sense of the loss they are experiencing.

As parents, our hope and prayer is that the losses our children experience will bring them closer to God. When our teens grieve, we want them to find comfort in their relationship with us and with God. When adolescents experience losses, they will need adults to help support and encourage them to explore their faith and their grief in an open and honest way.

Until the loss has been incorporated into teens' perceptions of the world and themselves, overwhelming thoughts, emotions, and physical sensations will continue to arise periodically. Teens have to determine how the death of someone close to them changes their view of the world and themselves. Even the loss of a relationship or a dream may change the way teens view themselves, others, and the world.

Even after teens have begun to incorporate the loss into their understanding of the world, they will occasionally feel profound grief. A significant loss accompanies us for the rest of our lives, because grief never ends. However, the way teens experience the intensity of emotions and the alteration in their world will surely change as they mature.

We stand in a unique situation with grieving teens: an opportunity to accompany our young fellow human beings in a position of trust as they go through difficult times. We can share with them that we have the ability to ride above those tides because someone helped us. It's a pay-it-forward situation.

"Praise be to the God and Father of our Lord Jesus Christ, the Father of compassion and the God of all comfort," Paul wrote, "who comforts us in all our troubles, so that we can comfort those in any trouble with the comfort we ourselves receive from God."[1]

Questions

1. When you were a teen, what were your experiences with grief? What did you feel? How did grief affect your other relationships?
2. When you were a teen experiencing grief or loss, what were the things that friends said or did that were most helpful?
3. Beth explains that teens experience grief differently because they are still developing in every aspect of their life: mentally, emotionally, physically, socially, and spiritually. Please

describe how a teen might experience grief differently in each of these aspects of their humanity.

4. How has your personal experience of grief changed over your lifetime? What are the things that you understand about grief now that you would not have understood in your youth?

5. How has your experience with loss or grief challenged your faith? How have these experiences affirmed your faith?

6. Beth tells us that minimizing a teenager's loss to help them "get over it" is a bad idea. Why? What is a more appropriate response to their grief?

7. In times of grief and loss, what are the things that people say or do that are the least helpful?

8. Just because we have experienced a loss similar to that experienced by a teen doesn't mean that we understand how they feel. How do we handle these similar, but not identical feelings? How do we talk about them with our younger friends?

9. Beth notes that some teens avoid grieving because the feelings are so overwhelming. What are some biblical stories we can use to help youth understand that it is okay to grieve?

10. In our connected world, it's possible for someone to learn of a death and post about it in minutes, perhaps even before the entire family knows. How could we help teens develop an etiquette that respects those closest to the deceased but empowers the ability of teens to communicate and grieve?

8

HUMAN SEXUALITY:
We Have a Lot to Talk About

Scott Talley

During my twenty-five-year youth ministry career, I authored two books designed to help parents communicate healthy sexual attitudes to their children and teens and to empower them with the skills to talk with their children about their sexuality.[1] I witnessed, then and now, teens struggling with sexual temptation and parents being reluctant and fearful about discussing anything related to sexuality. This is most unfortunate, since numerous studies show that the more positive, value-centered sex education children receive in their home, the less promiscuous they will be in life.

Parents have two important reasons to teach their children about their developing sexuality. First, if you do not teach your children about sex, someone else most certainly will. Second, God has given you the responsibility to train and teach your children about their sexuality. As parents, our goal for our teens is much larger than keeping them pure until their wedding day. The ultimate goal is a lifetime of sexual integrity.

Of course, a core belief in a lifetime of sexual integrity doesn't result from a one-time conversation or a sex education class. Sex education must begin at a very young age and continue as children grow. In reality, the sex education of children is an eighteen-year course of love, insight, and example. Overwhelming evidence suggests that parents who put their minds to it, and who have confidence and the right tools, can effectively teach their children about human sexuality. The focus of this particular book is guidance for parents as they help adolescents shape and form their lives in a godly manner. I hope you have already begun teaching and discussing sexual issues with your children long before adolescence. Sex education literally begins at birth, and many wonderful resources are available to guide parents through each developmental age before adolescence.[2] However, even if you have been somewhat remiss concerning sex education prior to adolescence, don't despair. Jump into the deep end of the pool now and remember: better late than never!

When I wrote my books during the mid-1980s through early 2000, teen sexual activity was at an all-time high. Since that time teen sexual activity has been slowly but steadily declining. However, even today, nearly 60 percent of sixteen- to eighteen-year-olds and nearly 30 percent of thirteen- to fifteen-year-olds have had sexual intercourse. Declining numbers of sexually active teens really don't matter much to a Christian parent whose child is on the wrong side of the statistics. Nevertheless, there is a bit of good news among the statistics: "In 2006–2010, the most common reason that sexually inexperienced teens gave for not having had sex was that it was against religion or morals."[3] Also, my work with families and teens during forty-two years of ministry has shown me that family closeness, expressed through open, honest sex education, can promote abstinence from premarital sexual activity. Additionally, religious training and church involvement can reduce sexual activity among teens.

Before discussing specific topics and making suggestions regarding what parents can teach their adolescents about sexuality, let me offer a biblical perspective—or a theology—of healthy sexuality. When one thinks about a moral and biblical foundation for sexual integrity, it is amazing how much the Bible has to say on this topic. Early in a child's life parents can begin teaching from Scripture the biblical foundational aspects of God's will for sexuality. A very good, complete, and concise treatment on a healthy theology of sexuality is found in Jim Burns's book, *Teaching Your Children Healthy Sexuality.*[4] He discusses many aspects of this topic, complete with scriptural references: God created sex, God sees sex as very good, what the Bible says about fornication and adultery, the union between a man and a woman, and bodily purity. I highly recommend this book as a guide to help parents provide a biblical framework for sexuality. Parents may use a variety of resources and Scriptures, but the goal is to lay a biblical background or theology of sexuality as a baseline for discussion and teaching with teens.

In a book with many important and difficult topics, and where space is limited, one can only briefly make suggestions, furnish ideas, and offer advice. The most important element is resources where in-depth information, analysis, and discussions can be obtained. Therefore, this chapter will include some specific topics, ideas, and suggestions as a general guideline, but more important, references will be provided for detailed and helpful resources, most of which can easily be found online. I encourage parents to use these mostly Christian resources when teaching teens about sexuality in an increasingly secular culture.

Earlier I mentioned that sex education with our children must begin at an early age and continue as they grow. Obviously, this education will include many formal and informal talks. During all such conversations it is very important to work on becoming what I call "askable." Parents must strive to be their children's primary source of information, especially sexual information, from a young age. The key issue then becomes, how do parents effectively communicate with their children? Are parents askable and approachable? Do children and teens feel free to approach their parents and ask questions? And, when asked questions regarding sexual issues, do parents answer immediately, truthfully, using age-appropriate language, and provide information that leads to the next logical question?

Children will not talk to parents about sex or anything else if parents are not askable and approachable. Becoming askable and approachable is a lifelong process. Parents must strive constantly to improve their communication skills, because they will never have a major influence on their child's sex education or any other significant matter unless and until the child feels comfortable, understood, and at ease discussing all matters with them.

Most communication with teens regarding sexual matters will be more informal than formal. The formal meetings generally take place prior to puberty, and sexual discussions with teens frequently result from parental initiative. These teachable moments can occur around natural physical and emotional changes like puberty, new babies, or everyday situations in the life of a teen (TV, movies, video games, inappropriate texts, etc.). Sex education opportunities are endless, and we need to seize them and not feel like sex can only be talked about with our children by appointment. When we calmly and lovingly use natural occurrences and situations as opportunities to discuss sex with them, we are taking the initiative and keeping the door open for future communication.

Puberty

We will begin making specific suggestions concerning appropriate topics for teaching and discussion with teens by tackling a child's unofficial entry into the teen years—puberty. Nothing strikes more fear in the hearts of preteens and parents than puberty—this time of massive physical, mental, emotional, and sexual changes. Unfortunately, because the onset of puberty appears at progressively earlier ages with each new generation, discussions preparing children for puberty may need to begin as early as ten or eleven. For example, in the 1870s the average girl first menstruated when she was sixteen or seventeen. Today, however, she is more likely to menstruate between age eleven and twelve. In fact, 95 percent of all girls show at least one sign of puberty between the age of nine and thirteen and a half. Boys are beginning to go through puberty between the ages of eleven and thirteen.

Puberty can be a fearful experience, even when young people are aware of what is happening. But children between the ages of ten and twelve typically don't have any conception of the tremendous changes that will shortly occur in their minds and bodies. Puberty is frightening at best, but if a child is totally unprepared for the traumatic events that accompany this developmental stage, major physical and emotional problems may be expected. Parents should take the lead, before puberty begins, to positively introduce their children to the wonderful and exciting changes that will soon occur in their bodies.[5] A parent's duty during the preteen years is to watch alertly for physical and emotional changes which signal the beginning of puberty and to communicate what's happening, under the umbrella of unconditional love and grace. Twila Pearson, in her great book, *The Challenging Years: Shedding Light on Teen Sexuality,* has a detailed chart depicting all the physical changes that occur during puberty and a good discussion related to those changes.[6]

One of the most controversial and traumatic issues encountered by preteens during puberty is masturbation. The very mention of the word causes people, especially parents, to cringe. An old joke says: 95 percent of all boys practice masturbation, and the other 5 percent are liars! Unfortunately, most surveys confirm these statistics. Most males, and an increasing number of females, masturbate during adolescence. Parents need to know that Christian writers, leaders, and professionals have widely diverse opinions and beliefs on the subject of masturbation. It is, however, vitally important for parents to carefully and completely study all sides of this issue and to discuss all aspects of masturbation, including the psychological, emotional, and spiritual effects, with preteens. My second book, *This Can't Wait,* has a large and broad discussion on this topic.[7] Also, see Jonathan McKee's exhaustive work, *More Than Just The Talk,* for another insightful viewpoint.[8] Of course, masturbation is only one of the many topics parents must discuss with preteens prior to puberty.

There are a variety of ways parents might have puberty-preparing discussions with their kids. For example, some parents, when their children begin displaying the first signs of puberty, arrange for moms and daughters or fathers and sons to spend a weekend away, talking about puberty issues in an uninterrupted and calm atmosphere. Another idea is for parents to arrange weekly discussions on different puberty matters. Jim Burns has written a book containing most of the issues parents need to discuss prior to puberty, and it is specifically designed to be read and discussed by parents and preteens together.[9] Choose whichever methods or resources best fit your situation, because it is vitally important that parents have frequent conversations with their preteens prior to puberty. When children have been thoroughly and adequately prepared for this stressful and traumatic stage of life, they will adjust and mature in a much healthier manner. Parents need to lovingly provide preteens with accurate information concerning all aspects of puberty. Of particular importance is parental acceptance of the confused feelings and emotions of adolescents during puberty. You need also to be generous with praise and encouragement and to be available to listen when they are ready to talk. With accurate information and the loving acceptance of parents, most children can successfully weather this stormy period of their lives.

Same-Sex Attraction

An issue that has recently exploded in the media and affects most adolescents and their parents is same sex attraction (SSA). Simply, SSA is a term used to describe the sexual feelings men and women have toward others of the same gender. Youth ministers, Christian counselors, and parents report a tremendous increase in questions, fears, and pleas for help from both teens and parents with concerns over SSA. This is a controversial and complicated issue requiring much study, insight, patience, and prayer. My purpose here is to define terms, provide a few details, observations, suggestions, and references of resources for further and more comprehensive study.

Let's begin with a brief discussion regarding identity. Identity formation occurs throughout childhood and adolescence and is the process by which an individual's environments and decisions lead to the construction of an identity. Gender-identity formation accelerates in children between the ages of six and ten, when they begin to figure out what it means to be male or female. During puberty or a bit later, sexual identity begins forming.

Sexual identity can be defined as how people choose to label themselves in light of their sexual attractions or orientations. Think about a young teen sorting through gender and sexual identity in a culture steeped in sexual-identity labels (heterosexual, homosexual, gay, straight, etc.). Add to this already confusing and puzzling mixture of identities the conflict that can exist between teens' questions about sexual identity and its relationship to their religious identity. Remember, teens are in the process of forming an identity and, as famous developmental psychologist Eric Erikson noted, the key developmental task of adolescence is identity versus role confusion.

Is it any wonder that adolescents are confused and bewildered? Of course, confusion is a normal part of adolescence, but between trying to sort through gender, sexual, and religious identities, teens can easily become overwhelmed. And when SSA feelings arise, the puzzle becomes really muddled.

Some mild SSA feelings and allures are relatively normal during adolescence, but if these fascinations lead to an orientation or experimentation, teens often feel trapped and believe they are destined for a life of homosexuality. This is simply not true: a number of studies demonstrate that adolescent SSA is not fixed, but fluid. A significant percentage of adolescents experiencing SSA as teens later identify as heterosexuals when adults.[10]

What does this mean for parents who have teens who might be experiencing or struggling with SSA? It emphasizes the importance of continual and multiple conversations and discussions with preteens and teens regarding all sexual matters in an atmosphere of grace, compassion, and understanding.

Adolescents who experience SSA aren't growing and maturing in a vacuum. They are hearing messages from parents, friends, ministers, and the media, all of them providing information, often conflicting, that influences thinking about homosexuality and faith. All this information and SSA feelings lead to questions about their sexual identity: Why do I feel attractions toward others of the same sex? What do my attractions mean? How do I make sense of my same-sex sexuality? Who am I in light of what I am feeling?

Questions about sexual identity are further complicated when asked in the context of a religious faith: How do I reconcile my same-sex feelings in light of my Christian faith? Where is God and why doesn't he heal me? Why don't I feel loved by God right now?[11] And parents are asking their own questions: What caused this, can it be changed, and what did we do wrong? Everyone wants to know—what causes SSA and/or homosexuality?

Questions concerning the causes of homosexuality are complicated and hotly debated. And unfortunately, since research done on this subject is viewed and discussed in a society immersed in cultural wars, it is difficult to get objective, dispassionate perspectives. There are those who believe homosexuality is completely determined by nature—completely controlled by one's DNA. This theory proposes that one is simply born heterosexual or homosexual. Others believe homosexuality is an absolute product of nurture—one's environment and the manner in which one was reared. Instead of seeing the cause as either nature or nurture or choosing between the two, most experts today believe that both contribute to sexual attraction and/or homosexual orientation. These contributions likely vary in strength from person to person.[12]

Dr. Francis Collins, Director of the National Institute of Health and former director of the Human Genome Project, and also a devout Christian, says:

> There is an inescapable component of heritability to many human behavior traits. For virtually none of them is heredity ever close to predictive. An area of particularly strong interest is the genetic basis of homosexuality. Evidence indicates that sexual orientation is genetically influenced but not hardwired by DNA, and whatever genes are involved represent predispositions not predeterminations."[13]

Nature and nurture may play a role in a sexual predisposition, but there is no evidence that either one determines it.

Another question closely related to the nature-versus-nurture dispute is the question: Is sexual orientation a choice? Dr. Steven Gerali, a noted counselor and expert in the field of adolescence and youth ministry, says:

> We need to correct a myth about sexual orientation. Some people mistakenly believe it's a choice. Teenagers are told they can choose whether or not to be gay. Yet scholars and medical professionals who hold to both the nurture and nature origin theories quickly dispel this belief. While sexual behavior is learned and chosen (one chooses to engage in sex acts), sexual orientation (one's drives, desires, and urges) is *not* chosen—although orientation can be reinforced through choice.

Gerali further asks: If homosexuality is a choice, then why is no help offered to teens regarding choosing a sexual orientation? No materials are written, courses taught, or even testimonials given about choosing a heterosexual or homosexual orientation.[14] After reading this information, parents and others concerned with teens struggling with SSA can begin to see the complicated nature of this problem and the feelings of helplessness and isolation many teens feel.

Let's shift from general information concerning SSA, to discussing what parents might do when suspicions or revelations of SSA exist with their teen.

Parents must begin thinking about such circumstances with understanding and help for both their teen and themselves. Initially, parents need to recognize, admit, and deal with their many feelings and understand a need to talk about these feelings. For example, parents in SSA situations with their teens almost always feel ambivalent—that is, they have a mixture of both positive and negative emotions and feelings toward their teen. Often ambivalence can lead to polarization when one parent reflects primarily positive emotions toward their teen and the other parent reflects mostly negative emotions toward the child. Being aware of a tendency toward ambivalence and polarization can help parents prevent such feelings and help provide the support their teen desperately needs.[15]

Also, parents from Christian families often react to SSA in their teens with guilt and shame. Some parents withdraw or isolate themselves from their church. This worsens the problem and their shame. Parents need to find a safe environment to openly discuss their feelings and emotions—perhaps a well-trained minister or, preferably, a counselor or therapist with experience counseling families in SSA circumstances.

Let's now discuss what parents can do to provide help and support for teens facing SSA issues.

Most Christian teens facing SSA issues experience guilt, trauma, and a host of fears and questions. It is vitally important that parents understand the need for creating an atmosphere of grace, which begins with compassion, mercy, and empathy. It is also tremendously important that parents understand their significance in the lives of teens with sexual-identity confusion. Parents can help teens by thoroughly researching the complexities of all the issues related to SSA and by facilitating a healthy dialogue with their teens. Steven Gerali's book *What Do I Do When Teenagers Question Their Sexuality?* has a helpful, comprehensive section: "Resources for Helping Teens Who Are Questioning Their Sexuality," with resources from a Christian perspective.[16]

Perhaps the most significant element parents can provide teens who are struggling with SSA is therapy with an experienced mental health professional or counselor. The goal of therapy is to help the teen identify the underlying causes and contributing factors of his or her SSA. Parents must find professionals with experience in treating adolescent SSA and other sexual-identity questions and furnish total support for the counseling process. Parents with teens who exhibit SSA indicators must consider therapy with a trained professional with experience in SSA and sexual-identity confusion.

This issue is extremely complicated and multifaceted. Parents who encounter SSA questions, problems, or suspicions should begin immediately to research this topic and consult a counselor or therapist for themselves and the teen. As I indicated earlier, the endnote section for this chapter provides many excellent resources for detailed study.

Other Topics

Now let's return to the previous subject and continue focusing on appropriate topics to teach and discuss with preteens and teens regarding sex and sexuality.

Our last topic was puberty and could be considered basic training. Now you are ready for combat—early adolescence (ages 13–15)! Actually, parents can eagerly anticipate a child's teen years and look forward to the rewarding opportunity to help teens grow and mature. Of course, a big part of that maturing process will focus on helping and guiding teens with their emerging sexuality.

Media

Early adolescence typically is a time of fear, anxiety, emotional feelings, and rapid development. Add to those the possibility of death of parents, divorce, bullying, and similar fears. Many adolescent worries and anxieties center around physical and sexual concerns such as their looks and their physical development. Unfortunately, teens find solutions and answers to anxieties and sexual concerns from the media—one of the primary sources of sexual information for teens. Neutralizing media influence is not an easy parental battle. But remember, our job as parents is not only education and discussion regarding sex, but also protection from erroneous and harmful influences. And the media has become increasingly harmful to teens in many areas, especially with regard to sexual matters. For example: "Studies show that kids with early exposure to sexually explicit media in TV, movies, magazines, music, and on the Internet were much more likely to have sexual intercourse than their peers who had a much lighter sexual media diet."[17] A preponderance of evidence documents the harmful effects of many types of media on children and teens.

The Cell Phone

A relatively new area of negative media influence on teens comes from their pockets—their cell phones. The average American uses a cell phone for over two-and-a-half hours per day, which is not nearly as much usage as that by the average teen. Many cell phones allow teens to access the Internet, take pictures, make videos, and make them instantly available on a variety of platforms. Cell phones also provide instant access to friends through calls and primarily through texting. The dangers are obvious and are exemplified by the emerging phenomenon known as "sexting" or text messaging provocative or nude photos of themselves.

I recently counseled a parent who was distraught over discovering nude pictures of a fifteen-year-old girl on her son's phone. She even found nude pictures of her son that he had sent to the girl. As we talked, I learned that this was not the first time she had made such a discovery. When I asked her why he still possessed his phone, her response demonstrated a need for parental guidelines and standards that neutralize and counteract the negative influence of media and avoid temptation.

Remember, our job as parents is to provide protection from harmful influences, even when our children probably will not welcome such protection. For example, before discovering such shocking activity as nude photos, certain procedures governing phone use must be in place. Teens need to know that possession of a phone is not a right but a privilege—it can be taken and locked away. I would suggest beginning with a policy with preteens and teens where all cell devices are taken to the parent's room at a designated time and deposited until morning. Also, let your teens know that you have the right and the responsibility to check their phone at any time and that you do so regularly.

Personal Appearance

For at least two decades, many child development experts, youth ministers, and parents have noticed that our society is encouraging and forcing children to grow up too fast and pushing them into adult roles and behaviors before they are mature enough to handle adult pressures. Nowhere is this more visible than our society's attempt to influence children and preteens to begin wearing make-up and revealing clothing at a much too early age. Parents who attempt to buy modest clothing for girls as young as nine or ten often are shocked by the skimpy nature of their choices. Abercrombie and Fitch marketed a line of thong panties decorated with sexually provocative phrases such as "wink, wink" and "eye candy," for ten-year-olds.[18]

Our culture is attempting to make our daughters too sexy too soon. Preteens and teens who dress immodestly and who are not prepared for sexual activity are inadvertently advertising or suggesting activities for which they are completely unprepared. As children grow and mature, parents have a responsibility to teach modesty and to explain the effects of immodesty.[19]

Dating

Early adolescence is a time when parents must begin thinking and planning for their teen's dating experience. During forty-two years of working with preteens, teens, and parents, one of the most often asked questions I have received is, "When should I allow my teen to begin dating?" This question generally refers to girls, because most males won't consider single-couple dating until they have a driver's license. Males consider it uncool to ask a girl on a date and arrive at her house on a bicycle or with their dad chauffeuring! This question is important, because ample evidence indicates a relationship between early dating and early sex. For example: of teens who began dating at twelve, 91 percent had sex before graduation, compared to 56 percent who first dated at thirteen, 53 percent who dated at age fourteen, 40 percent who dated at fifteen, and 20 percent who dated at sixteen.[20]

I recommend a gradual approach to dating—beginning with approved mixed groups, such as church youth groups, going places in groups. In most cases such groups are chaperoned by adults and can begin at thirteen or fourteen. At age fifteen, group activities not requiring the presence of adults, but with adults driving, could begin. Solitary dating can be allowed in certain circumstances and limited by curfews and activity restrictions beginning no earlier that age sixteen. My second book has an excellent section on purposes, guidelines, limits, and controls for dating that will help parents (it also has information about date rape).[21]

When young people reach late adolescence, ages sixteen to nineteen, they often experience dating and other potentially sexual activities. Our task during late adolescence is to help our teens sort and resolve options, responsibilities, and consequences of their behavior to help them experience good decision-making as they prepare to leave home. Teens are greatly influenced by feelings and emotions and often make decisions based on these sentiments. Parents need to help teens distinguish between romance, love, sex, and intimacy. It is often quite confusing for teens to understand that sex is not necessarily intimacy, because they live in a world that equates sex and intimacy. Helping teens understand the difference will help them avoid possible difficult situations and prepare them for marriage.

By far the most often asked questions by Christian teens, especially ones in relationships, are: "How far can we go?" or "How far is too far?" Parents must discuss this question openly and honestly with teens and help them set limits well before they experience situations where they need boundaries. Parents must help their older adolescent to realize that sex is a process that is progressive and begins well before intercourse. And parents must advise teens about how they can avoid beginning the process or going too far into the process. Most of the time parents have not talked with their teens about setting standards, and some teens end up going further than they intended.

There are three reasons teens go further than intended: (1) pressure to conform, (2) emotional involvement that exceeds their maturity level, (3) lack of value-centered sex education from home.[22] Good information on this topic can be found in my book (*This Can't Wait*) as well as Jim Burns's and Jonathan McKee's books. A second question late adolescents consider, even if they are not bold enough to ask, is: "Why wait?" Parents must begin answering this question by thoroughly discussing all that the Scriptures have to say on this subject. We ought to teach teens that everyone is created in the image of God and nobody should be viewed as an object for personal gratification. Selfish use of others for personal gratification violates the basic message of Christianity. Parents can also discuss and teach the many harmful results of casual sex.

Pornography

A topic that perhaps has the greatest potential to devastate the values and morals of our society is pornography. A perusal of the Internet reveals some statistics:

- forty million frequent pornography users reside in the United States
- 35 percent of all Internet downloads are from pornographic sites
- 2.5 billion pornographic e-mails are sent daily in the United States
- Internet pornographic sites generate 2.84 billion dollars annually
- 24 percent of all smartphone owners admit to having pornographic material on their mobile devices

Studies also indicate that pornographers primarily target adolescent males from fourteen to sixteen years of age because they believe these teens will become addicted for life. Pornography is both progressive and addictive.

Parents must not underestimate the powerful allure of pornography. They should look for opportunities to discuss this distasteful subject with their teens, especially males. Most importantly, parents must set standards and safeguards for their teens, which can help prevent exposure to pornography. As was discussed in the section on media, parents must proactively limit exposure to media and routinely monitor all their teens' mobile and home devices. If pornography is discovered, parents must openly discuss the consequences and increase standards and limits. Pornography, especially with the ease of Internet access, has far-reaching implications.

Birth Control

Another subject that can be broached with late adolescents is birth control. I say, possibly introduced, because of the contentiously debated views on this subject. Some reputable Christian writers, counselors, and parents believe that under no circumstances should parents ever discuss birth control with their children. These folk believe that such discussions promote promiscuity and send mixed messages. Other reputable Christians believe that if your teen is likely and determined to sin sexually, information about birth control might prevent the birth of an unwanted child, and even the possibility of abortion as an alternative.

My recommendation is that parents not dilute their own and God's view concerning sexual sins. However, having discussions with your teen about birth control and contraception cannot possibly undo all your previous teaching about sexual sin. Information is neither moral nor immoral, it is simply information, and it may prevent problems for them or others. I believe we can inform our teens about birth control while at the same time telling them that we pray that they will not use this information until marriage.

Pregnancy

The pregnancy of your daughter outside of marriage or the knowledge that your son is responsible for a pregnancy is one of the most emotionally painful events that can occur in a parent's life. The guilt is great for everyone in the family. How, then, should parents react?

Hopefully, your teen has been reared in an atmosphere of openness, mercy, and forgiveness. When children are raised in such an atmosphere, they are better equipped to make difficult decisions moving forward. Expressing forgiveness to young people in this situation is extremely difficult. Doing so requires parents to summon all their inner strength and emotional capabilities. But forgiveness is mandatory, both to heal the teen and to help them make intelligent, rational choices.

Do not despair—forgiveness is a gift from God, and when it's needed, God will provide the strength to forgive. Parents must also explain that although God always forgives his children, he rarely removes the consequences of sin. Your child will need your help and support through this difficult ordeal.

Final Thoughts

As I said at the beginning of this chapter, a parent's responsibility for their children with regard to sex education is to help them achieve a lifetime of sexual integrity according to God's word. There are essentially two ways Christians can approach teaching their teens about sex: the first is based on the fear of consequences; the second is rooted in giving God Lordship over our entire lives, including our sexuality.

Many of the books available today on the subject of teenage sexuality contain large sections devoted to the reasons teenagers have sex, and the reasons they should not have sex. These books can be excellent resources. I have, however, deliberately chosen not to focus only on such lists. Some benefit may be derived from examining causes, but in order to effectively help teens avoid pre-marital sexual involvement, parents must begin early teaching and demonstrating wholesome, godly sexual values and attitudes. When Christian values, attitudes, and accurate information are provided in an atmosphere of openness and love, children will be much less likely to succumb to sexual temptations. Our energy should be concentrated on providing positive, ongoing sex education for our children and teens.

Unfortunately, too many parents fail to provide early sexual training to their children, and later when the children reach adolescence, these parents attempt to use scare tactics and fear to prevent sexual activity. The use of fear becomes a substitute for continual and accurate sex education. I am not saying that teenagers should not be warned about the possible consequences of sexual sins. They need to know that if they engage in sexual intercourse, devastating consequences are a possibility. God will forgive sexual sins, but if pregnancy occurs, there will be a baby nine months later.

After many years of working directly with teens and preteens and helping rear two teens of my own, I am convinced there is only one sure antidote for sexual promiscuity: the Lordship of Jesus Christ. It is appropriate to use a certain amount of healthy fear to help your teens avoid sexual involvement. It is certainly a good idea to tell teens that if they are sexually active, possible consequences might involve pregnancy, AIDS, sexually transmitted diseases, and other physical and emotional problems. However, avoid the temptation to use fear as the only or primary teaching method. This distorts the biblical message of true sexuality.

Begin early in the lives of your children to teach the concept of the Lordship of Jesus. Christian teens need to be taught to avoid sexual sins because they have given their lives to Jesus. The apostle Paul says in 1 Corinthians 6:18–20:

> Flee from sexual immorality. All other sins a person commits are outside the body, but whoever sins sexually sins against their own body. Do you not know that your bodies are temples of the Holy Spirit, who is in you, whom you have received from God? You are not your own; you were bought at a price. Therefore honor God with your bodies. (NIV)

We must teach teenagers to avoid sexual activity because they have been "bought at a price." Their bodies have been purchased and house the Holy Spirit of God. Christian teens flee sexual sins because of the tremendous hurt such activity causes their Lord.[23]

Hopefully, I have persuaded parents to see the necessity of a lifetime of teaching and discussing sexuality with their children, especially teens. I have only briefly introduced many topics for discussion and conversation and provided some suggestions and recommendations. I highly endorse the reference material listed in the endnotes and believe you will find this a rich trove of information that will help you become the primary source of sex education and sexuality information for your teens.

May God bless your efforts to educate your teens concerning their Creator's will for their sexual integrity.

Questions

1. Scott tell us that "Parents must strive from a young age to be their children's primary source of information, especially sexual information." Why is this both important and challenging?
2. What are some ways we can maintain an ongoing conversation about human sexuality, even though it can be difficult to talk about?
3. How are you an "askable" or "approachable" parent? How could you get better at this?
4. What would be some teachable moments in your family's regular lifestyle that you could use to teach about good sexuality?
5. How have you prepared your children for puberty (or how did you prepare them for it)? Based on your experience, do you have any advice you would share with other parents?
6. What are your cell phone rules? How has the cell phone changed adolescent perspectives about human sexuality? Are you familiar with sexting acronyms? How should the Christian parent respond?
7. What plan do you have for your children about media use? For example, will you have or not have Internet and cable TV available in your children's rooms?
8. Since early dating is so frequently connected with early nonmarital sex, why might parents so often support dating at a young age? What are your dating guidelines for your children?

9. Dating questions and situations provide a really good place to practice discernment. How could you use "what if" scenarios to prepare your kids for dating?

10. How could you initiate informal times to talk with your children about the good and the bad things that come with dating? What will you do or say if your children ask you about your dating experiences?

11. How is the easy availability of pornography affecting human sexuality, especially for teens?

12. What are you doing to teach your sons to be holy and that women are not objects to be used for gratification, relationship, power, or status?

13. What are you doing to teach your daughters to be holy and not to use their sexuality for gratification, relationship, power, or status?

14. Although parents may discuss the consequences of extra-marital sex, what is the way that Scott feels better prepares teens for healthy sexuality and sexual integrity? How can we communicate this "better way"?

ADOPTIVE PARENTING: Coming to Understand the Heart of God

Ryan Fraser

I'm an adoptive father. This experience has shaped me as a man and impacted my self-concept and spiritual perspective in many ways. If you're an adoptive parent, you know exactly what I mean. If not, I hope you will at least be able to relate in some way to my reflections and will gain a deeper understanding and appreciation of adoptive parents. If you're an adult adoptee, you will no doubt look at the things described and discussed in this chapter through a totally different set of lenses. But I can only speak from my own distinct vantage point.

The Bible reveals to us that God is an adoptive parent. I believe this is more than just a clever metaphor. It's a spiritual reality. Romans 8:14–17 (ESV) tells us,

> All who are led by the Spirit of God are sons of God. For you did not receive the spirit of slavery to fall back into fear, but you have received the Spirit of adoption as sons,

by whom we cry, "Abba! Father!" The Spirit himself
bears witness with our spirit that we are children of God,
and if children, then heirs—heirs of God and fellow
heirs with Christ, provided we suffer with him in order
that we may also be glorified with him.

Spiritual adoption means complete acceptance and full rights, privileges, and obligations as God's beloved children. Paul reiterates this profound theological concept in Ephesians 1:4b–6 when he says, "In love he predestined us for adoption as sons through Jesus Christ, according to the purpose of his will, to the praise of his glorious grace, with which he has blessed us in the Beloved" (ESV). This has always been a part of God's plan and purpose for us. It was never an afterthought.

As Christians, we are beloved, adopted children of God. This theological truth means our heavenly Parent cherishes, nurtures, and protects us. Furthermore, we are blessed as joint heirs with our elder sibling, Jesus, of God's amazing eternal promises and inheritance. In return, God desires our love and loyalty, including our willing obedience to divine commands and personal sacrifices for the greater benefit of God's spiritual household. This deep reality should influence our self-understanding and increase our sense of inherent self-worth. In turn, it should also inform our grasp of the extraordinary human practice and divinely created institution of adoption. Adoption means acceptance and hope.

In my own life, I've discovered that foster parenting and adoptive parenting are unique challenges with countless surprises as well as blessings. It's an arduous journey—not for the faint of heart—with many twists and turns and ups and downs along the pathway. Very little can prepare adoptive parents for what's to come. There are mountaintop experiences as well as valleys of discouragement and despair.

Young people who grow up in adoptive homes are placed in a truly unique situation. Their family is related by spirit rather than blood. It is thus a spiritual rather than a physical kinship. Due to the backdrop and complex interwoven narratives leading up to the process of adoption, adolescent adoptees may struggle with a wide array of difficulties. Depending on the specific circumstances under which voluntary relinquishment or termination of birth parental rights occurred and the factors leading up to being adopted, some challenging emotional and spiritual struggles may be in store for these young people. There is also potential for great blessings and opportunities. Whatever the circumstances, it is important that they learn from an early age that God is faithful and ever present to help them, come what may.

Ultimately, the goal for both Christian adoptive parents and their adopted children should be acceptance—acceptance of self and of one another. Even more important is the realization that God accepts them as they are, and that divine love is unstoppable.

God-Image Concepts

Our "God-image" is our unconscious and conscious mental construction of God's personhood. This internalized concept begins to be formed in our mind at an early age. It consists of the complex amalgamation of our various feelings and perceptions regarding our primary caregivers and guardians, our birth parents, religious authorities, what we've been told about God from parents, grandparents, and Sunday school teachers, or what we have deduced or inferred about God from Scripture. It's a complicated process indeed. In reality, our personal God-image is likely a dim reflection of the true and living God, since our human perspectives are flawed and imperfect.

Adopted children have a special challenge in coming to terms with who God is—and what God's true nature is—in light of their formative experiences of relinquishment and adoption. They may struggle psychologically with unspoken confusion and ambiguity over a "God" who simultaneously rejects and loves, hurts and helps, abandons and embraces children. The shaping of their God-image will wield a tremendous influence upon the trajectory of their spiritual development as adolescents. Adoptive parents have their work cut out for them in facilitating the healthy spiritual formation of their kids. It requires intentionality, patience, and consistent effort.

What my wife and I have experienced, as both foster parents and adoptive parents, has caused us to grow as individuals and as a married couple in ways that nothing else could have. We have learned a lot about each other, about God, and about ourselves in the process. The highs and lows, excitement and anxiety, and joy and suffering we've experienced are hard to adequately describe in words. And our journey is still far from complete.

Our Foster-Adoption Story

It may be helpful if I share a few pieces of our story so that you may be able to better understand where I'm coming from. An important disclaimer is that I am risking some transparency and self-disclosure. To be honest with you, it makes me rather nervous to do so. I am a somewhat private person and usually don't like to air my dirty laundry. I'm not sure how you will perceive this information and how you may evaluate it or possibly judge me as a result. My purpose is not to solicit sympathy or make excuses for my own failures but to produce greater understanding and insight to help you grow. My prayer is that it will benefit someone in some way.

Due to serious health-related issues, my wife Missy and I decided to pursue adoption as the way to expand our family. Thankfully, God had already put in our hearts the desire to adopt a child or two even before we found out about these medical concerns. We were licensed as foster parents in the state of Texas from 1999–2005. We adopted two children, a boy and a girl. We also adopted an older child—a boy—but that did not work out.

Our beautiful daughter came to us through a private adoption agency prior to the beginning of our foster parenting days. Next, our youngest son and older adoptee came to us through the foster/adoption system of the state of Texas. The circumstances surrounding each child's adoption were unique. None of the processes were quick and simple, easy, or without some stressful complications.

Providing foster care for around five years was far more difficult than we ever expected it to be, and it took a heavy emotional toll on us individually and as a couple. Our private lives and home were laid bare. We felt exposed and vulnerable much of the time, and largely at the mercy of state government authorities. Dealing with the system was extremely frustrating because it was broken and needed to be fixed. I've come to realize that government bureaucracy is just that way. However, it's a necessary evil.

Interacting with various caseworkers, some who did a good—even exceptional—job, and others who seemed burned out and jaded and who acted unethically, was eye-opening and rather disappointing at times. Those social workers whose hearts were in the right place and who acted with the utmost professionalism, while also showing compassion and understanding, were an absolute breath of fresh air. They supplied us a lifeline.

Just for the record, let me state that social workers as a whole, especially those who work for children and family protective services, have a tough job. They are usually overworked, underpaid, and underappreciated. In fact, they are often caught in the middle of things and receive the brunt of people's anger and abusive treatment. They often get dumped on. Sadly, it seems to go with the territory.

Permanency planning hearings/meetings with judges, supervisors, and lawyers were always stressful events. It broke our hearts to turn loose of children we had grown to love. We worried about their safety and their future. We missed them and prayed for their well-being. It also affected our church family, who grew attached to the children in our care and formed an emotional bond with them.

Our two youngest adopted children came into our home when they were newborns, but our oldest child was nearly six years old and had lived in four foster homes prior to being adopted by us. This factor left irreparable physical and emotional scars on his body and mind, resulting in significant psychological damage, pathology, and dysfunction. His older, biological half-siblings were placed in a high-level therapeutic children's home designed for older "unadoptable" kids with deep psychiatric problems, usually stemming from severe abuse.

The Challenge of a Lifetime

I wish I could say that all has been roses—that our story has a happy, fairy-tale ending, but to do so would be a gross exaggeration of the truth. In fact, it would be a lie. While our daughter and youngest son managed to attach to my wife and me in a healthy way, our oldest son did not. Perhaps he could not because of his background. Or maybe he refused to allow himself to do so out of irrational fear and internalized anger. He erected an impenetrable psychological wall between us—a barrier we could never break through, no matter how hard we tried. Trying to connect with him was exasperating. Our former sense of competency and fulfillment as parents eroded. It put a great strain on our marriage relationship at times.

We often felt unfairly judged and harshly criticized by various acquaintances, friends, and parts of our extended family for either not being more strict or more patient, more firm or more loving, more consistent or more fair. They had no idea what we were going through at the time—not even an inkling. My wife was often the one under attack, and it hurt both of us deeply. Adoptive moms are an easy target for those who don't understand. They also become a transference object for displaced anger and a scapegoat for older children who cannot blame their fantasy-perfect birth mother.

From the get-go our older adopted son did not trust us. Given his history with irresponsible caregivers and cruel authority figures, this was quite understandable. He remained emotionally detached and refused to get close for fear of being betrayed and hurt again. It was a coping mechanism—a maladaptive survival tactic—that prevented us from forming any sort of healthy and mutually satisfying familial bond. It derailed our attempts to develop a good relationship. This invisible, impenetrable barrier was exceedingly painful for all of us. It caused tension and made things feel awkward and uncomfortable.

That adopted son came with much psychological baggage and brokenness. He resisted our parental love and role in his life. He remained suspicious of our motives and rebelled against us at every turn. He lied about practically everything—even things that didn't matter. This was his automatic, hardwired survival response to any question. He stole from us and from our relatives. He was a master of manipulation and made it a game to set up my wife and me against each other and then sit back with a smirk and enjoy the conflict he had set in motion. He seemed to thrive on drama that he created.

Now I am not saying that there were never any good times or glimmers of hope, but these would quickly become tainted by his destructive and deceitful behaviors. It was so disheartening.

As a sixteen-year-old, this troubled boy started making suicide threats, sending disturbing text messages to friends (both his and ours) and also to church members. Then, when he didn't like our rules or disciplinary consequences, he started running away for days at a time. This was the straw that broke the camel's back. We hung on as long as we could, but eventually, keeping him in our home ceased to be an option for us. It was unsafe for him and us.

All of this was humiliating to us as Christian parents and to me as a counseling professor and minister. Essentially, though, we felt helpless and recognized that we were not capable of providing the care and supervision our adopted son needed. We had done all we could. As time progressed, law enforcement got involved as well as the state. We were terrified at what might happen to our family, scared that our children might be taken from us. It kept us on edge most of the time. My wife struggled the most. The constant stress triggered severe depression and hopelessness in her. It negatively affected her physical, emotional, and spiritual health.

If I'm honest, living in our home must have been a difficult experience for our oldest son as well. He constantly got in trouble and felt singled out and unfairly judged and mistreated. He was suffering too. From early on, it became clear he wanted out of our home and family as soon as possible. Having been passed from one foster home to the next and being the victim of abuse had caused deep psychological damage. He had so many pathologies and problems, each of which fed on the other. He struggled to develop and maintain any type of healthy or normal relationships and friends. His peers often rejected him at school and even within the church.

We sought professional counseling help, enrolled him in group therapy, sent him to summer camps (church and otherwise), and tried to help him find a social niche with some positive peer influence. Whenever I thought we were making some real progress, he would quickly revert to self-defeating, self-destructive behaviors. Everything would unravel. It was one step forward, five steps back. He was his own worst enemy. After short peaceful periods of apparent progress, and the emergence of a false sense of security on our part, the truth of what was really going on behind the scenes would come out, and trust would be obliterated once again. It was back to square one.

Though I am the first to confess that we didn't do everything perfectly as parents—that we probably could have and should have handled some things far better than we did—I can affirm that we tried our best with him for twelve agonizing years (the longest time anyone had tried to parent him), and ultimately we still had to admit defeat. Our family's joy and sense of fulfillment were being eroded—vandalized—day by day. I feared they would eventually be totally destroyed. I've never been a quitter, so I really struggled with this admission of failure as a father. But I had to stand up as the leader of our family and make some excruciatingly tough decisions.

Finally I came to the point of recognizing we couldn't get through to him. I had to step back and think about the good of the family as a whole. We couldn't love our oldest son into changing his ways. He could never get beyond or overcome the foster child survivalist mentality. His unfortunate coping strategy was to reject adult caregivers before they had the chance to reject him. And it became a self-fulfilling prophecy.

With his willing cooperation, the state helped us find an appropriate residential treatment facility located two and a half hours away. It was an excellent full-service facility that was equipped to handle his severe psychological issues and provide a safe structure. He lived there most of his junior and senior years of high school. We visited him periodically and had peaceful interactions. Thankfully, he did graduate with a high school diploma before aging out of the treatment facility.

Sadly, coming home was no longer an option, due to significant physical and emotional risks to our family. I managed to get our oldest son accepted and enrolled at a Texas university during the summer following his release from treatment. All his tuition was covered. I got his housing set up and connected him with a good congregation and a Christian student center. Within weeks he had searched out his birth mother and reunited with her. Almost immediately, he changed his last name back to his preadoption name. Then he dropped out of college and entered into some unhealthy relationships which resulted in his fathering two children. He no longer considers us to be his family, and we do not consider him part of ours. Nowadays, contact between us is nonexistent.

I still pray for our former adoptive son, hoping against hope that somehow, some way, something will get through to him to produce needed changes in his life (to heal his relationship with his heavenly Parent, if not with us.). But that remains to be seen.

On a positive note, as a family we are in a much better place emotionally than we were a few years ago. Still not perfect, but far healthier, happier, and more whole.

Finding the Joy in Adoptive Parenting

The relationship we share with our two teenage children is extremely close and mutually satisfying. They have made a healthy bond with us, and we with them. We stick up for each other fiercely, enjoy spending time together, occasionally fight like cats and dogs (as in most families), support one another's interests, dreams, and personal endeavors, and cannot imagine ever being anything less than a loving family. Our children are mostly well-adjusted teenagers, though they certainly have their wild ideas, unique personalities, and quirkiness, just as most adolescents do. Okay, sometimes they drive us crazy! But, we love them and they love us.

We continue to leave the door open for each of them to establish a relationship with their birth families if they choose to do so someday, whatever that may look like. They have had some minimal contact with their birth families over the years, primarily through letter writing and photo exchanges. But, to this point, neither child has shown an interest in pursuing a more active relationship with their birth families. My wife and I try to remain neutral on the topic so as not to push them in any one direction. The message we consistently communicate to our kids, however, is that we will be fully supportive of whatever way they choose to proceed once they are eighteen years old.

We will be more than willing to help establish contact with their birth families if our children seek our assistance. But, in our opinion, that decision is totally theirs to make, and not ours or the birth families' choice. Our children understand that whatever decision they make will be just fine with us because we love and support them unconditionally. We believe our family love will withstand whatever storms are ahead. We want our children to feel secure in themselves as individuals and feel the freedom to live their lives in the healthiest way possible, knowing that they belong first and foremost to God, and not to us or anyone else.

From the time our children were old enough to understand, we have always spoken to them openly about their adoptions and birth families, and connected their individual adoption stories to God's story of redemption and love.

Challenges and Blessings to Adoptive Parents

Most adoptive parents I have met and worked with as a clinician over the years simply want to have as normal a parental relationship with their adopted children as possible. Adoptive parents generally don't seek to draw any special attention to their family and resist being put on some sort of pedestal. Our culture tends to vacillate between glorifying and demonizing adoption.

The narratives of adoptive parents concerning how God put their families together are generally inspiring and heartwarming, though they are often comprised of gut-wrenching pieces relating to miscarriages, infertility, failed adoptions, long waiting periods, and wrestling with God. The good parts go along with the bad. They're inseparable.

A few years ago, when I was conducting my doctoral dissertation research on the spiritual narratives of adoptive parents, I was struck by the powerful ways that adopting children shapes adoptive parents' faith stories and impacts perceptions within congregations.[1] Transracial adoptions seem to have a positive impact in correcting racial stereotypes and biases, especially in our churches.

For example, Lester and Gwen, a white couple, reflected on how the arrival of their first adopted son, who was biracial, paved the way for other biracial children who were later born to Lester's own biological siblings. Gwen wondered how their son's coming helped to turn around some of the negative attitudes the older generation of the family otherwise might have had toward these biological grandchildren. Here follows some of the interview dialogue:

> GWEN: At Christmas we were all there, and we were looking around at the two blond children and then the three dark-headed kids, and I said to Lester's dad—
>
> ME: What a mix! That must be fascinating.
>
> GWEN: I said, "Did you ever think your grandkids were going to be so colorful?" He said, "Colorful? That's a good word."

Later on in the conversation, the same theme of overcoming embedded racism was discussed in the church context. It was interesting to listen to the adoptive mother's description of the difference adopting transracially had made upon their home church.

> GWEN: I think for us, we get to help God teach some lessons because of Elijah. He is the first black baby a lot of people have held, because when he was little, he didn't care who you were. He was just Mister Friendly.

He'd walk up, look up, lift those arms up, and then what are you going to do? You either had to look at this beautiful baby boy and say, "No, I'm not going to pick you up."

And people would look at us and go, "What do I do?" It's like, "You can pick him up." And he didn't see black or white; he didn't see young or old. And I just have this picture of some old white man going, "Okay, I'm going to pick up this baby." And we have even had people say to us, "He has changed us!" We live in a city where there's a big race issue—and people have said, "He's changed my mind about the whole race thing."

ME: That is powerful!

It is conspicuous in this example how transracial adoption had a far-reaching impact not only on the adopting family but also on their entire faith community.

While the majority of the adoptive parents I interviewed held a basically positive view toward their experiences and their children, others showed signs of psycho-spiritual wear and tear in light of difficult circumstances they had been confronted with. Nonetheless, each of them had seemingly gained wisdom as a result of their journey.

God Is Pro-Adoption

The resoundingly unanimous vote of every adoptive parent I interviewed was that "God is in favor of adoption." Several adoptive parents observed that God is an adoptive Parent, since God adopted us, also making us God's adopted children (Rom. 8:15; Eph. 1:5). Barry explained that being adopted means that someone has said, "I will stand for you!" It also means that you have the same standing as anyone else in the family.

One adoptive father stated that God does not play favorites and that God's love for us is the same as for the "unique" or "one of a kind" (from the Greek word *monogenēs,* John 3:16) Son of God. Most of the English Bible translators did the church a great disservice when they translated *monogenēs* with the words "only begotten." Jesus was not the Holy One's only begotten son.

Adoptive father Phil stated he believes that adoption is close to what God wants in this life—for us to become family with those who do not have any biologically related family to nurture, care for, and love them. Phil compared the excitement and anticipation of the adoption ceremony and the pure joy of it for the adoptive parents to how God must feel when adopting us.

Alaina, a black adoptive mother, articulated her feelings about how in adoption we are able to experience something of the way God loves us, and in it how we experience a transcendent love for another human being who is not related to us by flesh and blood. She affirmed, "Adoption is acceptance!"

Each of the couples spoke about feeling a tremendous responsibility to set the proper Christian example for their adopted children and to teach them accurately about God. They yearned to prepare their children for a life of Christian faithfulness and commitment. Most of all, the adoptive parents often stated that their life's ultimate goal and the greatest desire of their heart was to have their children with them in heaven someday.

Bonding and Attachment Issues for Adolescent Adoptees

In my experience as a counselor, minister, and researcher, I have observed that the age of a child at adoption makes a huge difference. My research makes it clear that those children who are adopted beyond the age of eighteen months to two years generally struggle with attachment issues.[2] If they were in a series of foster homes prior to being adopted, they usually are going to exhibit some kind of attachment disorder symptoms from moderate to severe. As my wife and I discovered, these are extremely difficult issues to overcome. Showing genuine physical affection through hugs and holding their hand, no matter their age or gender, provides a sense of warm acceptance, belonging, family stability, and emotional security.

Grief and Loss

Many adoptees struggle with unresolved grief and personal loss over being relinquished by their birth parents. These feelings often surface during adolescence as they gain the ability to process the personal ramifications of the situation they were dealt before they were old enough to protest what was happening to them. They wonder why they were given up for adoption. While sometimes this important information is known and readily available, at other times it isn't.

Author Nancy Verrier has referred to this deeply profound trauma as the "primal wound."[3] Adoptees may sometimes fantasize over whether their birth mother or father is searching for them with the intent to come and "rescue" them. This secret fantasy can often result in emotional discomfort and their acting out in negative and unhealthy ways.

Adoptive parents will do well to facilitate honest conversations with their children about such things. Otherwise children may perceive them as taboo topics. Find tangible ways to honor their adoption story as well as to demonstrate love, appreciation, and respect toward the birth families. Acknowledge your child's right to feel sad, sorrowful, or angry about the loss of their biological parentage and blood-related family. Our love as adoptive parents must be strong enough to withstand their potential anger and grief. We must believe in the resilience and strength of our relationship.

Hidden Shame and Guilt

Adoptees also may feel hidden shame or guilt over their curiosity regarding their birth parents and their secret desire to search for them at some point in the future. Such adolescent adoptees may feel shame for being "disloyal" toward or seemingly unappreciative of all that the adoptive parents have done and are doing for them. Again openness, empathy, compassion, non-defensiveness, and understanding on the part of adoptive parents will go a long way in dissipating a young person's irrational, anxious thoughts. It is best to validate and normalize their feelings as making perfect sense. It may help to periodically initiate praying with your children for their birth families.

Many adoptees struggle with their fundamental sense of self-identity of who they are and where (or to whom) they truly belong. This is where patience is especially important. They find it confusing and challenging to find their place in this world. We must remind our children of their immeasurable value to us and to God, their heavenly Parent. One way we can do this is by listening non-judgmentally and affording dignity to their humanity and their God-imaged status.

Hope and Comfort in Adoption

For adoptive parents and adopted adolescents alike, God knew us before we were born. The Holy One foreknew the entirety of our complex life narrative before we took our first breath. Our Creator saw all the joys and sorrows that would come our way—the painful struggles, the profound losses, and the powerful victories. We can take comfort in this conviction of faith—this wonderful knowledge.

As adoptive parents, we hold a critically important place in our children's lives. Our unconditional and abiding love, commitment, consistency, belief in our children, and willingness to suffer for them and alongside them reflects the intimate relationship of

God with God's children. God has promised us, "Never will I leave you; never will I forsake you" (Heb. 13:5 NIV). The Holy One also promises that nothing can or ever will be able to separate us from God's perfect love in Christ Jesus our Lord (Rom. 8:39).

Hope is the fuel that sustains adoptive families. God, in infinite wisdom and providential care, is able to take and redeem our individual and collective stories. Our heavenly Parent gathers up the broken pieces of our lives and puts them back together again, creating something new and beautiful—a majestic mosaic that reflects the power of God's love, the glory of divine holiness, and the strength of intimate connection. God's matchless grace restores our souls and sustains our hearts for the journey ahead. Our shared destination is worth each struggle and every tear that is shed along the way home.

Questions

1. This adoptive parenting chapter is important for several reasons, one being that your children will be family or friends with children adopted from foreign countries (many from China and Ethiopia, to be specific). Diversity is present as never before. How should youth, parents, and the church community honor and celebrate this diversity?
2. We often picture adoption as smiling and tearful parents with happy, chubby babies; for those of you who've experienced adoption in your extended family, how is this true and not true?
3. How have you or will you go about explaining what adoption is to your adopted or biological children?
4. What are some ways that the church (or individuals within it) can better support the spiritual health of adoptive parents?

5. Ryan bravely tells his family's story of adoption. How would you personally reach out to families that might be going through some of the same processes and struggles?

6. How might your church or Sunday school class honor social workers, caseworkers, adoption agency workers, foster parents, children's-home workers, and others who care for "the fatherless and widows" in your city?

7. How can being adopted affect a child's view of God?

8. In what ways is being an adopted child like being a Christian (Rom. 8:15–17)?

9. How do we become the brothers and sisters and mothers and fathers to adopted and foster kids in our city? How do we treat them as we do others?

Connection and Community

LIFE AMONG THE PEOPLE OF GOD

Monty McCulley

Students are going to find community somewhere.
I want them to find it among followers of Christ.

Those two statements have had a huge impact on me as someone who spends his life trying to share the saving message of Jesus with teens. As our own children reached elementary, middle, and high school, these statements have also made a huge impact on how my wife and I are raising them.

I grew up going to church. My family didn't just go to church services sometimes. We went to church all the time. (And yes, I do know that you can't go to church, you are the church.) As a result of always going to church, I had a close group of friends and families from our church that made up a loving, faith-based community in my life. Some were old and some were young. They were the people I went to church with, and many of us (especially the ones my age) spent a lot of time together outside of church. Eating together, hanging out, backyard burger nights, family camping trips, retreats, and pick-up football games—these people helped me grow up, helped me grow to love the Lord, and helped me start to understand what real community truly is.

After I graduated from college and spent a year teaching math to eighth-grade students in west Texas, I started serving in full-time youth ministry at a church. As a young youth minister I assumed that all teens found community mainly at church. If they didn't have a close connectedness to people at church, then I assumed they didn't have it anywhere. I know—it's a crazy assumption. But at the time, in my young and naïve mind, it made sense.

About two years into my youth ministry career, a girl in our church lost her dad. She hadn't been involved in church or in youth ministry much at all, but she did go to church with us. My wife and I knew her a little, but not well. Losing a parent is hard at any age, but it is especially difficult for a young person. We offered as much sympathy, love, and encouragement as we could.

Soon the day for the funeral came. It was at a local funeral home instead of at our church building. I remember walking into a funeral chapel that had standing room only. Our church family was there, but we were outnumbered by a group of people who seemed so close and so loving and so supportive of the family. They were hugging and loving this family—and specifically the children of the man who died—including the girl from our youth ministry. I soon learned they were people who had known the dad through work and through riding motorcycles together.

Again, in my young and naïve mind, I thought, "Why isn't our church the ones who are being the supportive and loving people who are holding this family up during this really tough time?" The simple answer: this family didn't really need us. They had a community. They had people in their lives who had come alongside them during this difficult time. They had love. They had support. They had encouragement. Simply put, they had community.

Starting with this event, and with a few other defining events during my early years of youth ministry, I realized that almost every teen who was a part of our youth ministry had community somewhere. The ones who weren't very involved at church had a group of close people in their lives outside our church. Now, we could stop here and talk about the need for community in all of our lives, but I think we all understand that God didn't intend for us to live alone. God intended for us to live our lives in relationship and community with others. And almost every teen I know finds that community somewhere.

Teens find community at school, in sports, in extracurricular activities, in clubs, in common interests, and in countless other places. Community and friendship can be found based on where you live, what you like, or what you are good at. There seems to be no end to possibilities when it comes to finding a group of people to connect with. If teens can't find a community of people at school, they usually find it among friends outside of school. Scouts, robotics, video gaming, a band, or a variety of other activities offer community to teens. Many of these places are beneficial.

Still, it seems that teens choose to be closest to one or two communities in their lives. This doesn't mean there aren't other places they find community, but it seems that they will generally have one community which prevails over the others. Students will not *just* be in community. It goes deeper. They *need* community. It may be a sports team, scouts, band, choir, or any number of groups of people. Again, this isn't a bad thing.

However, I want my children to find their closest community among followers of Christ. For our family, it has always made the most sense for those people to be from our church. I want my children and their closest friends to find their closest community among those who love the Lord and choose to live for him. I want them to have a place to belong, a place to grow, and a group of people in their lives who will help them through the ups and downs they will experience in their lifetime.

God Created Our Teens to Be Relational

We were made to be in relationship with other people. This reality takes us back to Genesis. In Genesis 2:18, God says it's not good for man to be alone. This isn't so much speaking of Adam's loneliness as it is showing human nature as communal. All through our lives relationships are vital. During our teen years we have a huge need to be in relationship with others. In fact, these years are the ones when we form and shape how we will interact and relate to others for the rest of our lives. Some teens find this really easy; others have some challenges when it comes to relating to people. As parents, we have a great opportunity and obligation to guide our children as they learn and grow in relationships with everyone around them. We can guide them in learning how to best relate to others and who will be positive influences on them.

It is important that we don't overlook this journey they are on. It would be easier to simply let them figure it out on their own. In actuality, there are some teens who will excel in this area without help from parents. However, most teens need some help at some point along the way in relating to others and finding the right people to relate to. Sometimes the people they will find to relate to are not ones who will have positive impact on their lives. When our children need guidance toward the right kind of friendships and the right kind of community, we have a great opportunity to help.

As we look at our teens or at the teens in our church, we must remember that it's important for them to find a wholesome community, because teens will become like the people they spend time with. It is a biblical truth you have probably seen lived out time and time again. "Do not be misled: 'Bad company corrupts good character'" (1 Cor. 15:33 NIV). In other words, you will become like the people you spend time with. While we can't force our children to associate only with specific people, we do have an opportunity to lovingly and gently help them. I've heard it said that we become like the average of the five people with whom we spend the most time. It's true that the kind of people you surround yourself with has an effect on your life. It's important for our children to understand the importance of surrounding themselves with people who won't drag them down.

As a youth minister, I've had the opportunity to see many students move through middle and high school into college. I have watched as some have made great choices. Even after college they continue to do well. I have watched as others have walked a different path, one that led to hurt and disappointment and pain. This pain is not just felt by the teen but also by their family. Watching students grow and make these decisions, I have noticed that the words from 1 Corinthians 15:33 remain true in their lives: our teens become like the people they spend time with. So as I think about how I want to help my own children or the teens in our church, I know that one incredibly important thing is to help them have people around them who have positive impact in their lives. I want them to be surrounded by a community of believers who will help them to grow in the Lord and follow Jesus.

What Does Real Community Look Like?

When Jesus walked this earth, he showed us what community should look like. Specifically, the way he loved and cared for his disciples is something we can learn a great deal from. Jesus's disciples spent a large amount of time with Jesus and with each other. For the three years of Jesus's ministry, he and his disciples did life together. He brought them into a caring community where they

> Strong and weak, wise and foolish, gifted or ungifted, pious or impious, the diverse individuals in the community are no longer incentives for talking and judging and condemning, and thus excuses for self-justification. They are rather cause for rejoicing in one another and serving one another.
>
> —Dietrich Bonhoeffer
> *Life Together,* 93

found love, belonging, and significance. Jesus's love for his disciples was obvious through his acts of encouragement, along with his support and comfort for them. He took time to his main objectives, but he also loved them so much that he lived life with them on a daily basis. It reminds me of the words from 1 Thessalonians 2:8 when Paul writes that he, Silas, and Timothy loved the Thessalonians so much that they didn't just share the gospel of God with them, but they shared their lives as well.

Throughout the Gospels we see an unmistakable love Jesus had for his disciples. Paul, Silas, and Timothy had the same love for the Thessalonians. Both are examples to us. If we care about teens and want to help them have life among the people of God, it's important to note that this was a love accompanied by action. It wasn't a surface-level love, nor was it a love only present on Sundays or Wednesdays. It was a love that was always active, caring at all times, and obvious to everyone.

If we're to help today's generation of teens be connected to the people of God, if we are to take seriously our call to disciple them in their relationship with the Lord, we have to show them a love that far surpasses the love of this world. God's people should be able to offer a kind of love that is better than any love shown by a non-believer. God is the creator of love, and God's people will be known by their love (John 13:33–35). Because of the love we've received from God and through the power of the Holy Spirit, we should be able to love better than any other people in the world.

As a result, the teens in our churches and even the teens in our community should notice a difference.

Are the teens in your church feeling loved by the people in your church in a way that is noticeably different than the love they are being shown by the world? Or are they coming to a church building, sitting through a worship service, talking to a few people they know, and then going home without ever really feeling an atmosphere of love which should be present among God's people? Holy love is rare in this world. A church that offers an atmosphere of love has a powerful appeal to teens.

The opposite is also true. A church that has animosity or underlying currents of resentment will repel teens instead of attracting them. Even worse, a church with these negative characteristics can cause a teen to question whether they should ever go to any church. In the book *You Lost Me*, David Kinnaman shares research on why young people stop attending church. Statistically, he says, 59 percent of people ages eighteen to twenty-nine who grew up attending church regularly no longer go to church. For many of them, the questions they have about culture, lifestyle, sexuality, or science were not answered at church. What a tragedy.

It was about two years ago when a high school student and his mom moved to our town. Not long after he arrived, he was talking to one of our students in a class at school. As they talked, the student from our church mentioned our church. The new student had been in and out of church his entire life. One Wednesday night he showed up. The next week he came back and he brought his mom.

He found connection and he found community among the students at our church. About a year after he started coming, he was baptized. This fall he is headed to college at a Christian university with some of our other students.

There are answers to these questions, and we need to have the kind of relationships with teens in which these subjects can be discussed. This dialogue will come naturally when relationships between young and old are strong. So what are we doing to create the conditions where relationships can really take root and grow? What are we doing to lay the groundwork for teens to be able to ask questions that matter to them? We need to be intentional about the having the kind of relationships in which the truth of Jesus is shared and faith grows.

Teens need to see a love among those who follow Christ that is genuine and deep, believers who will show them examples of how to love and how to walk together through good times and bad times. Powerful sermons will be meaningless if teens see people who talk about loving each other but don't live it out. They need to see believers who are intentional about community and stay involved in each other's lives. Jesus showed this kind of love to his disciples not only through his words, but also through his actions. It created community among his disciples and it can create community among his followers today.

What Helps Teens Feel Connected to a Church?

Many teens will say they believe in Jesus, but they don't see the importance of being a part of a church. Others will say they love Jesus, but they do not want to go to church because they don't like the people there, or they simply don't like being a part of the worship services or classes. An increasing number of teens would identify themselves as "nones"—meaning they have no religious affiliation at all. All teens need a church family. They need to be a part of the body of

For more information about "nones" and how to reach them, check out *The Rise of the Nones* by James Emery White.

Christ. So how do we adults and parents help them connect and stay connected to a church family? And how do we help teens who would consider themselves to be "nones"?

A study done by the Barna Group found that most positive church experiences are relational. Teens who had a close group of friends or a group of people to connect with (whether old or young) were more likely to remain active in a church through college and into adulthood. This study found that seven out of ten Millennials who dropped out of church didn't have a close friendship with an adult and nearly nine out of ten never had a mentor at church.[1] This is a wake-up call about the necessity of developing relationships with the next generation of believers.

I have always known that relationships are important, but I didn't know how important until one Sunday morning a few years ago. Trying to help teens see the importance of joining together for worship, I asked the question, "Why did you come to church today?" There were no answers like, "I love Jesus and want to worship God," or "I know it is important to be among other believers on Sunday morning," or "I love your teaching and want you to teach me more." Instead they simply said they wanted to be with their friends. Their number one answer for why they wanted to be at church was to see their friends. (I'm sure my teaching would have been the number two answer had I given them an opportunity to give additional answers.)

At first I was surprised. Surely these mature, Christ-following teens would want to come together simply because they love God. Instead, they came together because they like the community they found at church. The disappointment I encountered by learning that they did not come for my teaching was soon erased by the realization that community was helping our teens want to come to church. The fact that our teens wanted to be together gave us an opportunity to share the life-changing truth of Jesus with them. There were even teens who didn't grow up coming to church but came just because their friends were a part of our church. They came to our church seeking community, they found relationships with students and adults, and they found an atmosphere of love.

One of the blessings of church family is the fact that it is comprised of people of all ages. Church is one of the very few places in our society that are intergenerational. In almost every other aspect of our teens' lives, they are surrounded by other teens and a limited number of adults. Adults stay to themselves and teens stay to themselves. At church, however, teens are surrounded by people young and old. Older people have a unique opportunity to encourage, inspire, and disciple teens.

Kara Powell at Fuller Youth Institute has done extensive research into the lives of students. Her book, *Sticky Faith*, reveals that students who had at least five meaningful relationships with adults were much more likely to continue in their faith after high school. She calls it a 5:1 ratio, where five adults are intentionally involved in the life of a teen. This is a significant discovery, especially in light of how teens are often separated from adults. Teens need adults in their lives. They need adults who will love, encourage, and disciple them as they grow into adulthood. Relationships like this can have a profound impact on a teen.

Yet, having multiple generations together is an often overlooked and underappreciated asset of a church. Consequently, it's one that we often don't use very well. We should be maximizing this blessing of having old and young together. Frequently, teens will see older people but not receive encouragement from them. Or they will be physically close to adults, but relationally distant.

In our churches teens need to know the older people, and the older people need to know them. Not only do they need to know older people, they need to see the older people living out their faith well. They need to see the joy of the Lord living in their lives. This goes beyond a Sunday morning worship time. Teens need to know how to live out their faith in their daily lives outside of a church building. We have such a great opportunity to connect generations if we are intentional about these relationships.

One older gentleman at our church is closely connected to many of our teens. He takes time to talk to them. He takes time to listen. He has done this for years. Last year he retired from his job. He has started going to school activities such as concerts and games to encourage and support our teens. As I have watched him interact with our teens, I have noticed that he takes time to get to know our students while they are still young. As they move into their teen years, he already has a strong relationship with them. He has their respect because he has taken time to know them, even while they were children. As a result, he does not just have a relationship with our committed students. He has a relationship with many of our students who are struggling in their faith. Many of our graduating seniors each year mention him as a person who had a significant impact in their life. They see his faith as a faith worth imitating because his love for God is visibly seen in his love for people.

We have a great opportunity to help teens grow in their relationship with the Lord simply by being intentional in our relationships with them. These relationships need to be more than surface-level relationships. They need to be relationships that can walk through questions of life and questions of faith. They need to be relationships in which students see real and genuine faith in God being lived out by those older than themselves. The deeper the relationships go, the more impact they will have. If students have at least five caring adults involved in their life, as the research from *Sticky Faith* discovered, they will be more likely to have a strong faith in high school that continues into adulthood.

Would Teens Find Real Community or Just a Sense of Community at Our Church?

Community doesn't just happen. A close connection between people doesn't form overnight. It takes time to build, yet it will have a lasting effect in our lives. Even though groups we find ourselves in will come and go, each one leaves a place in our hearts and a mark on our lives. The same will be true for our youth.

Many teens struggle to find a group of people who have the love, acceptance, and encouragement that a true community should have. They can easily find a group of people who they have things in common with, but when it comes to finding true community, that's often a difficult task.

Groups with just a "sense" of community can look like the real thing. There may be love and acceptance and encouragement found in these places, but it may not be a place of real community. Adults sometimes have a difficult time telling the difference too. Facebook, fantasy football, and other social media can provide a sense of community without providing real community. While adults sometimes struggle with this, teens often have an even more difficult time.

For example, teens can find acceptance and encouragement via social media and text messaging. Some teens spend far more time communicating this way than face-to-face. They've found it's much easier to type out a few words on a screen than to have a real conversation with someone. It's not uncommon for teens to say they feel more accepted and understood by the people they text than by people they talk to face-to-face. They feel a sense of close connection with people they don't see. In some cases, there can be a sense of close connection with people they've never seen. This may provide a sense of community, but it's not the life-on-life community that our teens need.

Sherry Turkle, renowned MIT sociologist, calls this "phantom community." Turkle's book, *Reclaiming Conversation: The Power of Talk in a Digital Age*, describes this digital connection as something that produces a sense of attachment that feels like true community, but it's not. While text messaging and social media provide many good things, they shouldn't be a replacement to real community.

Now, let's think about community in our churches again. Do teens experience community or just a sense of community when they come to church? For many years our churches did youth ministry in a way that separated the teens from the adults. We had teens who were physically present in the same building as adults, but there was no sense of connectedness between the teens and adults. It was as if we targeted one of the best ways to help teens, intergenerational community, and took it away. That was a mistake. Teens need adults who will be intentional about being in relationship with them and will disciple them in faith.

True community happens when some specific things come together. Because community involves people, it only makes sense to evaluate some things about the relationships between the people and to think about what those relationships should include. To help do this, consider some of the "one another" passages in the New Testament. Notice some specific things that are present among groups of people who exhibit true, God-honoring community. One component of a faith community would be to "honor one another above yourselves" (Rom. 12:10 NIV). "Serve one another" (Gal. 5:13 NIV). "Build each other up" (1 Thess. 5:11 NIV). Some additional things would be found in true community, such as "forgive one another" (Col. 3:13 NIV), and "pray for each other" (James 5:16 NIV).

Those things we just identified—honor, serve, build up, forgive, and pray for each other—are in addition to components you would find even in places of shallow community. Even in shallow community, things like "love one another" (John 13:34), "encouraging one another" (Heb. 10:25), and "accept one another" (Rom. 15:7) are generally found. People in shallow community generally have some sort of love for each other. It may be a shallow love, but there is still a semblance. The same would be true for encouragement and acceptance. Still, in places where true community is found, you would find more than simply love and acceptance and encouragement.

One more verse describes the kind of community we want our teens to find: 2 Timothy 2:22. In this verse, Paul instructs Timothy to "pursue righteousness, faith, love, and peace, along with those who call on the Lord out of a pure heart." In other words, be the kind of person who is committed to things like righteousness and find a group of people who are doing the same. Be the kind of person who loves God and wants to follow God, and be in community with people who also love and want to follow God. This is great advice for our teens, and for us. That's the kind of church family I want our teens to find: a group of people who are actively pursuing righteousness, peace, and faith, while also being in relationship with other people who are seeking the Lord with a pure heart. When our churches do this, we are becoming more like the true community God wants us to be.

What Are Some Ways to Help Teens Be Connected to the Church?

In our years of mentoring teens, we have learned that students who aren't involved at church by the time they graduate from high school will likely not be involved in church afterward. Therefore, we involve them in serving as much as we can before they graduate. We place a high value on service, and because of this, we have teens teaching classes, leading in worship, greeting, leading small groups, taking communion to shut-ins, and countless other acts of service.

In a Christian community everything depends upon whether each individual is an indispensable link in a chain. Only when the smallest link is securely interlocked is the chain unbreakable. A community which allows unemployed members to exist within it will perish because of them. It will be well, therefore, if every member receives a definite task to perform for the community, that he may know in hours of doubt that he, too, is not useless and unusable.

—Dietrich Bonhoeffer
Life Together, 94

We take this further within our youth ministry by trying to help our teens have a *desire* to serve in any way needed.

This doesn't just happen. It's possible, though, to create a culture of involvement and service. We stumbled onto a great way to do this one Sunday morning. During class I asked for a volunteer to read a Bible verse in class. No one volunteered. I thought to myself, "Who would not want to read the Bible?" The answer, evidently, was our teens. So we came back the next week and, through some fun and laughter, we had everyone volunteer to read the Bible anytime I asked for someone to read. Over the next few months, this turned into a room full of students volunteering anytime we needed someone to say a prayer. And now it has become a culture where everyone volunteers for whatever is needed. When it's time to put up chairs or take out trash or set up for an event, everyone volunteers. Well, almost everyone. With only two or three students who don't want to volunteer, we definitely have a culture of serving and helping anytime there is a need. Not only does this help teens connect with teens, but service opportunities also help our teens connect to others within our church.

In addition to building a culture of service, churches can do some simple things to help teens be more connected to others. We are intentional about building intergenerational community by providing opportunities for teens to get to know adults and vice versa. Most of the time we do this by inviting adults into the teen activities or setting instead of asking teens to go into an adult class or setting. We have had some successes and some failures, but we haven't given up on helping our teens connect with the different age groups. We aren't going to give up on this because it's too important.

Ideas We Have Used or Have Seen Other Churches Use

The ideas listed below will help provide more opportunities for relationships to develop and for community to form.

Come-Early Wednesday Meal

About once a month, have a meal before class for all middle and high school students. Share the responsibility between parents or other adults. The food can be homemade or from a local restaurant. Occasionally, include families of the teens or the entire church. It's fun and it provides a chance for teens to spend time with each other and with our adult volunteers.

Pray for Students

There are many ways to do this, but we like to pray for students as they go back to school. On the Sunday before school starts, we put the names of every kindergarten through twelfth-grade student on individual cards on the back walls of our worship center. Those names are taken by adults or families who will pray for those students throughout the school year. We have done this in a variety of ways through the years, but it always includes having adults pray for students.

One church I know of has adults occasionally praying for students during their Wednesday night class. As class starts, they have students write prayer requests on cards. Those cards are then taken to the room next door where adults will pray for those requests and for all of the students during the entire class. This helps students know adults care for them and helps adults know specific things to pray about for students. Having students and adults praying together would be even better. Students are more likely to share deep prayer needs in writing than in person; still, praying together is a great thing.

Provide Opportunities for Teens to Share Their Story

Teens are encouraged when they hear the stories of other people, especially people they know. Years ago we asked a few students to pick a favorite Bible verse, share it in front of our Sunday night youth worship, and tell why they like it or think it is important. We wanted teens to be comfortable talking about the word of God, and this was a simple way to help them do that. It went so well that we kept on doing it. Eventually we added something we call "My Story." This is where teens prepare a five-to-eight-minute talk about something they have learned from God lately, or they tell something about their relationship with God. We do this in the context of a youth-led worship night, and our teens are excited to share a Bible verse or tell their story. A few times a year we invite parents to join us, and it's always a great time of encouragement.

Serve Together

Serving others is always a great thing to do and it helps build community among those who are serving. We do a lot of service activities within youth ministry, but we also try to plan events where families can serve together or where young and old serve together. These events have a huge impact on building community and friendship. Yard work, helping at a food bank, baking cookies for firefighters, picking up trash at a park . . . think of a need in your community and use people in your church to help meet that need.

Greeters at Worship Services

A few years ago we recognized a need to have greeters at the doors of our auditorium. We helped our teens know how to greet, we put bulletins in their hands, and each week for the past five years we have had teens greeting before worship. We then coached our parents and elders to be super-encouraging to our teens when they walk through the doors. Occasionally we pair up teens and older folks at the same door. Now every person who walks into our church on a Sunday morning is welcomed by our teens.

Include Teens in Worship

Most Sundays we have at least one middle school, high school, or college student lead a prayer, read a verse, lead a song, or be involved in leading worship in some way. It's not uncommon for us to have three or four young people doing something of this sort on the same day. We set them up for success by mentoring them in this role before we have them up front. This helps our teens be involved, it is an encouragement to the church, and it is an example to our elementary and younger students.

Hopefully these ideas will get you thinking about some things your church could do to help teens feel more connected to the church. I recognize that none of these ideas are profound, but they have helped our church. They all come from a strong desire we have to help teens find a place to belong at church and find a group of people with whom they can connect.

Final Thoughts

Imagine a church where young and old feel closely connected. A church that feels more like family than simply a group of people getting together to sing songs and listen to a message. Imagine a church where teens feel an overwhelming presence of love and a sense of belonging. A place where adults realize that the teens desperately need a saving relationship with the Lord, and the planning of activities, ministries, and worship services happen with this in mind. We need our churches to be places like this—places where teens can come, grow, and be sent out with a faith in God that is strong and steadfast.

Whether you're a parent, an elder, or an adult who loves teens, I encourage you to help make your church a thriving place where teens are encouraged and inspired to belong. Help them find community and faith. Your church may be the last church a teen goes to before they start life on their own after high school. Keep in mind that all of this is about Jesus and helping teens to know him. Jesus's last words were "go and make disciples." In other words, help people become followers of me, just as I have taught you to become a follower of me. May our families and churches be places where this happens. May we be praying continually for God to help us do this and to help our teens to love God more. With God's help, it is something that can be done, and the lives of teens in your church, and your lives, will be forever changed.

Questions

1. Why do we need to be in community with others?
2. Where do teenagers find community? Which of these communities is likely to be more present throughout their lives? Which might have the greatest impact?
3. What are some ways that we can make sure our children's most enduring community is church?
4. How can we adults make sure there are other times for our children to hang out with good friends at church besides Sundays and Wednesday nights?
5. How is the adolescent search for personal identity connected with their choice of communities?

6. Are there questions that teenagers aren't allowed to ask in your church? What would it take for your congregation to become more open to these challenging conversations?

7. Monty talks about teens experiencing the "sense" of community and the real thing. What are the differences between the two? How can your church community become more authentically community?

8. Sherry Turkle calls connection via social media a "phantom community." How is phantom community both helpful and harmful to experiencing real community for adolescents and adults?

9. Monty tells us that the "one another" passages in the Bible mark true community. How do Romans 12:10, Galatians 5:13, 1 Thessalonians 5:11, Colossians 3:13, and James 5:16 shape community for youth and adults together?

10. How can you purposefully surround your children with adults from church who live out the command to "love one another"?

11. How intentionally intergenerational is your church? What specific activities are done intentionally to connect the different generations at church and away from church?

12. What are ways that we can significantly include teens in the regular practice of worship (and not just "youth Sunday")?

13. What could your church do to "train" adults to be available to the children and teens in the church?

14. Make plans in your family Bible times to share all of the "one another" passages of Scripture during the year (see www .teendisciple.org).

LIFE WITH PEERS

Brad Childers

"You see that mountain over there? Yeah? Well, one of these days I'm gonna climb that mountain."[1]

I had a friend who was at the top of El Capitan on Wednesday, January 14, 2015, cheering and pulling ropes when Tommy Caldwell and Kevin Jorgeson became the first to free-climb the Dawn Wall of America's largest rock. Free climbing means using one's hands and feet to ascend a rock's natural features, employing ropes and other gear only to stop a fall.

This same friend taught me how to backpack up a mountain. I still remember that first trip we took with our youth group out to the Rockies when I was in ninth grade. A decade later, he led the youth group I now minister to on our first weeklong backpacking trip on the Appalachian Trail. Over the past twenty years, as a youth group, we have completed over seven hundred miles of the trail—from Springer Mountain, Georgia, through the whole state of Maryland. We love to climb mountains.

A mountain that needs to be climbed can be viewed as an obstacle in the way of your destination or as the adventure of a lifetime. Adventures are not always safe; they are awesome—filled with highs and lows—but not safe. I am reminded of one conversation in C. S. Lewis's *The Lion, the Witch, and the Wardrobe.*

> "Aslan is a lion—the Lion, the great Lion."
> "Ooh," said Susan. "I'd thought he was a man. Is he—quite safe? I shall feel rather nervous about meeting a lion." . . .
> "Safe?" said Mr. Beaver . . . "Who said anything about safe? 'Course he isn't safe. But he's good. He's the King, I tell you."[2]

Because of the perils of beautiful vistas and awaiting pitfalls, the climbing of a mountain and the adventure of maturing into a Christian young lady or man require courage, perseverance, companionship, and intentionality. With some planning and vision, a walk in the woods can become an awesome expedition.

Studies by the Barna Group and others reveal the mountain of issues teens have to climb. Some of those problems include bullying, depression, substance abuse, cyber addictions, competition, grades, self-esteem, body image, eating disorders, sexuality issues, stress, and family issues. These are but a sample of the obstacles teens face as they climb through adolescence.

Because of these obstacles, an intentional plan for traversing the mountain of adolescence is needed. As with any good adventure, the journey is better made with others. The highs are higher and the lows are, well, not as low. Climbing mountains should not be attempted alone. It is the same with parenting teenagers. Don't attempt this alone. Other chapters in this book discuss the advantages of having multiple, like-minded adults in your children's lives. As we think of the spiritual journey that our teens are on, their peers can also play a positive role in that journey. We know that as our children reach middle school and high school, their peers become a bigger influence (a function of the quantity of time spent with them).[3] We know that peers can provide companionship, love and encouragement, identity, discernment, and accountability in the lives of other teens.[4] This chapter will explore how you as a parent can facilitate good peer relationships for your teenagers.

The Need for Companionship

Climbing a mountain is a great and humbling adventure, but not an easy task. It takes commitment, time, and training. The payoff includes fun, satisfaction, and beautiful vistas. All of that is great when the sun is shining or the stars are out. I am reminded, though, of a trip one July when we were about to cross a 1.4-mile bald mountaintop with a 360-degree view on a clear day, but this day wasn't clear at all. As we exited the tree line, thunder and lightning began. Then sleet hit us horizontally. The temperature dropped almost fifty degrees, and our group began to sprint (not the wisest thing ever) across the top of the bald terrain. By the time we reached the other side of the mountaintop, our teens began to show signs of hypothermia. We threw tents up and began putting them into sleeping bags to get their body heat up. Amazingly, all of this happened in the middle of July. That day I witnessed teens and adults helping their peers struggling with the cold. Good companions multiply the joys and temper the obstacles we face.

One of the major rules of climbing is that you never climb alone. In 2003, Aron Rolston headed into Utah's Bluejohn Canyon—alone—to complete what should have been an eight-hour hike (this story is now a movie titled *127 Hours*). During the hike Rolston dislodged an eight-hundred-pound boulder that pinned his arm. After he was held hostage by the boulder for five days, Rolston determined that the only way for him to survive was to self-amputate his arm to free himself from the giant rock. Rolston, an experienced hiker, was actually a member of a rescue council. But he didn't heed one of the cardinal rules of any outdoorsman—you never hike alone. A hiking companion is as much a necessity as food and water. Companions matter just as much to our youth. Our teens don't have to go through adolescence alone. We as parents can facilitate the connection with significant adults. We can also have an influence on the peers our sons and daughters run around with.

Let's squeeze another drop of truth out of the hiking meta-phor. Hiking with a friend provides bonding opportunities. On the Appalachian Trail, thirty of us may be spread out over a two-mile span as we backpack on any given day. However, you are never, ever, to be out of sight of another person on the trail. This maxim obviously provides safety, but something else usually happens—you talk. You pass the time. You share. You laugh. You bond. A companion is someone who spends a lot of time with others. Samia Nawaz emphasizes the importance of companions for adolescents:

> Peer influence is also considered a very strong and pow-erful aspect of adolescent life. They choose their friends who accept them, like them, and see them as encour-aging and helpful. Consequently, the impact of peers, whether positive or negative, is of critical importance for personality development during adolescence.[5]

The quality of peers and friends is of utmost importance for the success of the climb through adolescence.

I have watched teens over the years branch out in their rela-tionships and stray from those who are able to build them up. I remember one teen who became committed to the players and the influence of his high school basketball team to the exclusion of his Christian friends. You could tell immediately by his attitude, disposition, and language that he was acting differently. After a brush with an illegal substance led to a fight, the teen decided to return to his Christian friends. Confession, grace, and forgiveness were extended, and we saw a positive change.

You might ask, "Does that mean teens are to hang out only with good influences or Christians? I thought Jesus said we are to 'go into all the world.'" He did, but he sent disciples out in pairs (Luke 9 and 10). Each worker had a companion. It is not that God wants our teens to stay isolated in a holy huddle. The issue is that most of our teens, because of the lack of discipleship, do not depend enough on the Lord. In other words, they lack the faith to stand on their own and be the light God is calling them to be. This fact makes us ask why. Why are our teens not strong enough?

One reason teens are not strong enough is because many of them have an incorrect view of a relationship with God. That view has been taught by the church, modeled by parents, and in some ways resourced by youth ministries.[6] Whenever you plan a backpacking trip (at least section hiking on the Appalachian Trail), you have a beginning point, fifty miles or so of hiking, and an end point. The beginning point is called the trailhead. The end point is called the terminus. For many of our Christian teens, the trailhead is represented by the time they gave their lives to Christ and professed him as their Lord and Savior. This represents only the beginning, not the terminus.

I have had conversations with so many parents who, after baptizing their second of three children say, "Two down, one to go," as if they are almost finished. This special beginning time represents an important step in the discipleship process, but it is not the end, the terminus. During this important step, your son or daughter is publicly announcing their walk with Christ. They are still babes in Christ. It is your responsibility to help them grow into spiritual adults. You don't spend a ton of money on a backpack, boots, food, and gear to take your teen to the trailhead and say, "You made it. Now let's go home." No! Once you get to the trailhead, you are ready for a new step in the ongoing journey of discipleship. What lies ahead are many peaks, valleys, bruises, laughs, blisters, sleepless nights, harsh words, and glorious conversations. The terminus of the trail is when we die and go to be with the Lord. One reason our teens aren't strong enough to carry light into the world is because we've often mixed up the terminus and the trailhead.

The positive influence of peers can help on that journey. Researchers tell us, "During adolescence, close friends begin to rival and in some cases surpass parents as adolescents' primary source of social support and contribute in important ways to adolescents' self-concept and well-being."[7] The Bible speaks about this type of relationships. Remember the warning in 1 Corinthians 15:33 that says, "Do not be misled: 'Bad company corrupts good character'" (NIV). An old adage acknowledges, "It's difficult to soar with the eagles when you're scratching with the turkeys!" In a given teen's day, either eagles or turkeys could be the crowd the teen associates with in his or her environment. Many teens attend schools or live in neighborhoods that reflect, not Christ, but the world. Projects like "Sticky Faith" and others have revealed that the forces that have the most spiritual influence on teens are parents, grandparents, teachers, coaches, and ministers in that order. Richard Dunn and Janan Sundene remind us that "in every country and culture, the key factor that determines whether young adults are thriving or simply surviving is always the same: the availability and accessibility of teachers, coaches, pastors, friends, and mentors who are committed to investing in their spiritual vitality."[8] One could say that those whom teens spend the most time with are the ones with the most propensity for positive influence. It could also be stated that those whom teens spend the most time with are the ones with the most propensity for negative influence. The fact is, our youth are going to spend time with peers and friend groups. Who they hang out with matters immensely.

There is the opportunity for positive peer pressure as well as negative. Peer pressure becomes one of the biggest peaks teenagers have to climb. The external pressure peers apply is monumental. If parents aren't active in their teens' lives, peers and friends who do not hold the same values you want your teen to possess may become the negative influence all parents fear. Doesn't Romans 7:21–24 speak of this climb? "So I find this law at work: Although I want to do good, evil is right there with me. For in my inner being I delight in God's law; but I see another law at work in me, waging war against the law of my mind and making me a prisoner of the law of sin at work within me. What a wretched man I am! Who will rescue me from this body that is subject to death?" (NIV). Surrounded by bad influences, even a teenager who knows what is right and wants to do well may give in to the temptation of the moment. This fact magnifies the importance of parents knowing their teenager's peers and friends. Invest time in them. Have them in your home. Pray for them. Acknowledge and thank your teenager for choosing good peers and friends.

As you can see, as teens climb the mountain, their peer relationships are incredibly important because of the impact they make.

Influencing the Choice of Friends

So how do parents intentionally influence their teen's choice of peers and friends? Over fourteen thousand books on Amazon have something to do with parenting teens. Just 157 of them speak about "intentionally" parenting. No matter how old your children are, as you read this, please remember that you are in charge, and you are charged. Good research about families helps us understand the dynamics of relationships. Even though you may feel sometimes that your teen is listening to his or her friends more than to you, you are still the major player. You must be intentional about the journey your teen is on. We know that parents can influence their children's peer and friendship networks by

1. choosing the environment that their family is part of;
2. monitoring their children (although avoiding being a drone parent);
3. modeling desirable behavior;
4. simply teaching good social skills; and most important,
5. maintaining a quality relationship with their teen.[9]

What would these five practices look like in your home?

Choosing the Environment

Well, for starters, let's go back to our mountain-climbing analogy. When I prepare for a hike or climb, I get the maps out. I bring in my trusted companions who have traveled miles with me. We choose trails that will give our teens a good challenge and a good chance of successfully completing their task. This is the kind of smart planning all parents should do for their teens. Currently, most of us in North America can pick where we live, where we go to school, and where we go to church. It may not seem like it, but these choices are critical logistics that should be taken seriously, especially if you are having trouble with your teenager. Many parents have moved to have their children in a different school district to take advantage of specific programs that were not available at other schools. Environment does have an influence on all of us. Some folks, though, may be stuck in places they can't escape. You can still counter any bad influences in the environment by working on the items mentioned above and described in more detail below.

Monitoring Teens

When researchers discuss monitoring children and teens, they are usually referring to more of a supervising role (not helicopter or drone parenting, which is detrimental to our children[10]). While our goal as parents is to launch our teens to be independent, they still need guidance, especially in their choice of peers and friends. Good monitoring includes simple things like knowing who your teen is hanging out with, knowing they are where they say they are, having them call if there are changes, knowing the parents of your teen's peers and friends. being available 24/7 to come to their side if they need to be rescued, making sure that *your* home is a safe and hospitable place for your teen to hang out with peers. These and other suggestions have been documented by the CDC (Centers for Disease Control and Prevention). This government agency brought together a panel of researchers and put together a book entitled, *Parental Monitoring of Adolescents: Current Perspective for Researchers and Practitioners.*[11] Following are some of the suggestions from that book on monitoring teens.

- Talk with your teen about your rules and expectations, and explain the consequences for breaking the rules.
- Talk and listen to your teen often about how he or she feels and what he or she is thinking.
- Know who your teen's friends are.
- Talk with your teen about the plans he or she has with friends, what he or she is doing after school, and where he or she will be going.
- Set expectations for when your teen will come home, and expect a call if he or she is going to be late.
- Ask whether an adult will be present when your teen is visiting a friend's home.
- Get to know your teen's boyfriend or girlfriend.

- Get to know the parents of your teen's friends.
- Talk with your relatives, your neighbors, your teen's teachers, and other adults who know your teen. Ask them to share what they observe about your teen's behaviors, moods, or friends.
- Watch how your teen spends money.
- Keep track of how your teen spends time online, and talk about using the Internet safely.
- Pay attention to your teen's mood and behavior at home, and discuss any concerns you might have.
- If your teen does break a rule, enforce the consequences fairly and consistently.
- Make sure your teen knows how to contact you at all times.

So once again, peers and friends are a crucial part of your teen's life. The adolescent years speed by quickly. They are a time for exploring, for taking risks. That is one reason we do backpacking trips with our teens. It lets them explore and teaches them how to take calculated risks alongside their peers, with experienced adults near. Be near your teen during this exciting climb up the mountain.

Modeling

When I think of Deuteronomy 6:4–9, I think more about intentionally being *around* my children, mainly so they can *watch* me being the role model they need in their lives. This is intentional modeling of how I lie, sit, and walk around with God. Every day our kids see the model of how I treat my spouse. This is an opportunity for them to see "the greatest commands" lived out in the flesh. The old adage "I'd rather see a sermon that hear one" certainly rings true here. I need my children to see me with my peers, to see how I interact with my peers. I have a friend who has climbed some of the highest mountains in the world. Before attempting these climbs, he trained for them and sought out people who had been there and done it—and lived. He wanted to talk and plan with folks who were good models for climbing those specific mountains. You can buy many books about mountain climbing, but there is no substitute for finding successful climbers and modeling yourself and your climb after them.

Social Skills

When our children choose peers, the resulting relationships become some of the tightest friendships they have. Typically they become friends because they "fit in" or have things in common, which is important to teens. Good social skills are a great gift you can give your teen to help empower them to fit in. Teach them how to meet and greet people. Teach them how to be interested in others (teach them altruistic values). Teens that don't "fit in" usually feel like loners, or losers, or misfits. They end up hanging out with negative influences—fringe groups, deviant groups, gangs—because there they are accepted, given purpose, and rewarded. Research on gangs demonstrates that even in the face of the powerful attraction of these groups, the practices mentioned here can be used to help teens make better choices about who they have as their community. I realize that Jesus chose to hang out with the "least of these," yet I am thinking that he was a wise, mature man, and we are talking here about teens. And, of course, Jesus was God—we aren't!

Teaching your children and teens good social skills equips them to know people better and to make better decisions about who to hang out with. When Jesus was asked what the greatest command was, he didn't hesitate to say, "Love the Lord your God with all your heart and with all your soul and with all your mind." He immediately added that the second greatest command is, "Love your neighbor as yourself."[12] Most of the time we think there are two parts to this passage of scripture. There are three parts. "As yourself" is critical. If a person doesn't love themselves (though not in a narcissistic way), they will not love others. Teaching our children social skills helps them to better know themselves and the people around them. It helps them to "love others." You will empower your children to make good choices if you equip them with skills that focus on listening, managing conflict, being part of a group, caring about others, communicating, being able to express what they feel, and learning how to stand up for themselves. These skills will point them toward good choices in peers and friends. Please see our companion website for this book (www.teendisci ples.org) and check out the resources about teaching social skills.

Maintaining a Quality Relationship

Finally, in this list of ways to influence your teen's choice of peers, maintaining a quality relationship with your teen may be the most important factor of all. We are so busy. Many of us work with people all day long and when we get home, we are peopled-out. We need our space. Our teen notices this, because teens need their own space too. Please remember that even though this chapter is about peers, we as the parents are still high on the influence list of our children. Keep baby pictures of your teen in your wallet to remind you that this child is the same one you brought into life a few years ago, the same child that has God's fingerprints all over him or her.

Quality and quantity aren't the same thing, but both are needed. Figure out at least one time a week when you can have some one-on-one time with your teen. Find something you both like to do and do it together. Find out what your teen is interested in and learn something about it and talk about it. Your teen might even be able to teach you a thing or two. Watch your attitude. The fallen world often makes adults bitter, stressed, cynical, and downright mean sometimes. Don't bring this home. Lighten up. Watch a funny movie together. Keep laughter in your home. Make sure you *do* your faith in front of your teen. Forgive, love others, serve others—and take your teen with you. We all have rules to live by. Teach that to your teen. Don't try to be your child's peer or friend. They need you to be an adult.

The period of adolescence represents a time of transformation in social relationships. Adolescents spend increasing time in activities with peers without supervision of adults such as parents and teachers. This provides opportunities for teens to be themselves as they test their faith in making godly decisions with their new freedom. However, as Engles, Deković, and Meeus remind us, "Despite the increasing relevance of peer relationships, parents do not . . . become less relevant in shaping adolescents."[13] As teens experience more risk, it is the quality of the parental relationship that continues to be a positive factor in a teen's decision-making processes. As teens traverse the Appalachian Trail or climb the mountain of spiritual maturity, it is important to have intentionally intergenerational relationships that can speak into their lives in a non-threatening way while they climb to new plateaus. As Karen Choi notes, "Since youth pastors and teachers are limited in their capacity to build deep relationships with many adolescents, it seems crucial that more adults from the congregation become involved in YM [youth ministry] functions to spend time with youth, hear their stories, and love them."[14]

An Extended Family

As we bring this chapter to a close, I am reminded of ongoing studies about teens and faith, some of them mentioned by other contributors in this book. As we become a global society, our families are spreading out. No longer, like my grandparents, do our families settle down with all of our extended family living in the same neighborhood or town. "Parents who are not blessed with grandparents, siblings, and cousins nearby may need to do a bit more work to form a web of relationships, but opportunities abound at church, in the neighborhood, at your child's school, or at your child's activities."[15] The first thing my climbing friend did when he began teaching me about rock climbing was to teach me the importance of a harness. That harness is connected by a carabiner to a rope. That rope is connected to my climbing friend. He provides a *web* of safety for me. One of our jobs as parents, youth workers, and peers is to—like a carabiner—link people to our teens. "Often the best web is created when you can give as well as receive support for your children."[16]

The spiritual journey of the life of a teen is as beautiful and daunting as climbing a mountain like El Capitan. Even though my climbing friend does really great things (like holding the web of safety ropes at the top of El Capitan for the world-record climbers), he continues to teach me to be a better rock climber. The Quakers have a peer-group process that is designed for friends to discern together how to carry out life. They feel this is a ministry process. The idea is that your teen and his/her peers get together anyway, so why not approach those times from a spiritual perspective. With little adaptation, your teen and his/her peers can teach each other how to listen, how to pray about things that matter, and how to hold each other accountable (all of which sounds like making disciples). Once again, we use the word *intentional*. We parents need to provide the space in our homes or churches for peers to have this type of interaction. Our youth are going to get together somewhere. With a little direction and given the freedom to run their own peer group, this method may be valuable to some. Much information on this method and other spiritual information can be accessed on the Internet.[17]

Colleges and universities are well aware of the power of peers. Some even have peer chaplains. These students are trained to listen, to be nonjudgmental, to practice radical acceptance, and to provide a ministry of presence.[18] The advantage of being a peer advisor at one school[19] is evident in the following training areas:

Leadership	Supervision	Dependability
Assertiveness	Ministry/Service	Referral
Listening Skills	Coordination/Planning	Time Management
Delegation	Program Development	Helping Skills
Responsibility	Confrontation	Self-Management
Conflict Mediation	Team Building	

Great skills and traits for any teen. This should give you an idea of some areas you could address while spending quality time with your teen. Doing so will help them help their peers.

While schools recognize the importance of peers influencing peers, we as parents are concerned on a much different level—the spiritual. Good churches recognize the peer-to-peer relationship and its importance. Some churches have specific peer ministries that realize the need to teach the young. David Kinnaman of Barna Research reports that Millennials (our teens) want to put skills to use with their peers. Specifically, he discusses the concept of "reverse mentoring," where our young believers discover their own mission in the world *now*, not later when they are adults.[20]

Peers are important; they are a critical piece of our mountain-climbing gear. "The key factor that determines whether young adults are thriving or simply surviving is always the same: the availability and accessibility of teachers, coaches, pastors, friends, and mentors who are committed to investing in their spiritual vitality."[21] The Lord has created the church to function as a family, a sticky web, if you will. This web is created not by blood relation, but by the blood of Christ. Climbing the mountain of spiritual maturity is hard stuff. To reach the summit, the web of love needs to be connected to: 1) peers who have the same values you have instilled in your teen, 2) parents who are teaching their teens good peer skills and, 3) other significant adults who realize the value of peer-to-peer relationships.

Most of our teens are going to have friends. Most are going to have close friends. Helping them choose good ones will be a giant step toward keeping our teens on the transformative journey toward owning their own faith as they begin their lifelong hike to heaven.

Questions and Exercises

1. Brad points out that one way we help our children find peers is by "choosing the environment." What does he mean by this? What are the challenges in these choices for Christians aware of their mission?
2. How can we "monitor our children" without becoming helicopter parents? Talk about some specific practices.
3. Write down the names of your children's best friends and in what context they know them.
4. How do our interactions with our peers, our business associates, or our social circle model healthy peer relationships for our youth?
5. Brad mentions bullying, depression, substance abuse, cyber addictions, competition, grades, self-esteem, body image, eating disorders, sexuality issues, stress, and family issues, as challenges that our teens face today. What help does your church offer you and others in any of these areas?

6. What are the key social skills that youth need as they enter adolescence? What are the more advanced skills they will need over time? How can we monitor and coach these?

7. What do you think is the significance of Jesus sending his disciples out in twos? What lessons can we learn from that method for our teens today?

8. What might a teenager teach us about quality relationships?

FRIENDS, MENTORS, HEROES:
Connecting with Other Generations

David Fraze

The call came on the first day of my 2008 research with the Fuller Youth Institute (FYI). "David, I need some advice!"

After almost twenty years of experience in youth ministry and education, I came to study with FYI because I couldn't shake the feeling that something was not right about how we were teaching and practicing youth ministry. The evidence suggesting that 40–50 percent of our students leave Christianity after high school graduation heightened my concerns.[1] So my wife and I loaded up our family, packed them into a Pasadena apartment, and spent two months thinking deeply about youth ministry. Specifically, I was at Fuller to research intergenerational strategies for youth ministry—youth ministry practices designed to create opportunities for spiritual growth across generational lines. The youth leader seeking advice on the other end of the phone call was a dear friend, a veteran youth worker, and a youth ministry professor whose experience eclipses mine by at least ten years (he's old!). Our conversation went something like this:

> "I am not sure it is working," my friend volunteered.
> "What's not working?" I asked.
> "The way we are programming and teaching youth ministry."

He continued to explain how the kids he knew who were part of the 50 percent that "made it" would probably have been okay with or without the youth ministry programming that had been offered them. Sure, the youth ministry had strengthened the faith of those students and provided them with valuable learning opportunities and great relationships. But, in his opinion, the students who developed into and remained committed disciples ended up that way because they had come from strong, intact, and engaged families who were themselves connected to strong, intact, and engaged communities of faith. His concern was with the other 50 percent and the way youth ministry education must change in order to equip future youth workers to reach the students whose faith is not nurtured by strong, intact, and engaged adult relationships.

Does any part of this conversation sound familiar?

Has your experience with youth ministry led you to the same line of questioning?

If so, "Welcome!"

If we step back from the youth ministry carnival of activity for a moment, many of us might come to a similar conclusion. Ask yourself this question: Out of all the programming teenagers have participated in through the years, what has worked to build long-term, committed followers of Jesus? (Go ahead, ask yourself the question.) Follow up with a second question: In all that programming, how many times was the "real ministry" moment a conversation on the car, van, or bus ride back from an activity? The crazy thing about discipling teenagers is that we don't always know when those real ministry moments are going to occur. We expect them to occur after the emotional youth conference appeal, but they are just as likely to occur after the annual baby oil/shampoo slip-and-slide contest (I'm not making this up; this really happened to me). Perhaps the best programming is that which creates moments for meaningful experience and conversation. If your experience is anything like mine, your favorite real ministry moments may have been facilitated by a certain programmatic event but are ultimately memorable because of the parents, adults, and other members of the community of faith who shared the moment with you (Appendix One provides a great resource for solidifying the impact adults have on spiritual formation).

I suggest that an evaluation of traditional youth ministry practice reveals our unintentional tendency to undervalue the role of parents and adult volunteers. It also explains the separation of age groups at church. To be fair, many parents and adult leaders seem to prefer and support this type of segregated youth ministry practice. They prefer opportunities to participate in classes and worship services specifically targeted to their own adult interests, while someone else is "watching" the kids. However, if my friend on the phone call is right and the teenagers who continue in a long-term, committed discipleship journey are those who come from strong, intact, and engaged families and/or are connected to adults who provide supportive, familial relationships, then youth ministry teaching and practice may need some major retooling in order to support and foster more vibrant teen/adult relationships.

What Does Intergenerational Mean?

People often joke that I cannot conduct a youth ministry training without using the word *intergenerational* at least one time during the presentation. Well, the joke has validity because the term is important in understanding how adults connect with students in student ministry.

Intergenerational youth ministry. An intergenerational youth ministry approach views the roles of parents *and* the surrounding adult community as the *primary influence* in a student's spiritual formation. As a result, intergenerational youth ministry programming is designed to create opportunities for spiritual growth across generational lines.

Intergenerational ministry should not be confused with *family-based youth ministry.* The family-based approach, while closely related (and valuable), focuses primarily on the nuclear family unit. An intergenerational approach, while honoring and working with nuclear family units, focuses on employing the *entire* adult faith community in youth ministry strategies.

Intergenerational youth ministry should likewise not be confused with *inclusive youth ministry programming.* Inclusive strategies work towards eliminating age-specific ministry programs altogether. Intergenerational strategies work to bring the generations together in meaningful ways while still offering programs that meet the specific age-appropriate needs of adolescent believers.

Intergenerational youth ministry should also not be confused with *multigenerational programming.* Multigenerational puts the generations in the same ministry "space" but does little to put the various age groups into meaningful contact or dialogue.

With these definitions out of the way, let us move on to better understand the evidence that we need a renewed engagement with adults so that we turn them into the friends, mentors, and heroes of our youth ministries.

Support for Intergenerational Programming

If you think back to your elementary school days for a moment, you will probably remember you or someone else giving the four-word challenge: "Oh yeah? Prove it!"

The essence of the "prove it" challenge is the need we all feel to back up our words. Well, it is time for those of us who have been proclaiming the importance of intergenerational youth ministry to back up intergenerational youth ministry as more than just another programming fad (yes, it is going to seem like a classroom—keep reading and notice the endnotes).[2]

Support in the Old Testament

As we think about scriptural patterns for educating children, it's logical to start with the Old Testament. At least twice in previous chapters of this book my fellow writers have quoted Deuteronomy 6:4–9. With good reason. These foundational instructions gave the people of Israel their most basic cues as to what was expected of them in the spiritual formation of their biological children as well as the children of their community. Let me repeat it here, since these words form the basis of our thoughts on the pages just ahead.

> Hear, O Israel: The LORD our God, the LORD is one.
> Love the LORD your God with all your heart and with all
> your soul and with all your strength. These command-
> ments that I give you today are to be on your hearts.
> Impress them on your children. Talk about them when
> you sit at home and when you walk along the road,
> when you lie down and when you get up. Tie them as
> symbols on your hands and bind them on your fore-
> heads. Write them on the doorframes of your houses
> and on your gates. (NIV)

Most of us have probably read, sung, contemplated, and written this section of Scripture. A deeper examination of these verses reveals two principles that support intergenerational philosophy and programming for youth ministry.

Principle #1

Parents and the surrounding community of adults are expected to exemplify what it means to be fully devoted followers of God.

This expectation of total devotion is indicated in several portions of the Deuteronomy 6 passage. First, to declare "The LORD our God, the LORD is one . . ." is no small matter. It is a covenant agreement in which the people of Israel agree to follow the "one and only God" with absolute loyalty and obedience.[3] This pledge of allegiance, often read aloud, starting with the words, "Hear, O Israel," is a "summons to those who would be Israel in any age"[4] to align themselves with the work and will of the Lord. Following the pattern of the Near Eastern ruler/subject relationship (also known as the suzerain/vassal relationship), the Israelites (the subjects) are agreeing to give three parts of themselves to the Lord: their undivided loyalty (their heart), their physical assets and talents (their might), and their own lives if necessary (their soul). In other words, Israel is entering into a legal, covenant agreement when they recite these words.[5]

What is the connection between wholehearted devotion and a theology of intergenerational youth ministry? Research shows, whether for good or bad, that children follow the spiritual lead set by their parents and the surrounding adult community.[6] The results of less than wholehearted devotion from parents, community members, and, to be fair, children are highlighted in the book of Judges. Recalling the failure of the generation who originally received the Deuteronomy 6 admonition, Judges 2:10–11a records: "After that whole generation had been gathered to their ancestors, another generation grew up, who knew neither the LORD nor what he had done for Israel. Then the Israelites did evil . . ." (NIV).

At a fundamental level, the positive example of Deuteronomy 6 and the negative example of Judges 2 remind us of the impact of modeling in our intergenerational relationships.

Principle #2

Adults, starting with parents, are commanded to be active participants in their children's spiritual formation.

Several portions of the Deuteronomy 6 passage indicate parental and community involvement in a child's spiritual formation. First, "*impress them on your children*" is a phrase that indicates the parents' responsibility and agreement to teach their children about the Lord. At the time when Moses authored this passage, the spiritual formation of children included the use of both formal and informal opportunities to teach, and it centered on the telling of family, tribal, and national historical narratives of the Exodus and the experience of living in covenant relationship with the Lord.[7] Second, the words "talk . . .walk . . . lie down . . . get up . . . tie . . . write," are action verbs that indicate constant process. The phrase "on your forehead" indicates the Lord's desire that, through formal teaching and the witness of right living in the lives of parents and the surrounding adult community, God's ways remain "between the eyes" of children.[8]

Deuteronomy 6:4–9 specifically mentions the responsibility of parents in the spiritual formation of children. So what level of responsibility does the overall community have in the process? Historically in Israel, families carried out their formational responsibility in the context of the broad community. Supplementing the education received in the home was a sequence of festivals and observances that provided instructional opportunities for the whole Israelite community.[9] Read the following verses and imagine the impact such an occasion would have had on the children in attendance.

> At the end of every seven years, in the year for canceling debts, during the Festival of Tabernacles, when all Israel comes to appear before the LORD your God at the place he will choose, you shall read this law before them in their hearing. Assemble the people—men, women and children, and the foreigners residing in your towns—so they can listen and learn to fear the LORD your God and follow carefully all the words of this law. Their children, who do not know this law, must hear it and learn to fear the LORD your God as long as you live in the land you are crossing the Jordan to possess. (Deut. 31:10–13 NIV)

I believe Eugene Peterson casts an appropriate vision for the ongoing interface between family and community in kids' spiritual formation in his paraphrase of Deuteronomy 6:4–9:

> Attention, Israel! God, our God! God the one and only! Love God, your God, with your whole heart: love him with all that's in you, love him with all you've got! Write these commandments that I've given you today on your hearts. Get them inside of you and then get them inside your children. Talk about them wherever you are, sitting at home or walking in the street; talk about them from the time you get up in the morning to when you fall into bed at night. Tie them on your hands and foreheads as a reminder; inscribe them on the doorposts of your homes and on your city gates. (*THE MESSAGE*)

Support in the New Testament

The experience and teachings of both Jesus and Paul mirror and often intensify the principles of intergenerational ministry already highlighted from Deuteronomy 6.[10]

Principle # 1

Jesus lived life as a fully devoted follower of God.

Jesus demonstrated the significance of Deuteronomy 6:4–9 by quoting from it when asked by the Pharisees to identify the greatest commandment (Matt. 22:35–40).[11] Akin to the "with all your soul" dedication of Deuteronomy 6, Jesus demonstrated his obedience to God unto death (Phil. 2:8). Jesus requires the same full, cross-bearing devotion from those who make the commitment to follow him (Luke 14:26–27).

Principle # 2

Jesus's spiritual formation was impacted by his parents and surrounding adult community.

This impact is seen in the various temple dialogues, his temple experience as a twelve-year-old, his "lost experience," and his submission to his parents' will (Luke 2:21–52). Jesus's knowledge of the Law and his ability to read Hebrew indicates that he may have been a participant in the local school system established by the high priest in the first century.[12] This would be a further indication of the community's involvement in Jesus's education.

Principle #3

Jesus spoke of adults as active participants in a child's spiritual formation.

Jesus strongly opposed[13] the disciples who were attempting to keep children away from him (Mark 10:13–14). Jesus welcomed children into his crowded schedule and urged others to do the same in his name (Matt. 18:5). The use of the term "in my name" in Matthew 18:5 highlights Jesus's desire that his disciples accept children because that is exactly what he would do.[14] So passionate was Jesus that he said of those who cause children to sin that it would be best for them if they would jump into the sea with a large millstone tied around their neck (Matt. 18:6).

Principle #4

Paul was a fully devoted follower of Jesus.

The apostle Paul, highly educated in the Jewish education traditions (Acts 22:3–5) and the New Testament's most prolific writer, demonstrates similar connections to the principles highlighted from Deuteronomy 6:4–9. Paul's wholehearted devotion to God is seen before and after his conversion. He demonstrated his devotion to Christ by remaining faithful through tremendous persecution and knowledge of his own impending martyrdom (2 Cor. 11:22–30; 2 Tim. 4:6–8).

Principle #5

Paul called his hearers to live and model a fully devoted life in Christ.

Paul speaks of his efforts to deepen his relationship with Christ as a race to be won. This level of devotion, demonstrated in his own life, Paul expects "mature" believers to possess (Phil. 3:12–21).[15] For Paul, modeling demonstrates the harmony between doctrine and lifestyle choices. Harmony (practicing what one is preaching) assures that the watching "younger" audience understands that the source of all moral behavior centers on Christ and not on societal standards of conduct.[16]

Principle #6

Paul's own life and faith journey was shaped by adults.

An examination of the Scriptures highlighting Paul's religious and cultural upbringing demonstrates the impact Paul's parents and community had on his spiritual formation.[17] The impact of Paul's parents and surrounding adult community is implicit in Paul's defense before Agrippa (Acts 26:2–23). Here Paul highlights his extensive religious training and experience that led up to his conversion to Christianity. Furthermore, Paul claims his training and experience has been evident to the Jewish community from his childhood (Acts 26:4).

Principle #7

Paul spoke of parents and adults as active participants in a child's spiritual formation.

Paul's admonition to fathers in Ephesians 6:4 that they raise their children "in the training and instruction of the Lord" indicates his expectation that fathers be major players in their children's spiritual formation. It is clear that Paul wants the older Christians and those in authority to teach younger Christians (either by age or experience) what it means to follow Christ in word and action (Titus 2:1–15). His emphasis on familial and familial-like relationships in the body of Christ is evident when he describes the respect and honor he expects each believer to give across generational lines (1 Tim. 5:1–21).[18] As in Deuteronomy 6, passages such as Titus 2:1–15 and 1 Timothy 5:1–21 indicate a continual process that makes the most out of both formal and informal opportunities for intergenerational interaction.[19] (Appendix Two provides a great exercise for evaluating how well your youth ministry is embracing an intergenerational theology.)

Support in Current Research[20]

Parents and Adults Matter in the Spiritual Formation of Kids was the not so surprising find of sociologists Christian Smith and Melinda Lindquist Denton. As sociologists paying attention to adolescent issues, Smith and Denton noticed a gap in contemporary research on teenagers and their faith. As a result, Smith launched the National Study of Youth and Religion with the goal to "develop a better scholarly and public understanding of the religious and spiritual lives of American adolescents"[21] and provide "stimulus for soul-searching conversations."[22] While the study's findings extend beyond the scope of intergenerational relationships, this article focuses on those findings that are most relevant to intergenerational youth ministry.

Finding #1: Parents and Adults Are the Primary Influencers of Spiritual Formation

> *Even though agents of religious socialization do not appear to be wildly successful in fostering clarity and articulacy about faith among teens, it remains true that parents and other adults exert huge influence in the lives of American adolescents—whether for good or ill, and whether adults can perceive it or not—when it comes to religious faith and most other areas of teens' lives.*[23]

While a significant number of teenagers take religious faith and practice seriously, Smith and Denton came across a much larger number of teenagers who were "remarkably inarticulate and befuddled about religion."[24] In their study they found "little evidence that the agents of religious socialization in this country [parents/adults] are being highly effective and successful with the majority of their young people."[25] Even so, the study identified parents and other adults as the *number one influencers* of teenage religious faith and practice. The influence of parents and adults was found to be so strong that Smith and Denton refer to the common cultural assumption that a teenager's peer group is more influential than that of adults in teenagers' lives as "badly misguided."[26]

Finding #2: Youth Ministry Programming Is Important

In the absence of parental encouragement by example to attend religious services, religious congregations that offer teenagers organized youth groups—particularly those with full-time, paid, adult youth group leaders—seem to make a significant difference in attracting teens to attend congregational religious services. Well-developed, congregational-based youth groups with established youth leaders likely provide teens who lack parental support appealing doorways into and relational ties encouraging greater religious participation in the life of religious congregations.[27]

As a professional youth worker, I particularly like this finding. It demonstrates the importance of youth ministry programming in the body of Christ. With that said, Smith's and Denton's comments need to be examined so that the significance of "youth ministry" is properly understood.

"*In the absence of parental encouragement . . . .*" Even though important to the attraction of teenagers to religious services, the role of youth ministry is of secondary importance to that of parents.

"*. . . appealing doorways into and relational ties encouraging greater religious participation in the life of religious congregations . . . .*" According to Smith and Denton, the role of youth ministry in situations where a teenager lacks parental support is to provide "*appealing doorways*" for significant relationships to develop.

Personally, I have been a part of some incredible youth programs. These programs have been able to attract large numbers of students and lead many students to a saving relationship with Jesus Christ. However, when I reflect back on the students who lacked strong parent support, I see that our impact was not through our programs; it came through the ways we offered meaningful relationships with other adult believers that continue to be sustaining influences in their discipleship journeys to this day.[28]

Finding #3: Teenage Spirituality Is a Reflection of Adult Spirituality

The religion and spirituality of most teenagers actually strike us as very powerfully reflecting the contours, priorities, expectations, and structures of the larger adult world into which adolescents are being socialized.[29]

Teenagers pick up their religious cues from the surrounding adult culture. As a result, Smith and Denton found the religious world of teenagers quite like that of the adult world.

Alarms have been sounding for what seems like decades that churches and young adult participation in these churches are in rapid decline. Finding #3 alone provides a major jumping-off point for church leaders to begin discussions on what can be done to reverse the decline. Any substantive correction has to begin with addressing the depth and direction of adult spirituality. In other words, the *first* move is not correcting youth ministry *programming* (needed but secondary) but assuring that the adults connected in relationship with our students are fully devoted followers of Jesus.

Do you hear the theme and see the circle closing?

The principles of Deuteronomy 6:4–9 are coming into focus once more.

Practical Steps for Providing Intergenerational Relationships between Adults and Students

Do you remember the game Mercy?

In this game, two competitors stand face-to-face, join inter-woven-finger hands and at "go", try to bend the other combatant's hands backwards until the defeated yells, "Mercy!"

You may feel a bit defeated at this point in this chapter. "David, we get it!"

"Adults are more than *safety police* and *van drivers*—mercy!"

"Parents and other surrounding adults are the *primary* spiritual influencers—mercy!"

"Looking at today's teenage culture, we need to be better *influencers*—mercy!"

Good news. The answer to moving forward is rather simple and involves little or no programmatic change (okay, there will be some kind of programming change, but you will easily know what to change when you make the first move).

The *first* step toward intergenerational relationship building begins with a *mindset change,* and you have already experienced that in your reading: *Adults are the primary influencers in the spiritual formation of students!* Like a new pair of glasses, this mindset change allows you to view all ministry programming, from announcements to zoo trips, with renewed focus. This allows you to ask the question, "How is (INSERT ANY CHURCH PROGRAM) helping students see Jesus, equipping them for life and eternity, and assimilating them into the body of Christ?" The questions will now be answered with a focus that the best method for fulfilling these three ministry purposes involves meaningful, relational connection with adult believers.

Be prepared as you ask these questions with renewed, intergenerational concern. Like many modern churches, you will discover many strategies that are at best multigenerational (go back to the definitions) but few that are truly intergenerational. Kids stay in their space, teenagers stay in their space, adults in theirs, and the connection is not often strategic. Do not be discouraged. My friend and mentor Chap Clark always reminds his students, "Change should be viewed as a large ship with a tiny rudder—it happens slowly." Don't concern yourself with the pace of change. Be patient! Soon, your renewed vision will begin to make a practical impact so that intergenerational relationships are developed and pursued by adults and teenagers alike.

Why am I so confident? Because the Bible, the research, and the experience of most church members confirm that the greatest influencers in their own spiritual journey were the adults who took the time to notice and speak into their life eternity-shaping truths. We all need to play a little game of Mercy from time to time in order to remind ourselves that God's program *is* people. *First step taken*.

What do I do now?

Take a *second* step. *Communicate* with other adults the truth(s) that led you to take the first step (you can even use this chapter as a discussion starter). This will be more difficult than imagined. Because, amid all of the supporting research, modern youth ministry continues to deliver the message to parents and surrounding adults that they should leave the "youth ministry" to the professionals. The goal of the second step is to get other adults talking about and then embracing the idea that they are indeed the greatest asset in your youth ministry programming.

Communication is a funny, complex, and often frustrating thing. For instance, no matter how many e-mails, texts, fliers, web announcements, bulletin announcements, tweets, Facebook postings (the list of media could continue) you send out, someone, usually a parent (just speaking the truth), will say "*I did not know about* (INSERT ANYTHING HERE)!" Even so, it is important to communicate the need for intergenerational youth ministry programming clearly and passionately. (Appendix Three provides helpful suggestions for getting in front of adults and providing a great classroom experience.) We are now moving from mind-set change (first and second steps) to programmatic change.

Take a *third* step. Actually, like a child learning to walk (step, stumble, fall, and repeat until walking), the third step involves a few steps. **Re-vision, Reorient, Repeat** is a simple process designed to make intergenerational programmatic change move from stepping to walking to running.

Re-vision

A move toward intergenerational practice involves an intentional effort to *re-vision* the role of adults in your youth ministry. This is the first programming shift that brings significant course correction to the ship of ministry change. Instead of being your sponsor and police force, adults in your church need to hear from you that they are the most influential and crucial friend, mentor, and hero force you have in your ministry toolbox. Re-visioning also means to widen the volunteer pool by inviting all adults (young, old, single, married, athletic, unathletic, creative, uncreative, cool, uncool, etc.) to engage in the youth ministry of your church. Here are some of the practical moves you can make to re-vision the role of adults in your ministry:

- *Change your vocabulary as a staff.* We no longer solely target parents of teenagers for service in youth ministry. As a staff we are making appeals for workers across generational lines.
- *Invite the entire church body.* In other words, we are going to more than just the "parents of teenagers" class to ask for volunteers. We may not get too many new workers through the mass appeal, but this encouragement

highlights our desire that the entire adult community
play a role in the spiritual formation of teenagers.

- *Encourage your current adult leaders,* especially those who
  are not parents of a teenager, to get additional workers
  from a wider range of adults (young professionals, parents of small children, parents of grown children, singles,
  and senior adults).
- Partner with your senior-adult ministry to provide
  opportunities for senior adults to participate in youth
  ministry (hanging out in the youth area, serving food,
  joining a small group, sharing their story of faith are
  simple ways to employ senior adults).
- With the wider range of adult volunteers, simplify your
  volunteer processing (background checks and volunteer
  opportunities forms, etc.) and provide more volunteer
  training opportunities. This takes the fear and uncer-
  tainty out of working with teenagers, a fear that can lead
  potential adult volunteers to opt out of serving teenagers.

The word to keep in mind is *intentional*! It can be difficult to gather
the entire, multigenerational church together for youth ministry
service, but it is possible. I have found that a number of people are
waiting and wanting to be involved in the lives of teenagers. It is
our job to be *intentional* in how we target diverse generations of
volunteers and give them the skills needed to succeed (Appendix
Four provides helpful ideas to help adult volunteers and the church
body re-vision their role with students). Now we move ahead to
the second and more noticeable programming shift.

Reorient
Bringing intentional change to youth ministry programming
is easier than you think. Instead of adding another event to an

already busy church ministry calendar (Stop the madness. Erasers are a church leadership's friend), take an already existing ministry (youth ministry or otherwise) and give it an intergenerational emphasis. For instance:

- Do you have church dinners—potlucks? Mix up the age groups and make them go through the line together and sit together (no youth and adult tables). Place questions on the table for the intergenerational group to answer while eating (nothing serious but more like "What was your favorite band in high school?" type of questions).
- Do you have back-to-school prayer times? Instead of offering up one prayer for the kids, parents, teachers, coaches, and administrators in a service, dedicate an entire service to seasons (times) of prayer throughout an assembly. Pray separately for each group and include a church leader's targeted blessing for each group.
- Do you have a "student section" at your church? (Caution: this one can be controversial.) Get rid of it! Have adults sit right in the middle of the student section and students in the middle of adult sections. Really.
- Do you have church ministry teams or committees? Invite students to be fully functional members of those teams. No, I am not advocating children elders. I am advocating a fully functional body of Christ. You will be surprised what happens when an adolescent is asked their opinion on how to make a mission emphasis better.
- Do you have men's or women's retreats/conferences? Get rid of the youth ministry version of these and work together (young and old together on ministry teams/ committees) to build one, intergenerational men's or women's event.

Yes, people could be upset if you intergenerationally reorient their favorite church program. Remember, you have already taken two steps at this point, and the church has gone through (at some level) a mind-set change that has prepared them for this difficult moment. Also, because you have involved all of your new and improved volunteer pool, you have chosen the easiest program to reorient.

Repeat

It takes a strategic, often small, dedicated hand to turn the rudder and get the ship of change course corrected. If you fail, try reorienting something else. Don't give up.

If you succeed, build on the experience, tell the stories,[30] and find another program to reorient.

No matter the outcome of the reorienting, commit to the last process of step three, *repeat.*

Summary

After my 2008 year at Fuller Seminary, equipped with a renewed dedication to the priority of adult involvement in a student's spiritual formation, I conducted a *Parenteen* Seminar in the Houston area. The parents, youth ministry volunteers, and community professionals who participated in the seminar generated great dialogue and insights. Being in NASA country, I was thrilled to have an actual NASA team member in the crowd. I waited strategically until the end of the seminar when the need for authentic parental and adult engagement of the abandoned teenage culture was being discussed, to use the phrase, "It's not *rocket science.*" The laugh was cheap but the point clear. In the midst of a society and American church that tends to isolate kids from adults, God calls kingdom followers to a different path. Throughout Scripture and validated in current research, God paints a picture of kids being raised by parents who are working hand in hand with the broader adult community.

First Step: *Change your mind-set*. Adults are the primary influencers in the spiritual formation of students.

Second Step: *Communicate*. Other adults need to hear about and embrace the mind-set.

Third Step: *Commit to the process of programmatic change*. Re-vision, Reorient, and Repeat.

Visit www.teendisciples.org for a case study of a church that went through each of these three steps and made friends, mentors, and heroes out of the adults in their church.

Questions

1. David defines a term for us: "An intergenerational youth ministry approach views the roles of parents *and* the surrounding adult community as the *primary influence* in a student's spiritual formation." What are the surprising parts of this statement? How might this mean that our current youth ministries would have to change?
2. How are intergenerational, family-based, inclusive, and multigenerational ministries different?
3. In what ways do youth, parents, or leadership resist change in youth ministry toward an intergenerational approach?
4. David observes that the spiritual formation of Jesus "was impacted by his parents and the surrounding adult community." How is our obligation different (or not) from that of Joseph, Mary, and the people at the synagogue in Nazareth?

5. Why is it essential for youth to see harmony between doc-trine and lifestyle for the adults who serve as their models?
6. If adult and parental influence is so important, then why does David (and the researchers in the NSYR) affirm that youth ministry programming is vitally important?
7. If "teenage spirituality is a reflection of adult spirituality" as David tells us, then what does our reflection over the last decade say about our congregation?
8. How might your church need to "re-vision" its connection, communication, and relationship with the teens in its midst?

13

BRINGING IN THE OUTSIDER: Hospitality in the Way of Jesus

Cari Myers

After ten years in full-time youth ministry, I left the church staff to enter public education. It wasn't until I stepped into that seventh-grade language arts classroom with a disco ball hanging from the ceiling that I began to seriously think about "hospitality." When I became a teacher, my students represented a different racial and socioeconomic demographic than mine, and I began to see them in every aspect of my life—the mall, movies, restaurants, as I was driving—everywhere. Every place except for one; I never saw any of my students at my church. Even though my church was well known and close to their community, none of my students were regular members. A few had visited and thought our game room and concession stand were "awesome," but the interaction was superficial and they never returned. I was deeply troubled by this and asked them why they stayed away. Was it a denominational difference? Were people unfriendly? Was it too hard to find a ride?

None of these were the answer. They just felt uncomfortable: "No one there looked like me."

So I began to study two cultures—the culture of my students and my own. Over time, as I listened to the stories and life-experiences of my students, I began to hear my own culture with new ears. At first I was very defensive for my people and myself. None of us wanted to be a part of hurting people. It was unconscious but ubiquitous—we didn't mean to do it, but we did. I could hear the insider language. I could hear how our concerns and worries sounded to them. I could hear distinct differences in the things that kept us up at night and gave us anxiety. And I could hear how our perception of people like my students sounded to them. They were keenly intuitive and could hear and sense the way my people reacted when they walked in the building. They saw our glances, they heard our murmurs, and they saw our clothes and cars and phones. They understood "different."

At one point, one of our adult volunteers, Joe, discovered a passion for prison ministry. He decided he wanted to help provide a soft place for juvenile offenders to land once they left the juvenile detention center: he helped them find jobs, he helped them with their school work if they went back to school, he helped mediate conversations with their parents, but above all, he wanted them to come to church. So on Wednesday nights he would take a van and drive around and pick up five or six boys and drive them to Wednesday night church. These fellows never created any problems—they were respectful, polite, and as well dressed as they could be. Regardless, when some of the parents found out what Joe was up to, they expressed concern about their children attending church with these boys. These parents were worried about their children's safety, what kind of language they might be exposed to, but mostly they were worried that these boys might flirt with the girls. "We've been members here for nine years, and we love it," one concerned mother confided in me, "But I'll tell you this: If those boys keep coming here, we are going to go somewhere else." In response, the church increased security in the youth center, and Joe was asked to explain a few rules and expectations to the boys. Needless to say, a certain message was sent and received, and this experiment was short-lived.

The thing is, we really wanted to be a place for kids who didn't have other places. We talked about that quite a bit—how we could be more thoughtful about welcoming others in, how we could use language that could be understood without a church pedigree, what kind of incentives we could give kids who brought friends from school, what kind of concerts "unchurched" kids might like, and so on. When we hired new staff, we thought a lot about the different groups of kids who might lean toward the candidate's personality, style, and cultural representations so that we were a varied staff and could reach more kids. When we started a ministry for teen mothers, we delighted when one showed up at our door, explaining that the church down the street recommended she come to us, because, they thought, "They'll take anyone over there." We really thought we were being intentional about outreach and hospitality—so what happened?

When you decide to throw open your doors to whosoever may come, you run the risk of collecting those who may not know "the rules." As one of a few women on a largely male staff, I spent a significant amount of time policing girls' dress. We were on the constant lookout for what was too tight, too short, or too low. When someone drew some inappropriate figures on one of the bathroom

A community which refuses to welcome—whether through fear, weariness, insecurity, a desire to cling to comfort, or just because it is fed up with visitors—is dying spiritually.

—Jean Vanier, *Community and Growth*, 267.

> We worry about damage, theft, or misuse. Those of us with substantial material wealth can also be embarrassed by our abundance, especially when we live close to others in need. Rather than deal with our discomfort by making changes, we sometimes choose to keep our distance or to find new friends whose resources more closely match our own.
>
> —Christine Pohl,
> *Making Room*, 117.

stalls and someone scuffed up the wall while sitting on one of the window ledges, we began placing adult volunteers in strategic vantage points around the youth center. When the kids would text and giggle all through the worship service, we began placing adult volunteers around there too. We got our very own security guard in the youth center, and we produced a video explaining our expectations and showed it each week before class started, and we posted signs around the building communicating these same expectations. I understand and remember clearly our reasoning behind doing this—we made the presentation fun and funny, but we were serious about these restrictions. I just feel like it could have been quite damaging for those juvenile offenders to enter into another highly policed situation in a place where they were told they would be safe, and I'm pretty sure that the last thing that sophomore was looking forward to that night was me pulling her away from her friends and explaining why she had to change shirts.

We've all become familiar with the idea of helicopter parents—parents who "hover" over the lives of their children and are overprotective and excessively involved. This is a problematic label for a few reasons. For example, more schools are requesting that parents be more actively involved in the educational experiences of their children, but then these parents who attempt to engage their children's schools are told they are "hovering." It's a mixed message. A few years ago, the term "lawnmower parent" emerged. Lawnmower parents "clear a path for their child before they even take a step, preempting possible problems and mowing down obstacles in their child's way."[1]

Popular thought might tell us that a child who never faces resistance or never has to overcome any obstacles will be a weak child for whom adolescence lasts well into their twenties. They'll be like a caterpillar whose chrysalis is interrupted or broken. The caterpillar can never fully form into a butterfly without the struggle. I find both of these parenting images troubling, because the parent in them is either *above* the child or *ahead* of the child. At the end of this chapter I will propose some suggestions of communal hospitality where the parent and the child walk side by side, both facing forward with common goals, the child safe but challenged.

Theologians and philosophers surely come first in line among those who like to make up words to explain concepts, and Jacques Derrida is possibly my favorite. He used the term "hostipitality" in an attempt to explain why we will never be able to really understand true hospitality, that true unconditional hospitality is an impossibility.[2] He suggests that the opposite of hospitality is hostility, and while it is the right of a stranger to not be greeted with hostility when he arrives in someone else's territory, this is often the message that is sent. In the traditional sense, the very act of hospitality requires those offering hospitality to feel ownership of "the house." In order to offer hospitality, we must have the power to host. Those we are inviting in are not owners or masters, so they are present in a lower

> To practice the virtue of hospitality assumes the 'house' belongs to the one practicing this virtue, who is sharing her or his resources with the Other, who has no claim to the possession.
>
> —Miguel De La Torre, *Latino/a Social Ethics*, 27.

position of power. This dynamic gives the host a measure of control over the guests and gives the "master of the house" the power to control the behavior of the guests, or to attempt to control the behavior of the guests, even to the degree of refusing admission to the house or closing the doors to certain potential guests, especially uninvited guests.

Derrida argues that our version of hospitality is not actually hospitable, but it borders on hostility. Hospitality always includes limits and boundaries where the guest may not wander (the master bedroom door is closed, the offices are locked), where the guest is not welcome. In the way we traditionally think about it and practice it, hospitality is rather inhospitable, or hostile. When a guest trespasses into the master bedroom or wears inappropriate clothes to church, they experience the inhospitable side of hospitality—hostility. If we accept that hospitality in a sense means a welcoming of whoever comes, in whatever state and need of our hospitality, the host must accept a measure of loss of power and an abandoning of claims to ownership of "the house."

We seem to have forgotten that we are not the owners of the house. The house of worship is not ours—it is God's; we are just as much guests in the house as anyone else. In Mark 11:15–17, Jesus clears the temple courts with a whip after discovering a misuse of God's house:

> Jesus entered the temple courts and began driving out
> those who were buying and selling there. He overturned
> the tables of the money changers and the benches of
> those selling doves, and would not allow anyone to
> carry merchandise through the temple courts. And as
> he taught them, he said, "Is it not written: 'My house
> will be called a house of prayer for all nations'? But you
> have made it 'a den of robbers.'" (NIV)

Jesus clearly has some ideas for the correct use of God's house, and the selling of livestock and the exchange of money don't seem to be among them. He also has very clear ideas on ownership of the house—it is God's house. If God is the master of the house, what are God's concerns for the proper use of the house? How do we join in God's plan for the use of the master's house?

If we conditionally welcome someone into our house of worship with restrictions, rules, and expectations of the type of person they will become within our walls, that is "hostipitality." We are controlling the conditions of hospitality. In Derrida's description of hospitality, one welcomes the stranger, even though one will not fully know who one is welcoming. So in this sense hospitality is opening one's self to the stranger, and in Derrida's view, to all that the stranger has to offer. True, impossible hospitality is an openness to the radical other, but also to the other who is always already there. Hospitality then is this provocative kind of openness to both stranger and not-stranger. Derrida exposes us to this notion that we're always confronted with the in-breaking of the other, because a truly hospitable house would have no doors or windows, no boundaries or thresholds to cross. In this way it can no longer be privately owned territory but equally accessible to all. What does this unbounded hospitality look like in reality? How does a church show hospitality and welcome without doors to open?

> The will to give ourselves to others and 'welcome' them, to readjust our identities to make space for them, is prior to any judgment about others, except that of identifying them in their humanity.
>
> —Miroslav Volf,
> *Exclusion and Embrace,* 29.

To be fair, Christian communities have been struggling with acceptance of the outsider for thousands of years. In Luke 7, Jesus is dining in the home of Simon when an unwelcome guest enters, throwing the house into awkwardness. The guest is a woman "who lived a sinful life"[3] who carries with her an alabaster jar of perfume. While Jesus is reclining at the table, she kisses his feet and weeps onto them, cleaning them with her tears, then drying them with her hair and pouring perfume on them. These actions are sexualized by nature of their intimacy and her gender, and apparently by her personal history. The other guests (the Gospel of Luke specifically mentions the host) are unsettled by this and think it is inappropriate for Jesus to be touched by a sinful woman. This woman does not follow the rules. She enters uninvited, she interrupts the dining experience with her profession to Jesus, she humbles herself before all present, she lays her lips on the bare feet of a man she does not know, she is weeping—she does not follow the rules of proper dining etiquette. The congregation present responds as we might respond if this were to happen at a dinner party today. But what does Jesus do? How does Jesus respond to this woman who challenges the prescribed limits of acceptable social behavior? Does he jerk away from her, embarrassed? Does he pull her to her feet and show her out? Does he ask the host to do so? Does he reprimand her? Does he read her the list of rules and expectations for entering the house or sit her to the side and ask a disciple to keep an eye on her? Does Jesus express concern for how this will affect his image? Does he call for security? No. He meets her needs—her greatest need. He forgives her sins and speaks peace over her.

Further, it is important to notice that this woman apparently isn't trying to cause trouble and shake things up. She wasn't performing a direct act of resistance against the status quo or wealth inequity or religious privilege. She wasn't trying to steal from the host of the dinner or even asking for special treatment or favor from Jesus. She was, quite literally, throwing herself on the feet of Jesus and hoping for the best. It is safe to assume that she knows this is an "inappropriate" act. She knows that it is socially unacceptable to barge into a dinner party where you are uninvited and kiss, weep over, and anoint the feet of the guest of honor. She knows she might be thrown out or hurt or worse. What must be going on in the life of this woman to make this an option for her? These actions seem like a last resort, a final act of desperation. What might have happened to her had Jesus reprimanded her and had her thrown out? What happens when an inappropriately affectionate student has come to us

> With sure artistry, and great power Jesus depicted what happens when a man responds to human need across the barriers of class, race, and condition. . . . Neighborliness is non-spatial; it is qualitative. A man must love his neighbor directly, clearly, permitting no barriers between.
>
> —Howard Thurman,
> *Jesus and the Disinherited*, 89.

as an act of last resort and is met with rules and regulations that she might not be able to meet? Do we dismiss her or seek to meet the deeper need?

Jesus is not the owner of this house—in fact, as far as we know, Jesus owned no house. He models for us a carrying of hospitality out into the world, of impossible, unbounded hospitality. Wherever he was, that was the place for hospitality. Even if it was territory that technically belonged to someone else.

Before any acts occur, perhaps some soul-searching is in order. Have we created our houses of worship to be safe enclaves for the saved? Do we like the fact that "they" might not feel welcome here because we intentionally/unintentionally create an inhospitable environment? What assumptions are we making about our surrounding communities? Are we assuming that "poor" or "different" equals "dangerous?" Do we throw outreach events so we can say we are trying to reach unchurched people, but we are secretly relieved

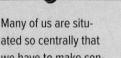

> Many of us are situated so centrally that we have to make conscious decisions to experience marginality in our lives."
>
> —Christine Pohl,
> *Making Room,* 123.

when we don't have to worry about a flood of unindoctrinated outsiders invading our walls? Truthfully, bringing in the young outsider requires a lot of work and a lot of upheaval. Like so many potential reforms for youth culture, it will require a lot of effort on the part of peripheral adults. If we can come to a point where we agree that we really are serious about bringing in adolescent outsiders, that a youth minister who teaches about recognizing Jesus in the stranger is worth her salt, and that we are willing to put in the work and time, then I believe we need to take the following steps:

Confession—We must admit that we have not done this well, that maybe we are a little terrified of unknown youth and what issues they might bring in our doors. That maybe we have been primarily concerned with protecting our own and providing a space of comfort and commonality instead of honestly living our professed mission of seeking and saving.

Repentance—We are now willing to sacrifice our claims to power and ownership and change our behavior so that we are the vulnerable and risk-taking ones instead of requiring that of the outsider. Remember Jesus's prayer? "My prayer is not that you take them out of the world but that you protect them from the evil one . . . As you sent me into the world, I have sent them into the world" (John 17:15, 18 NIV).

Act anew—The first step will be a slow creaking open of
the church doors and a tentative step out into the larger
world on the part of members. We must recognize that this
will be uncomfortable and probably painful, that we will be
awkward and we might be laughed at, and we will surely
see and hear things we might not want to see and hear, and
we will undoubtedly say or do something offensive and
uninformed. But we will ask forgiveness and try again.

If the outsider has not experienced true hospitality inside our walls,
what might hospitality look like outside our walls? How do we
bring hospitality into the larger community instead of expecting
the unchurched to come to us and get it?

One idea might be that we don't extend an invitation into
God's house as much as we venture into the world and behave in
welcoming ways. What if we go to them instead of always expecting them to come to us? I'm suggesting some engagement beyond
the donation of funds or school supplies. While those things are
nice and necessary, they often serve to keep us at a distance from
our communities. We don't have to look in someone's eye or take
someone's hand. We are saved from the prospect of examining why
things are the way they are, and what our role in that might be, or
at least how we are benefiting from the normative standard (the
ways things are) when others so clearly are not. I am suggesting
embodied engagement with those outside our church walls in new,
radical, and uncomfortable ways.

When we partner with our communities in other ways, perhaps
our communities will want to partner with us in our churches. As
family units, as ministry partners, one of the ways we help our
youth understand and express the radical message of hospitality
is living it out in other areas of life in ways such as these:

- Buy houses in neighborhoods where the student demographic is not represented in our youth groups. As our churches get older, what if we continued to live in the neighborhoods surrounding our churches instead of moving farther and farther into the suburbs? On one mission trip, I took a group of sophomores to St. Louis to run a VBS at a neighborhood park. This neighborhood consisted largely of youth representing a different race and class than the ones in my youth group. A church from Oklahoma had sent a man and his family there as domestic missionaries to love the people in this neighborhood. He and his wife and two elementary aged children lived in a house and attended schools in the neighborhood where we held our VBS, and he had earned the trust of that community in doing so. As a result, he was able to love and speak to them in ways that were inconceivable to those of us who were "just visiting."

- What if we sent our children to the public schools in the neighborhood serviced by the local schools instead of sending them away to elite private schools? What kind of friends might they make? Have we raised our children to be strong, faithful, and resilient enough to attend the schools in their local neighborhoods?

- Are we serious enough about bringing in outsiders to change the way we vote? Are we willing to cast a vote that assists someone who has less than we do—a vote that doesn't directly help us, or protect our financial interests, and might require us to give up some privilege or power? To this day, the lower gym in my sixty-plus-year-old school still floods every time it rains because the bonds suggesting an upgrade, or a new school, are always tied to addendums that serve the larger (wealthier) district. So people vote it down, and the kids have to play on warped floors for the rest of the school year.

- We could choose to shop a little more inconveniently and support our neighbors by spending our money in private, locally owned businesses and farmer's markets instead of giving our money to anonymous international corporate conglomerations.

- We could choose to surrender our elite gym memberships and attend a local recreation center or gym instead. Through these facilities our children can join sports teams with children from the neighborhood; we can join basketball leagues and take Zumba classes with neighbors and build social relationships. If you live in a nice neighborhood and are already attending a local gym or rec center, what if you chose to travel a bit and join a gym or rec center in a neighborhood you would like to welcome into church community?

- Finally, perhaps the best way to embrace the outsider in your area is to learn and master another language. Welcoming another in their language of greatest comfort is a profound act of neighbor-love and speaks volumes about the posture of your community toward those outside its walls.

> The church and "Christians" are only authentic to the extent that they represent and embody this surrender to Christ through discipleship; and this surrender to Christ brings both the church and individual Christians in contact with suffering through gospel-demanded work on behalf of others.
>
> —Anthony B. Pinn,
> *Beyond the Pale: Reading Ethics from the Margin,* 138

> One of the dangerous by-products of living in community can be separation. It's an unintended consequence of community. To counter this tendency, the next Christians intentionally overlap their lives and their service with the networks that already exist in the wider world around them.
>
> —Gabe Lyons,
> *The Next Christians,* 159.

We must decide who we are, and we must act based on what we decide. As a community are we more concerned with gospel outreach or are we more concerned with enclave protection? Or are we trying to create some kind of hybrid? In that case, how do we get our actions to match our message? The church staff, the students, and the parents must all be on the same page: Are we okay with potentially losing some members who are frightened by the outsider? Will those who leave abandon the kingdom entirely or just go to another congregation? Are we humble and courageous and faithful enough to potentially adopt out some members if we risk bringing in a true outsider? Are membership numbers our truest sign of success and potency? The body must be united in this.

Questions

1. What kinds of teens sometimes scare or intimidate adults? Why?
2. How do our fears for ourselves, or for our children, create outsiders?
3. Every community has its rules and, behind every rule, there's almost always a story. What kind of story do adolescents read when new rules, policies, or procedures appear shortly after they do?

4. How do helicopter parents complicate bringing in outsider youth, who don't yet know or understand the community's behavioral standards?

5. If the "house" we worship in is really God's house, then how should that shape our rules (written or understood) about dress, language, questions, or behavior for outsiders? How does our perspective change if we understand God is the one doing the inviting?

6. Cari talks about conditional and unconditional welcome; please explain the difference. If conditional hospitality is on one end of the spectrum and unconditional is on the other, where on the line is your congregation? Where should your congregation be? What would it take to get where you need to be?

Preparing for Launch

MAINTAINING A HOLY IDENTITY WHILE WHOLLY IMMERSED IN A CULTURE

Walter Surdacki

J avier is a freshman at NYU. Ever since he got his first guitar from his parents in seventh grade, Javier has spent almost every free minute practicing. His bedroom is papered with posters of his favorite bands. He has milk crates filled with vinyl records lining his room. When not playing guitar, Javier is generally listening to his music collection and trying to figure out the guitar part in his head. His wardrobe consists of jeans and concert T-shirts. Music consumes his life.

Mei is a fifteen-year-old in La Jolla, California. She loves working and volunteering at the local animal shelter. Her passion for animals is evident within the first fifteen minutes of meeting a new friend. It is almost impossible to have a conversation without her talking about some animal that is in her life. Her friends refer to her as "Dr. Mei, future vet." She is comforted by the fact that there is *something* others know about her.

Caleb is seventeen years old. His hero is Michael Phelps. He spends as many hours in the pool as his schedule allows him. He has a lot of natural athletic talent, and he might be able to earn a college scholarship if he continues to work hard. Most of the conversations Caleb has with others revolve around swimming. His nickname around town is Flipper. He likes this attention because it lets him know who he is and where he fits in.

Caleb, Mei, and Javier are all tremendously active in their youth groups. They are all students any parent would want for their son or daughter. So what is the problem? There is something in each one of these student's surrounding culture that has equated their identity with their activity. When you ask any one of their friends about them, the first thing that comes to their mind is, "Oh, Caleb? Yeah, he's a swimmer. Javier, the musician? Mei, the Cat Girl?" All of these students are *defined* by what they do rather than *who* they are. If you were to ask them to talk about themselves, the first thing that comes to mind is the activities they participate in. Granted, the things they are participating in are all good things. The problem lies in the fact that the surrounding culture has played such a dominant role in defining the identity of our students based on what they do. When this ever-so-subtle shift of identity from *imago Dei* (the image of God) to one's activities happens, it is easy for these students to forget their true identities.

How does a teen understand that one's identity comes from who God created them to be in the image of God rather than the image of what they do?

Teenagers have access to almost every aspect of popular culture from around the globe and any product that culture produces. Teens can take a virtual tour of the Louvre via Google Maps, get the newest album from their favorite Indy rock band, as well as download the latest episode of their favorite reality television show in just a few seconds—all from the smartphone in their pocket. The barriers of access to pop culture like time and space that once existed in their parents' world have disappeared. The ease of accessibility has brought with it an exponential rise in culture's ability to influence a teenager. Students have far easier access to unholy influences than ever before.

How does a student who is called by Jesus to be salt and light maintain a holy identity with all of these competing forces at play?

For a parent, it seems as though culture is changing at breakneck speeds.[1] What is popular right now is already passé by lunchtime. It seems as if it would take a staff of forty people working full time to keep up with what is in right now and what it out. Staying on top of the latest trends seems useless.

How does a parent stay on top of the latest trends and what is popular? Or at least be aware when something is looming large in a student's day, like SnapChat or YikYak or YouTubers they watch daily and follow on Twitter?

In the meantime, as culture seems to play a larger and larger role in the lives of young people, those adults surrounding them are wringing their hands and wondering, "What does one do? How do we protect our children?" as it appears that the world is going to hell in a handbasket. We don't want popular culture to have such influence over our students. This isn't a new concern. From the moment Elvis Presley gyrated his hips on the *Ed Sullivan Show*, parents grew concerned over the detrimental effect rock 'n' roll had on their innocent sons and daughters. This concern hasn't ceased. Consider the questionable morality espoused by Madonna in the 1980s, sexual promiscuity of *Friends* in the 1990s, the possible witchcraft influences of *Harry Potter* and *Twilight*. Parents feel the almost insatiable need for worry.

How does a parent equip the teens in their lives with the tools to discern how to maintain a holy identity in the midst of this culture without being engulfed by it?

This chapter is concerned with helping students maintain a holy identity inside a deluge of culture. Our three tools are: a biblical foundation youth workers can use, awareness of the changing roles of youth pastors, and theological guidelines for discernment.

A Bigger Story for Identity

There is a common story for life that is popular. It goes something like this: "As a teenager, you need to work hard to get good grades. Get good grades so you can get into a good college. Work hard in college so that you can graduate and get a good job. Get a good job so you can make lots of money. Make lots of money so that you can enjoy life and have security. The end." It is a common narrative that is propagated in homes, schools, and churches. The problem with this story is that it is far too petty for our students to get excited about.

Christian Smith illustrates this in his book *Soul Searching*. Smith found through the National Study of Youth and Religion that the narrative prevalent in many churches is one that he calls Moralistic Therapeutic Deism (MTD).[2] The creed of this narrative is:

1. A God exists who created and orders the world and watches over human life on earth.
2. God wants people to be good, nice, and fair to each other, as taught in the Bible and by most world religions.

3. The central goal of life is to be happy and to feel good about oneself.

4. God does not need to be particularly involved in one's life except when God is needed to resolve a problem.

5. Good people go to heaven when they die.[3]

Smith argues that MTD has supplanted the narrative of Scripture as the primary story that is being told in our faith communities. Our students want to be part of a metanarrative that is much bigger than the behavior-modification-be-happy-stay-out-of-hell life that Moralistic Therapeutic Deism offers. The biblical narrative offers a story that, when presented accurately, is far less safe and predictable. It is dangerous. It is challenging. It requires effort and sacrifice. It is risky. The late longtime youth worker Mike Yaconelli put it this way: "God is the master of surprises: frightening clouds of smoke and fire, earthquakes, windstorms and firestorms, donkeys that talk, pillars of salt, oceans splitting apart, using a little boy to kill a giant, the Messiah in swaddling clothes and dying on a cross. No one can follow God and be comfortable for long."[4] *This* is the kind of story that challenges and stretches adolescents to be holy and set apart no matter what culture surrounds them. This is the narrative that empowers our students to live as God intended when God said, "Let us make mankind in our image" (Gen. 1:26 NIV).

Imago Dei Identity

Woven into the fabric of every human being is the foundational identity marker—the *imago Dei*, the image of God. Sadly, many adolescents have tremendous difficulty acknowledging that they possess this *imago Dei*.

Carl is a sophomore at his high school in El Paso, Texas. Carl has become enamored with the surfing and skateboard culture. His wardrobe consists of Tony Hawk T-shirts, Santa Cruz sweatshirts, and Vans shoes. Even though he lives hundreds of miles from one of the nearest surfing beaches in Texas, Carl is trying on the identity of a surfer to see if it fits him. Every few months Carl tries a different clothing style, hair color, or piercing, only to abandon the change a few months later for something else.

Through this journey for identity, many adolescents "try on" different identities to figure out which one of them "fits" their authentic self. It is not uncommon to see teens mimic various externals in surrounding culture; this is the power that culture holds in offering choices of identity. It is imperative that the adults around a teen work tirelessly to equip them with appropriate tools they can use to navigate culture's impact on this process.

Biblical truths get lost in the ocean of cultural messages. The biblical foundation ought to provide the basis upon which to build one's identity. The creation account in Genesis 1 describes to a teen how she possesses a divine connection with Creator God. As the Godhead is building the creation, beginning with light and ending with humanity, there is one inescapable fact as it relates to humanity—we are made in the *imago Dei*, the image of God. No other being or heavenly body is created with this unique quality. This is further reinforced in the creation account in Genesis 2 when God breathes into humanity *Pneuma*—God's Spirit. Encoded in the DNA of humanity is a divine connection with the Transcendent. Nothing else in the universe shares these two unique qualities.

Adolescents live in a world where untruths scream at them: they lack value, they are not important, they are not special. These messages contradict the basic truth that they possess God's image and Spirit.[5]

Embark upon this exercise for the next twenty-four or forty-eight hours: walk through your regular daily life and imagine that you are fifteen years old. When you see an image of a teen, ask yourself if this is a positive or negative portrayal. When you hear others speak about teens, do they paint them in a positive light? How are teens displayed on magazine covers? What is the average age of the actor or actress playing a teen? Chances are, most of the messaging you see portrays students as lazy, apathetic, lacking intelligence or judgment, disrespectful . . . a myriad of negative stereotypes. Are there any messages that reflect her as God's image bearer?

As parents and youth workers, it is our task to endlessly echo that reminder to the teens in our lives that they are special, they are beloved by God, they are uniquely shaped in God's image, for they rarely get that message anywhere else in their lives.

Salt and Light Identity

Perhaps the most difficult part of the adolescent journey is a nagging feeling that you are different from everyone else. That you stick out. Jesus's proclamation for us to be salt and light may exacerbate this feeling. The social capital it takes to be Salt and Light is an enormous sacrifice for many teens. Standing out is not a virtue. Many students prefer to stand in the shadows or just blend in.

Calling as Identity

Calling and vocation often prove to be the most important determiners of one's identity and purpose in this world. Many times adolescents have varying expectations and roles thrust upon them by the surrounding culture. When this occurs, they aren't afforded the space to be able to investigate or determine what their true calling is. Teens find it extremely difficult to answer the questions, "Why am I here?" and "What am I supposed to do?" from the core of who they are in these situations, when grades, sports, or fine arts are the things that draw praise from those around them.[6]

For example, Sujata is a starting forward for her high school's soccer team. Sujata gets adulation for her performance on the field from her coaches, parents, teammates, and classmates. Sujata does not seem to get any praise for her honesty or integrity. If she does, it is generally only in passing. Sujata, then, naturally begins to define herself as a soccer player. When the adults around tend to value only her external production, it is then natural for her to believe her mission and purpose is defined by her actions. Sujata believes that her mission is to succeed at soccer, rather than seeing her soccer team as her missional community—the community where she ministers to others.

David Kinnaman makes the following observation in *You Lost Me,* regarding many church communities:

> Millions of Christ-following teens and young adults are interested in serving in mainstream professions, such as science, law, media, technology, education, law enforcement, military, the arts, business, marketing and advertising, health care, accounting, psychology, and dozens of others. Yet most receive little guidance from their church communities for how to connect these vocational dreams deeply with their faith in Christ.[7]

I would argue that a student's true vocation, that gentle whisper from the Divine, ought to be a foundational pillar of identity.

There is life-altering power in coming alongside teens and discerning with them God's gifts of unique talents, skills, and passions in their lives. Churches and parents have a tremendous responsibility to engage in these vocational discussions and to do so without requiring or ruling out any particular identity. Perhaps we could wonder with a teen how—with their passion for languages—they might work alongside God in international missions or serving immigrants in their community. Or we might imagine with our soccer player Sujata reasons God would give her athletic gifts. What if this missional perspective helps Sujata to be an example of the gospel—through her actions when things go wrong, her sportsmanship when others are behaving poorly, her work ethic even when she is tired, her care for other team members who don't treat her well? For Sujata, her mission as a successful soccer player becomes secondary to who she is called to be as a disciple. Through involvement of the adults around her, Sujata comes to view *everything* she participates in as a facet of who she is becoming as a follower of Christ.

The church can serve our students better by helping them recognize their giftedness is not some cosmic random set of arbitrary characteristics, but a carefully *designed* set of particular gifts freely given to be utilized as part of the mission of God. When a student recognizes their gift for technology or music or athletics, we can serve as a trail guide, not by imposing an outcome, but by asking, "Where do you think your gifts could be used?"

Navigating Culture through Listening

Popular culture is a multifaceted beast. When adults interpret popular youth culture, it is almost inevitable that they will misinterpret it. It is art—beauty is in the eye of the beholder. When an adult makes a snap judgment, especially about a YouTuber band or game that is close to the heart of a teen, that adult risks losing significant credibility with that teen. Adults often give ourselves permission to make comments that demean, judge, or label things that loom large for our sons or daughters.

Let's take Brad, for example. Brad is talking with his teenage daughter Brianna about the music that she is playing on the local radio station as they drive to the grocery store. The music is not the genre that Brad prefers. In the course of the conversation, Brad makes an offhanded stinging comment about the lyrics of the song and how it must reflect on the character of the artist. What Brad does not realize is that Brianna is a tremendous fan of this musician. Actually, Brianna finds the artist's lyrics to be deeply moving; they speak to the core of who she is. Brianna quietly shuts down the conversation to save her pride and avoid expressing her anger on behalf of the artist, whom she views as a creative genius. Brad does not even notice that the subject has been changed. It is irrelevant now if the lyrics are controversial or the behavior of the artist objectionable. By too quickly judging, Brad has lost the opportunity to find out why the artist is so appealing to Brianna. Furthermore, Brianna likely internalizes his disdain and assumes that Brad would feel the same towards her if he knew how she felt.

Listen First—Then Listen More

Teenagers are sophisticated interpreters of culture. For the most part, they carefully curate the stories they consume. These stories may be told in music, Twitter feeds, poetry, or YouTube channels. Teens follow creators of content who speak to their idea of their own individuality or a role they'd like to play, a resolution they'd like their life to reach: a story of an adolescent girl becoming a hero in a post-apocalyptic world, a rap song in which someone overcomes tremendous obstacles and succeeds, a story of a young boy on a distant planet becoming a man of substance as he embarks upon a grand adventure to save the galaxy. It is incumbent upon adults to better understand what it is about these stories that is attractive, because the alternative is to invalidate our teens' search for meaning in the world, and by association invalidate them personally.

These content creators play a tremendous role in the identity development of many of our students. Andrew Root puts it perfectly in his book, *Unpacking Scripture in Youth Ministry*.

Adolescence is a time where our interpreted experiences become the building blocks that create who we are. Adolescents interpret everything, both because the very human journey is still new and because the meaning they give to their experiences will be the material to construct their very selves. Kids are always asking their friends, "Is my outfit stupid?", "Is my butt too big?", etc. We human beings are all hermeneutical animals; we're always interpreting. But adolescents are hermeneutical animals on steroids—they are interpreting (overinterpreting) everything. What does that look mean? What does this shirt say about me? And adolescents particularly are not only interpreting things for themselves, but to show the intensity of the hermeneutical blood that runs through them, they are almost constantly wondering how they are viewed by others, how others interpret them.[8]

The teens we work with notice everything about others. They assign meaning to virtually everything they bring into their world. Clothes proclaim who they see themselves to be. Music creates the emotional state they want to sustain.

We must seek first to understand before we allow ourselves the freedom to comment. "Can you tell me more about that?" can open up a conversation that affords deeper knowledge. "Where did you first hear about that artist?" might illuminate a meaningful moment in her life that you were unaware of. "Can I listen to that with you?" may allow you to gain a more nuanced understanding of your son's idea of what is important in the world.

Imagine how different the scene in the car would be if Brad asked Brianna, "What is it about that song that speaks to you? What do you hear when that song is playing?" Imagine the tremendous insight into the heart and soul of his daughter Brad would have discovered. Also, in asking these questions Brad builds some credibility in the Brianna's eyes by displaying genuine interest and not rejecting outright the content that Brianna knows he might be suspicious of. Instead, Brad can engage Brianna in meaningful discussion about the salient themes of the song rather than having the conversation shut down.

Furthermore, imagine what Brad might learn about the song, the artist, and the lyrics that he was unaware of before his comment. What if Brad engaged in the spiritual discipline of listening? Dietrich Bonhoeffer reminds us, "It is God's love for us that He not only gives us His Word but also lends us His ear . . . Christians, especially ministers, so often think they must always contribute something when they are in the company of others, that this is the one service they have to render. They forget that listening can be a greater service than speaking."[9]

Before commenting on teen culture, let us first lend our ears to hear the insight and wisdom that our teens possess.

The Shift from Sage on the Stage to Guide from the Side

The explosion of the Information Age has shifted the role of the teacher. There was a time not so long ago when the teacher possessed the knowledge and her role was to impart this knowledge to students. The knowledge of the teacher was a commodity of incredible value. Information generally had a barrier to access in the form of library research, reference volumes, or specialized industry journals. For example, if a student wanted to learn about something like Malaysia, she had to venture to the library, locate a book in the card catalogue, locate the book in the stacks, and then read about Malaysia to learn about her subject. The Internet has changed all that. Information is no longer difficult to acquire. A student literally has the world at their fingertips with a smartphone. Now if students want to learn about Malaysia, all they have to do is ask their phone, "Tell me about Malaysia," and up pop 878 million different articles to choose from, attached to pictures, maps, virtual tours, 3-D models, and videos. There is less of a need for the teacher to be a distributor of knowledge. Now the teacher is called upon to come alongside and help students interpret and understand the information they are accessing. Instead of being a "sage on a stage" the teacher is to serve as a "guide from the side." Parents of adolescents are now to be this cultural guide for their teens. This is a difficult transition for many parents because, for most of their sons' and daughters' childhood and early adolescent years, the "sage from the stage" role has worked wonderfully. Actually, many parents mourn the loss of this type of authority.

The new role is to recognize blind spots, avoid pitfalls, show them healthy paths to take in their encounters with cultural idols, artists, and trends. This role is frightening because it requires allowing our teens to fail, but it can be fulfilling because it allows failure to be the more effective teacher. Teaching fades to the background as we begin walking with our students. As they fall, we help them to frame their thoughts and responses when they get back up again.

Discernment

As students are bombarded with a myriad of competing worldviews, they need discernment to identify which views to accept and which to resist. Two tools for this journey are a value sieve and creative engagement.

Develop a Value Sieve

Perhaps the most important factor for discernment might be a sieve that is based on foundational values: a tool to determine what to let in and what to let go.

Imagine you are sitting at an all-you-can-eat buffet. The easy choice is to eat and eat and eat, and before we know it we feel uncomfortable and regretful. The same happens when we are faced with the endless buffet of popular culture choices. Simply eating without regard to what we are consuming leads to unhealthy choices. This lack of strategy does not end well. However, if we came to the buffet with a set of values that guided our consumption, our actions would be quite different. Instead of eating whatever came into view, values would guide our consumption. For example, if we had the value that we are going to eat foods that are healthy, we would stay away from the fried chicken (or at least eat a reasonable portion) and spend a lot of time at the salad bar.

It would be helpful for us to engage our students in dialogue and ask, "What are our foundational values? What are the principles that we will use to determine what it is we let in and what we don't?" We might decide that one of the values of our sieve is education—we want our consumption to teach us something. Maybe that something is a documentary on the Civil War or a cooking show that teaches me how to make a soufflé or a reality show based in a pawn shop that helps me determine how to negotiate better.

Helping our sons and daughters determine the value of what they have consumed, or the lack thereof, gives them another tool in their toolbox for spiritual health.

Culture Engaged Creatively

For generations, the church has wrestled with how to engage with culture. Many times faith and culture are at battle with one another. Is our role to change culture? Should we eschew culture and remain completely separate? H. Richard Niebuhr posits that culture and Christians may stand in paradox even with one another by presenting the dualistic nature of life.[10] I suggest that we train and equip our students to engage culture creatively. From the Genesis creation account we learn the first act that God commands humanity to do is to "be fruitful and increase in number" (Gen. 1:28 NIV). God commands humanity to participate in creative action. Further in the Genesis account of Adam and Eve, one of Adam's first tasks is to name the animals—another creative action. Part of our engagement with culture is to be creators, rather than merely consumers.

What if instead of scrolling endlessly down a social media feed, we write, compose, photograph, paint, draw, tell stories? For centuries the church was the leader when it came to the arts and music. People of faith set the cultural standard through participation in the creative process.

Grace is a teenage girl who is consumed by social media. Grace has accounts on three of the most popular social media sites. She spends hours checking her feeds, responding and reposting the thoughts of others, and noticing the number of likes and comments her posts receive. Grace is concerned with consuming what others are saying, and it sometimes devolves into voyeurism.

However, through a conversation with an influential adult in her life, Grace's engagement with social media shifts from consumer to distributor. She identifies her calling to use these powerful tools to create something beautiful.

A student's photography skills illuminate a daisy on a spring morning, and her Instagram feed proclaims its beauty to the world. A gift for writing short stories brings a blogger's followers to a better understanding of the plight of refugees he just read about. A YouTube video shares a musician's latest composition in process. A friend takes the opportunity to encourage through Twitter feeds and Facebook posts. Technology allows teens to be tremendously creative. Let us encourage students to reclaim their creative nature through the technology they love. Let one another be encouraged through those creative gifts and recognize God's image in those creations.

Tension with culture will always arise. Rather than being reactive to the encroachment of popular culture, remind teens that they reflect the image of God in how they interact with the world and use their gifts. God can and will use the faith community to create capable and dynamic young adults who will contribute in powerful and unique ways to the kingdom of God.

Questions

1. What are the different ways that our culture (and sometimes even the church) seeks to put a label, an identity on adolescents and adults? How do these identities shape our relationships and our behavior?

2. Walter stresses that a Christian's identity should come from the reality that we have been created in God's image, called *imago Dei*. What, though, does it really mean for us to be the "image of God"?

3. Walter notes that our culture has a narrative that is pressed onto the lives of our young people: "Work hard to get good grades. Get good grades so you can get into a good college. Work hard in college so that you can graduate and get a good job. Get a good job so you can make lots of money. Make lots of money so that you can enjoy life and have security. The end." What is untrue in this story? How does this story potentially betray the *imago Dei* for a Christian?

4. This chapter describes Moral Therapeutic Deism (MTD) as a false narrative, a false version of the Christian faith that researchers have found teenagers (and adults) too often substitute for the real thing. How is the MTD narrative different from a biblically-based faith narrative? Why is this important?

5. Walter challenges his readers to consider for twenty-four to forty-eight hours the ways that they talk about teens. If you were to think back over the last day or two about the things that you have said about teenagers, what words and thoughts been positive? Which one have been negative? What would teens hearing your words think of themselves if they heard your words?

6. Walter tells us that one of the most effective ways to navigate culture is listening. If we are to be good listeners, what conversational bad habits must we learn to avoid?

7. Since teens know current culture much better than we do, how can we ask them to help us better understand when the conversation moves to culture?

8. How can the spiritual practices of discernment help in considering culture matters? What are the ways that faith can engage culture besides head-on conflict?

15

DREAMS, VISIONS, AND REAL LIFE

Earl Lavender

Raising children who embrace a life of lasting faith is a daunting challenge in today's world. God not only grants parents the opportunity of co-creating life, but assigns them the responsibility to shape and help develop that life into its full potential in the kingdom of God. Who is capable of such a task?

We cannot do this without help. Life according to God's design offers a community of wisdom that allows one to learn how to flourish in every aspect of one's life, including parenting. Most, if not all, of the Bible assumes oral reading to communities of faith. It is to our detriment that the English language has lost its second person plural pronoun: *ye*. Over five thousand times, in both Hebrew and Greek, "you" is plural in Scripture—but in our individualistic culture, we instinctively hear the singular "you." The rampant individualism of our age encourages us to isolate ourselves and solve our own problems. Many have even individualized salvation itself, embracing the idea of Jesus as their "personal Savior." Jesus did not come to save us as individuals—he came to save the world (John 3:16).

What does this have to do with raising faithful children? This challenging topic is at times reduced to seminars and how-to books on how to build strong nuclear families, with children who "succeed" in the world. This success, of course, includes a strong faith. It is easy to fall into the trap of being more concerned about others' impressions of and thoughts about our children (after all, that does reflect on me) than God's purpose for them. God offers a far better story. The key to an enduring faith is identifying and pursuing God's purpose for our children and for us in God's redemptive narrative.

Writing Our Story

Any question concerning life and its direction necessitates a context. Consider this analogy. Each of us is writing a story as we live day to day. Many elements of our stories are givens over which we have no control—where we were born, to whom we were born, the culture into which we were born—you get the idea. However, at some point in our early development, we became coauthors and co-directors of our life story. As we grow, we subconsciously develop a particular view of the world as a whole. This, over time, develops into a legitimating narrative or metanarrative (big story) into which we invest our personal lives.

We live in a world of competing narratives, each vying for our allegiance, time, and money. Inevitably, we choose one, and then behave according to the expectations of that narrative. Every morning we wake up with a storehouse of energy metabolized during the night. We will spend that energy (even thoughts burn stored fuel) where we believe we will receive the highest return. Daily we inevitably answer this question: "In what story will I live today?"

That particular story functions as our true faith. In this sense, faith is a deeper concept than belief. Belief can be simply intellectual acknowledgment or agreement. Faith is actually living according to that belief. In other words, saying "Jesus is Lord" is one thing. Living that belief changes everything, including how we choose to raise our children.

Every institution or group has a legitimating or constitutive narrative. Without a differentiating story, there is no reason for a group to exist. Every group tells and perpetuates a particular story. That story sets the expectation of participation within the group. Observe any group for a while, ask questions about its origin, ask people why they are a part of it, and you will be able to piece together its legitimating narrative.

I teach a doctoral course in missional leadership. One of the pre-class projects I have assigned is to use appreciative inquiry to identify the legitimating narrative of one's particular faith community. The results are often surprising. People behave as they do because it is the expected behavior of the church's narrative. Leaders often express frustration because more people do not actively participate in the ministries of a church. The research done in this course has shown that a majority of members view the church as an entity that exists to meet their spiritual needs. Extra service beyond attendance and financial contribution is considered extraordinary and even unusual rather than normative. The legitimating narrative focuses on the members' needs and comforts. Members behave accordingly.

Families function in the same way. Each family has its own legitimating narrative. It is a complex combination of stories being woven together into a particular narrative. When families get together, they tell stories. The stories told not only reveal a lot about the family's past, but also about what they expect life yet to be. Unfortunately, some of those stories are oppressive (often not intentionally). Certain past events are retold in such a way that they limit the potential development of the one about whom the story is told. A child's identity is significantly impacted by the stories told about her or him.

We have both individual and corporate stories. While each member of the family is writing their own story, they are functioning within the larger family story. The family's legitimating narrative reveals the beliefs, values, and desires of that family. It is within the family narrative that dreams are born, pursued, and sometimes crushed.

While I have the great opportunity of teaching courses on the levels of doctoral studies, masters, and undergraduate—and I enjoy them all—my passion is undergraduate courses. I have students of all different disciplines of study and religious backgrounds, including atheist and agnostic. I am aware that each brings a different story into the classroom. However, the story is not written in its entirety; in a sense it has just begun. Many of the courses I teach to undergraduates are required courses such as The Story of Jesus, The Story of the Church, and The Story of Israel. They are designed to present the biblical text as a story into which all are invited. I encourage the students to consider allowing their personal stories to be woven into God's story.

This is an amazing teaching opportunity. I love watching many students gradually come to the realization that their lives are exponentially more meaningful than they previously thought. My teaching theme: while the world offers many legitimating narratives, only one story allows the reaching of one's full potential—God's story. I identify it as a "theology of creation" (more about this later). Every class I teach at every level is clearly set in this context. It is an invitation to life in its fullest potential. This is what Jesus referred to when he declared, "I am the way and the truth and the life" (John 14:6 NIV). It is only through embracing and pursuing

Jesus's invitation into God's legitimating narrative that we can find life in its fullest meaning. In perhaps the best-known verse in the Bible, John identifies this as the purpose for which Jesus came (3:16). Allow me to paraphrase; "God loved the world so much he sent his only Son so that those who believe and embrace the life he offers will no longer perish in the false stories of the world, but will live the eternal life for which they were created." John's Gospel identifies "eternal life" not as life after physical death, but as life in Christ (John 17:3) that begins at obedience and never ends.

The purpose of this chapter is to explore how we, as influential adults, whether parents, church leaders, or friends, might help launch young people into a life of mature discipleship. How do we support their dreams, help them maximize their gifts within the body of Christ—the church—and learn to lean on the Lord in all times, especially in times of trouble? The answer to these thought-provoking questions is both simple and complex. The simple answer is "Jesus." Living out the life of Jesus in today's culture is, or at least can be, complex.

Story and Creation

Let's return to the idea of a "theology of creation." The Genesis story of creation provides a challenging protology for the entire biblical story. "Protology" is the study of beginnings, but it is more than a simple introduction. It provides the meaning and trajectory for the epic story that follows, from creation to new creation. The story begins with God preceding all material things; then, God "begins" to create. God created realms (days one through three) and then populated the realms (days four through six). In the end, all was "very good." It was functioning exactly as God intended. Each of the first six days ends in "there was evening and there was morning." On the seventh day, this pattern is broken. God rests. There is no evening and morning at the conclusion of that day. It seems as if God's seventh day rest continues.

God graciously handed over his creative work to humankind. We were called to work with God in forming and filling the earth, tending the garden, and exercising responsible rule over all living things. It is as if God was saying, "I have created a wonderful universe. Now I am assigning humanity the responsibility and joy of taking what I have created and working with me to continue to create." Humankind was and is created in the *image of God* to do what God would do if he were working through our specific gifts and abilities.

Note carefully how all of creation functioned at this point. All things were working together for the purposes (the glory) of God. Adam enjoyed an unbroken relationship with God, with Eve, and with creation. Adam and Eve were working together in perfect harmony. There was no competition; it was value-enhancing complementarianism. This was God's perfect design in action. This was and is life as God intended it to be. Plants of all kinds were producing infinite varieties of fruit and grain, all creation was praising God by functioning according to its given purpose, and man and woman were ruling the garden in peace.

What happened to this blissful paradise? The story was derailed. Satan (surely the one behind the action and words of the serpent) convinced humankind that the gifts and possibilities of life could be used more satisfyingly in the context of another legitimating narrative. They did not have to serve God; they themselves could be God! They could use their God-given attributes to gain limitless knowledge and build kingdoms for themselves. Why did they need God?

Genesis 3–11 tells the difficult story of the fall of humankind, which ultimately developed into full rebellion against God with the attempted building of the tower of Babel. Then, in Genesis 12,

God begins to work again to rescue creation. God chose a man named Abram to begin a story of faith that would ultimately lead to the healing of the nations. The promise included a blessing for all the nations of the world.

The Holy One freed Israel from slavery in order to show the world God's purposes for life. Israel's legitimating narrative was based on their being set free to again walk with and worship the true God of the universe. They were to remember that they once were slaves, but they were set free by the mighty action of God in order to serve God's purposes as a model nation for all. Disappointingly, the same counter-narrative derailed the story once again. Israel wanted to be great by the world's standards instead of through faithfulness to God. Therefore, Israel suffered defeat and ultimately exile. The prophets lamented the loss of Israel's place in God's story, but they spoke of One who would deliver them from their self-inflicted plight. A Messiah would come and restore God's purposeful narrative for Israel.

The story of Jesus must be placed firmly in the hope of Israel or it will be misunderstood. If we disregard him as Israel's Messiah, we lose the purpose of his coming. Jesus did not come to die for our sins so that we can go to heaven (as too many assume); he came to redeem the broken story of all humankind. Jesus embodied the model human, one living fully in the image of God (see Heb. 1:3; Col. 1:15, 2:9; 2 Cor. 4:4). Jesus came to present true righteousness—a word that reflects life in its fullest expression. Jesus personified the life of faithful trust in God that we were all created to live. His death and resurrection not only provide forgiveness for our sins; they vindicate every word Jesus spoke about the true nature of life.

The church is called to continue the ministry, teaching, and invitation of Jesus to life in its fullest expression. One of the greatest challenges levied in Scripture is the vision of the church vividly described in Ephesians 4:11–16. Jesus Christ is pictured as the victorious king, having vanquished his enemies through his death and resurrection. As he ascends into heaven, he gives the gift of leaders to his church. The gift is not the "gift of leadership" but rather the gift is apostles, prophets, evangelists, and teaching pastors themselves. The ascending Christ gifted and gifts his church with leaders. Their identified role in this text is very specific. They are to equip the saints for works of ministry by helping them mature to the full stature of Christ Jesus. In fact, every saint, every member, is to be a living embodiment of truth, growing up in every way into Christ (Eph. 4:15).[1] As the result of this spiritual maturity, all members realize their needed purpose or function within the body of Christ. Each "part" contributes its essential working component to the body, resulting in healthy growth.

As parents and/or influential adults, we are called to introduce to our children this legitimating narrative, identified in Scripture as God's kingdom or rule reestablished on earth. This is the "good news" Jesus came to bring; we have been enabled by Jesus Christ and the Holy Spirit to live in and under the reign of God. How do we do this? By being equipped in the ways and teachings of Jesus, being challenged to grow toward full maturity in Christ. All saints (those set apart for God's purposes) are called to be fully engaged in "ministry." This is a very important word. We know that it means to serve others. More specifically, the word means that we are to be a "go between." In God's narrative, we have been entrusted with certain gifts and/or abilities in order to use them for the good of others. We steward our gifts for the good of the world. This is "the theology of creation" in action through the full participation of every member of the body of Christ.

Without this understanding of the church, it is difficult to encourage meaningful visioning in our children. I have been teaching in a university environment for over twenty-five years. I am constantly amazed at the creative genius of our students. I am also deeply troubled by how little of their creativity is spent for the expansion of God's kingdom. It is not their fault. The church, in its present form (there are exceptions), provides almost no possibility for our youths' creative contributions. The truth is that most churches are not structured for creative imagination in any form, much to their detriment. Ministry programs often stifle what could be the meaningful contribution of all by limiting what the church does to a few "good works." What might the church be if it were a place where one could hear the true legitimating narrative of life and explore the possibilities of utilizing one's specific passions in a unique and meaningful way?

I believe this is the basis of the stirring rendition of God's gracious story of redemption in Ephesians 2:8–10: "It is by grace you have been saved, through faith—and this is not from yourselves, it is the gift of God—not by works, so that no one can boast. For we are God's handiwork, created in Christ Jesus to do good works, which God prepared in advance for us to do" (NIV). Think about the implications of this great text. Imagine the "twinkle" in God's eye when God handcrafted your child. What dreams did God have as God lovingly and creatively wove together the DNA that ultimately determined what capacities, gifts, and abilities she or he has?

Walking into God's Story

With this in mind, I would love to have the opportunity to raise our children again. It is my hope that I might help others with their children by what I share next.

Rebecca and I have been blessed with three amazing children, now married adults. We have been blessed with six amazing grandchildren. I am deeply grateful for another opportunity to help in the shaping of those precious lives. One of my spiritual disciplines is to never miss an opportunity to share thoughts on Jesus with our grandchildren. Every time I am with them, I speak of Jesus in some way that is appropriate to their level of understanding. Hopefully I am also patterning his life in all I do and say.

What has changed since we raised our children? I have come to understand more fully the amazing redemptive narrative into which we are each invited to fully participate. I acknowledge that while Rebecca and I have always been involved in missions, church planting, or teaching, for much of that time I was living in a faulty legitimating narrative. Life was still about me. While I never doubted the existence of God, I was raised without an understanding of God's intimate guiding presence in my life.

I was taught that one figured out life by reading the Bible and putting it into practice, but my focus was on doing church right so I could go to heaven after death. My spiritual life had little consistency. I knew better than to "stray into a major sin," but I could be a different person in varying environments. I could act like an idiot at a sporting event, but I was remarkably kind and loving in a church environment (my job depended on it!). I believe I modeled an egocentric life with a strong "Christian" commitment. I repent. I have found an exceedingly better story. What was once an awkward conversation with my children (how to live faithfully) is now the joy of my life. I want to share a completely new vision of life that the world could never give. The challenge of wanting to be more like Jesus every day is replacing what was once compelling to me; I am understanding Paul's comments in Philippians 3 more every day.

God was gracious to me as I struggled to understand the meaning of my life. Our children have developed into amazing adults (I will credit this to the Lord and Rebecca) in spite of my selfishness. To our great joy, they married amazing, faithful followers of Jesus. So, by God's grace, all is well. But I need to admit that in my former self-focused legitimating narrative a portion of my concern for our children's faithfulness to the church was because that reflected positively on me. That was not the complete motivation—clearly, I wanted them to go to heaven—but good parents somehow convince their children to walk as they walked in matters of faith (so I thought). I choose not to beat myself up for any of this. It was all I knew. Even my efforts at evangelism as a missionary and church planter had much to do with a personal success narrative. Once again, God was gracious and worked through me in spite of my many failings.

What changed? Through difficult struggles (including being fired—that has a way of getting one's attention), I slowly came to discover a much better story. I turned away from a narrative of self-reliance to one of trust in God. Of course, it was not quite that abrupt or clear-cut. Rebecca, my amazing wife, was extremely helpful in this transition. When I journeyed out of my story and walked into God's story, everything changed. Creative imagination returned. My joy gained from teaching increased exponentially. I was no longer performing for approval; I was now free to invite students and other believers and nonbelievers in Jesus to join me in the adventure of participating in God's redemptive narrative. I could help them with missional imagination—new ways of serving God. More and more students came into my office because they wanted to envision what they could do with their lives. I began allowing them to negotiate their medium of expression at the end of a course of study. Rather than just writing a three-page essay (they could choose this if prose was their preferred medium), they could express themselves through art, dance, video, music, or even Legos! My office now looks like a museum, full of art offered as expressions of praise. What could have been an essay taking less than an hour to write was exchanged for a piece of art that took weeks to create.

Creative Participation

My experience with hundreds of college students a year has convinced me that many in older generations have misjudged them completely. I hear careless comments such as "young people have no interest in spiritual things" or "these kids only care about themselves." While admitting that some fit these characterizations, what generation does not display such attitudes and behaviors? Egocentricity and narcissism have been around since the Fall. I am deeply impressed with our present generation of youth because of their deep longing for meaningful participation in something that will improve our world.

The church, as presently constituted, does not provide much opportunity for this kind of contribution. Some object by saying, "We offer a lot of different ministry opportunities!" Giving someone a job to be done is much different from inviting one into creative participation based on giftedness. While current church practices and standard ministry offerings might be deeply meaningful to those of us who have learned to be content with sitting and listening and "doing what needs to be done," our younger generations find little or no meaning in this kind of scripted participation. They have been raised in an environment that is audibly, physically, and emotionally stimulating.

Some of my students have actually begun their own businesses while in school, and are doing quite well. It is difficult for many of them to comprehend why praise and service to God, the greatest possible Being, should be expressed in somewhat quiet, almost passive behaviors in worship or ministry confined to jobs that "need to be done." We can cheer wildly at an athletic event, applaud loudly at multiple performance venues, but our worship to God remains somewhat reserved and restrained. We can be creative entrepreneurs in business, but not in service to God and humankind.

Dreams and Imagination

The importance of meaningful participation of our youth that allows for expression of one's giftedness in a contributive way cannot be overstated. One of the guiding principles of the Christian life is the giving of self for the good of others.

One of my favorite activities is leading our students in mission opportunities and watching them give themselves away to people they do not even know. I realize the limitations of short-term missions, but I also see the potential of expressions of ministry that would otherwise not be available. I am fascinated and encouraged by the number of creative ministry expressions that result from opportunities to dream and imagine. I am deeply impressed by our students' willingness to maintain relationships through social media after the mission effort has ended. During a recent mission trip with students, I was amazed at the influence of one young woman who collected a small congregation of "disciples"— relationships that had grown over the three years of her repeated participation in the same mission. Her influence in their lives is simply amazing.

For a number of years I have taught a master's level class entitled, Missional Strategies in Emerging Culture. It is an intensive study of a comprehensive theology of mission that ends in proposing a specific way of reaching into a specific context with the gospel of the kingdom of God. Some projects have been somewhat predictable, but the vast majority have been very encouraging. Numerous new ways of proclaiming the gospel are now in existence because students were given the opportunity to openly assess their passions and imagine where those might meet a need in the world.

I take no credit for this. It is the outcome of studying the story of God and allowing one to dream how they might participate in that story in meaningful ways. Regretfully, several of these had to enter the world of not-for-profit organizations because the church was not capable of embracing their creative ideas. While there is certainly a place for not-for-profits, I would love to see the church become a place for creative imagination to flourish with no fear of failure.

Coping with Disappointment without Fearing Failure

One more aspect of the biblical story I believe to be essential to this discussion. It has to do with helping our children develop coping skills for life's disappointments, teaching them to lean on the Lord in times of trouble. We need to reconsider how we teach the text. In the Western world, we long ago sold out to the idea that education comes through disseminating information. The Enlightenment convinced us that rational thought is the key to understanding life. This is a left-brained approach to education. Teach and test facts. Returning to the Hebrew idea of learning wisdom through experience is essential to developing our children into mature adults.

This is one of the reasons why narrative is so important. Most of the Bible is narrative. Paul instructs Timothy to continue in what he has learned from the God-breathed Scriptures—useful for teaching, rebuking, correcting, and training in righteousness (2 Tim. 3:14–17). Paul here is clearly referring to the Hebrew Scriptures or Old Testament. The Scriptures are also able to make one wise for salvation through faith in Christ Jesus. We know these words of Paul, but we often do not read the very texts to which Paul refers. And if we do read the Old Testament, we do not read it as Paul would have read it. The Hebrew approach to Scripture is right-brained; it is experiential, not informational. We need to read the stories, all of them, good and bad. We need to enter into the stories, experience the stories—and not just the good parts. The Bible is full of stories of broken people making huge mistakes, yet God is longsuffering and loving. God patiently works through them in spite of their failures.

Look at the Psalms. We love the psalms of praise but seem to skip over the psalms of lament. We certainly don't want to read the imprecatory psalms! If we "enter the story," we learn there are times in life when God seems absent. Sometimes the stories do not end well. But the main story line continues, uninterrupted.

One of my favorite classes to teach is The Story of Israel. I unapologetically teach it as the prequel to the coming of Christ Jesus (as I believe Jesus did in Luke 24). However, we look at all the story in all its messiness. One of the remarks I often receive in student evaluations is how surprised they are with the brokenness God chooses to work through. Many are encouraged because it shows them that God will not give up on them. Some of the projects turned in at the end of the course intended to summarize what a student has learned have brought me to tears. One was a broken mirror. A badly broken mirror. Carefully glued back together, letters of non-uniform size and font simply said, "Broken, but loved, I can still reflect God's light." Then below, the Hebrew word "*hesed*" —the word most often used in the Old Testament to describe God's unfailing love.

Embracing God's Story

Raising faithful children in today's world can only be done by offering them a different legitimating narrative for their lives. Only God's story will truly allow our children to live. Help them discover the beauty of the story. Help them dream about what God could release them to do with their lives. It might not be our dream, but we need to let that go. There is a better story.

I conclude with a quote from a presentation I was asked to give at my son's high school graduation (you can imagine how nervous he was!).

"My friends, what lies before you is a lifetime of possibilities. What will you do? Where will you go? I beg you to
remember this. Whatever dreams you might have, God's
dream for you is greater than any this world could ever
create. My prayer is that you will embrace God's story
and allow God's Spirit to transform you into exactly
that which God had in mind, when you were lovingly
formed in his hands."

Questions

1. Earl reminds us that each day we answer the question: "In
   what story will I live today?" How does the way we as adults
   answer this question affect how the adolescents in our lives
   will answer that question?
2. What is your family's "legitimizing narrative?" What is the
   story that gives your lives together meaning, and where is it
   going?
3. Earl tells us that, as he has his students work through their
   life stories, they discover that "their lives are exponentially
   more meaningful than they previously thought!" How might
   this be true in the lives of the teens in your life? How does
   connecting these life stories with the story of God make
   them even more powerful?
4. How would the church be different if every teen saw themselves as stewards of God-given gifts for the sake of the
   world, instead of gifted for personal safety or wealth? How
   can adults help them see this stewardship?

5. What are some of the apparently righteous but false narratives that Christians can be tricked into following?
6. How do you "fund" or "empower" the imagination and dreams of the youth you know? How can the local church do this better?
7. Why do we falsely fear failure?

APPENDIX ONE

Understanding Adult Impact

To solidify the impact adults have on spiritual formation, try this exercise.

Make two lists:

1. First, write down all of the sermons, lessons, and devotionals you remember that had a deep spiritual impact on you as a teenager.

2. Second, write down the names of all the people you remember who had a deep impact on your spiritual journey as a teenager.

Question: Which list is longer and/or do you consider more influential in your present spiritual journey?

More than likely, the answer to this question illustrates the value of intergenerational relationships in youth ministry.

APPENDIX TWO

Evaluating Your Intergenerational Effectiveness

To evaluate how well your youth ministry is embracing an intergenerational theology, use the simple scale below, record your answers to the following questions, and then discuss them as a team.

1: Strongly Disagree, 2: Disagree, 3: Not Sure, 4: Agree, 5: Strongly Agree

____ Our youth ministry teaches that declaring Jesus as Lord is a total-life commitment that is evident in both word and action.

____ The parents and adult sponsors assisting in our youth ministry are expected to be devoted followers of Jesus (they practice what they preach).

____ Our youth ministry publicly acknowledges and encourages the role and responsibility of parents in the spiritual formation of teenagers.

_____ Our youth ministry publicly acknowledges and encourages the role and responsibility of other adult community members in the spiritual formation of teenagers.

_____ Our youth ministry offers worship opportunities and other rituals designed to engage both adult and child audiences.

_____ TOTAL SCORE

Spend time discussing and praying over the results of this evaluation.

What ideas do you have to make progress in these areas?

What practical steps can you implement in your ministry?

APPENDIX THREE

Suggestions for Adult Involvement

Here are a few practical suggestions for getting into the adult education realm and providing an exceptional classroom experience:

1. *Ask!* This may sound simple, but it is important to ask the preacher, adult education director, class coordinator, or whoever is in charge for the opportunity to speak to the class. Tell them you want to speak on the need for adults to be involved in the spiritual formation of students.
2. *Prepare well!* Visit www.stickyfaith.org for a lot of great resources and curriculum ideas.
3. *Follow up!* After you teach, what is the follow-up plan? What do you want your audience to do with the information you have just given them? Give them something tangible like:

   - Challenge adults to meet at least five students they do not know and start up a conversation.
   - Challenge adults to have a spiritual conversation with the teenager(s) living in their home.

- Challenge adults to walk through the youth center area (or area where teens hang out in your church) and say hello to a few students on the way to the adult areas of church.
- Give them something tangible to look forward to like an intergenerational event or opportunity on the horizon.

APPENDIX FOUR

More Ideas for Youth Volunteers

Ideas that have worked to help adults **re-vision** their role as volunteers in youth ministry:

- *Invite* adults to participate in the ministry and provide a clear path in which to volunteer in the youth ministry (a simple, but often forgotten step).
- *Expect* the adult's first "job" in the youth ministry to be visiting with and geting to know students (amazing what putting this expectation in a volunteer job description does for Sticky Faith focus). Furthermore, the following statement clearly places the expectation for a student's growth at the feet of parents and other adult community members: "We can't out-teach what happens in the home and surrounding adult community—we are not that good."
- *Train* the adult volunteer with skills to understand today's teen culture and how to have "relational wins" with students in the ministry.

- *Celebrate* the role of adults in your youth ministry. We constantly thank and brag about our parent volunteers. Provide times of prayer and support at major retreats and camps. Host a yearly banquet in which we eat, have fun (babysitting provided), and share stories from the past year's ministry.

Ideas that have worked to help an entire church **re-vision** their role in the life of kids and youth ministry:

- Students who possess the giftedness and maturity are *welcomed* as fully functioning participants on church ministry teams and committees, worship leading, technical/fine arts crews, various church stage productions, teaching roles in children and student programming, and other traditionally "adult only" areas of church work.
- Once a year the *Youth Minister preaches* a "Sticky Sermon" to the church body. This typically works best at the first of each school year and highlights the role of the church and biological family in the spiritual formation of students.
- Senior Ministers use *language of inclusion* when speaking about student ministry programming. For instance, when a preacher speaks on missions, student and adult projects get highlighted with the same level of importance and excitement.

CONTRIBUTOR BIOGRAPHIES

Ron Bruner (DMin, Abilene Christian University) has served as the executive director of Westview Boys' Home in Hollis, Oklahoma, since 1999. He co-edited *Along the Way: Conversations about Children and Faith* with Dana Kennamer Pemberton. Because of his interest in practical theology—especially in the fields of intergenerational, children's, and youth ministry—Ron edits the e-journal *Discernment: Theology and the Practice of Ministry*. He and his wife, Ann, enjoy life with their three adult children and four grandchildren.

Dudley Chancey (PhD, University of Tennessee) has served as professor of youth ministry at Oklahoma Christian University since 1998. He is involved in several professional organizations including the National Council on Family Relations, Groves Conference on Marriage and Family, Association of Youth Ministry Educators, and the National Conference on Youth Ministries. Dudley is dedicated to Honduras family mission trips at OCU. He loves all the sponsors, parents, and youth ministers who have brought teens to Winterfest for the last 30 years. Dudley is married to Vicki and has two adult children and two grandchildren.

Brad Childers gave his life to Jesus at the age of fourteen when his mentor Jim Moss shared the gospel. After attending Lipscomb University, he married his college sweetheart Margaret. They now have four kids: Margaret Grace, Charles, Annie Cage, and William. For twenty-three years, he has served as the youth minister at the Providence Road Church of Christ in Charlotte, North Carolina. He has served on the boards of National Conference on Youth Ministries, Breaking Chains, and Carolina Teen. Brad is an avid golfer and is currently getting his masters from Liberty University.

Ryan Noel Fraser (PhD, Brite Divinity School, Texas Christian University) has taught in the graduate counseling program at Freed-Hardeman University since 2006. He is a pastoral therapist in private practice. Ryan also serves as the pulpit minister and an elder for the Bethel Springs Church of Christ in Bethel Springs, Tennessee. He wrote *The Spiritual Narratives of Adoptive Parents: Constructions of Christian Faith Stories and Pastoral Theological Implications* (Peter Lang, 2013). Ryan is a pastoral theologian with expertise in marriage and family issues, as well as ministry and mental health concerns. He and his wife, Missy, are blessed with two adopted children.

David Fraze (DMin, Fuller Theological Seminary) was drawn to Lubbock Christian University in 1987 to pursue his life's calling in youth ministry. Fraze began working as a part-time college minister at Greenlawn Church of Christ in Lubbock, Texas, in 1989; he and his wife, Lisa, were hired full time for student ministry from 1991–2002. He served as an adjunct professor at LCU from 1994–1999, then as full-time faculty beginning in 2001 until he and Lisa moved to Dallas-Fort Worth in 2007 to lead a large student ministry. David completed his Doctor of Ministry at Fuller Theological Seminary. He is now the special assistant to the president of LCU.

Houston Heflin (EdD, Southern Seminary) spent twelve years in church ministry before moving to Abilene, Texas, where he is an associate professor at Abilene Christian University. He is the author of *Youth Pastor: The Theology and Practice of Youth Ministry* and *Teaching Eutychus: Engaging Today's Learners with Passion and Creativity.* Houston and his wife, Karen, are youth ministry volunteers at their church and are thankful to be raising four adolescent and elementary-aged children.

Earl Lavender (PhD, Saint Louis University) has taught at Lipscomb since 1990 and for the last thirteen years has served as Director of Missional Studies and professor in the College of Bible and Ministry. He has led mission and education events in Europe, Australia, India, Russia, Brazil, Ghana, and China. Earl also serves as the founding director of the Institute for Christian Spirituality, established at Lipscomb in the fall of 2009. He and his wife, Rebecca, have three grown children. Rebecca and Earl have planted churches in Italy (1978–1984) and Illinois (1986–1990).

Johnny Markham has been a full-time youth minister since 1985. He served the McGregor Boulevard (now Gulf Coast) Church of Christ in Ft. Myers, Florida, from 1985 until 1990. He has been with the College Hills Church of Christ in Lebanon, Tennessee, since 1990. In addition to his responsibilities at College Hills, Johnny serves on the boards of Winterfest and Impact (Lipscomb University). He and his wife, Vicki, have three children: Mary Beth, John, and Katie. Johnny completed his quest to attend a complete game at all thirty current Major League Baseball stadiums.

Monty McCulley has served as the Youth and Family Minister at A&M Church of Christ in College Station, Texas, since 2006. He began serving in full-time youth ministry at Georgetown Church of Christ in 1999. Prior to his full-time role in youth ministry, he taught eighth-grade math in Abilene, Texas. He is a graduate of Abilene Christian University. Monty is married to his college sweetheart, Heather, and they have four children. He loves spending time with his family, doing anything outdoors, and helping students grow in faith.

Cari Myers is studying Religion and Social Change in the joint PhD program at the Iliff School of Theology and the University of Denver. Her work resides at the crossroads of social ethics, postcolonial theory, Latino/a studies, adolescent development, and public education. Specifically, Cari's dissertation will focus on the ways Latino/a youth negotiate life on the United States-Mexico border, especially in the context of the colonized classroom and the Christian church. Of particular interest are the "survival narratives" Latino/a youth receive about how to survive and succeed in the United States. Currently, Cari is serving as a Faculty Fellow in the Religion and Philosophy Division at Seaver College of Pepperdine University.

Robert Oglesby is the director of ACU Center for Youth and Family Ministry and a professor of youth and family ministry in the Department of Bible, Missions, and Ministry. He also works with the Ministry Support Network and is a consultant with the Siburt Institute for Church Ministry. He was the youth and family minister at Southern Hills Church of Christ in Abilene, Texas, from 1984 to 1999, when he came to Abilene Christian University full time. Whether riding his Harley or climbing a 14,000-foot mountain peak, he is not risk-averse. Robert and his wife, Jenny, have three adult children.

Dave Pocta (MS, Lubbock Christian University) presides over three ministry training academies in Africa and one in Texas. He has served as chairman for the international youth and family service team in the International Churches of Christ for the past six years. He and his wife, Beth, have been in full-time ministry for twenty-five years and have spent the last seventeen years working with teenagers and their families. They currently minister in San Antonio, Texas, and spend a fair amount of time training church leaders about family-based models for youth and family ministry. Dave also runs a Christian resource publishing company named GROUNDED Resources (www.getgroundedforlife.com). Both of their daughters are currently in college in Texas.

Beth Robinson (EdD, Texas Tech University) is a professor in the Pediatrics Department at Texas Tech University Health Sciences Center. She is a licensed professional counselor, an approved supervisor for licensed professional counselors, and a certified school counselor. Dr. Robinson has written several books and developed therapeutic coloring books for foster children. She has worked with traumatized children, as well as foster and adopted children for more than 20 years. Dr. Robinson also holds academic appointments at Harding University and Lubbock Christian University.

Walter Surdacki (DMin, Fuller Theological Seminary) is an associate professor of youth and family ministry at Lipscomb University in Nashville, Tennessee, where he teaches various youth ministry and practical ministry courses as well as spiritual disciplines and spiritual formation courses. He has served in full-time youth ministry for over sixteen years, working at churches in Torrance, Malibu, and Campbell, California. He currently volunteers with the youth ministry at the Otter Creek Church where his daughters are in the youth group. He is a regular speaker and teacher at events all over the country. Walter and his wife, Amy, have two daughters,

Madeline and Abby. Walter loves to travel, cook, snowboard, read, write, and ride roller coasters.

Scott Talley is the executive minister at the Crestview Church of Christ in Waco, Texas, where he has been on the ministry staff for thirty-nine years. Scott also served as youth minister three years at Central in Amarillo and twenty-three years at Crestview in Waco. He authored two books providing practical guidance for parents and youth workers concerning communicating and modeling godly sexual values for children and teens. In 1990, he published *Talking with Your Kids about the Birds and the Bees* and *This Can't Wait: Talking with Your Kids about Sex* in 2000.

ENDNOTES

Chapter One—You're Not Supposed to Do This by Yourself

[1]In ten presentations to parents and other interested adults in ten different church settings of an *Almost Christian* seminar, some participants would respond afterwards in every setting with, "We don't know how to spiritually form our children," or "We don't have time." Christian Smith and Melinda L. Denton, *Soul Searching: The Religious and Spiritual Lives of American Teenagers* (New York: Oxford University Press, 2005).

[2]See: Mark Oestreicher, *Youth Ministry 3.0: A Manifesto of Where We've Been, Where We Are and Where We Need to Go* (Grand Rapids: Zondervan. 2008).

[3]Mark DeVries, *Family-Based Youth Ministry* (Downers Grove, IL: InterVarsity Press, 2004); Oestreicher, *Youth Ministry 3.0*.

[4]DeVries, *Family-Based Youth Ministry*; Richard Dunn and Mark Senter III, *Reaching a Generation for Christ: A Comprehensive Guide to Youth Ministry* (Chicago: Moody, 1997); Richard A. Hardel, *Passing On the Faith: A Radical Model for Youth and Family Ministry* (Winona, MN: St. Mary's, 2000); Kenda Creasy Dean, Chap Clark, and Dave Rahn, *Starting Right: Thinking Theologically about Youth Ministry* (El Cajon, CA: Youth Specialties, 2001); Kara Powell and Chap Clark, *Sticky Faith: Everyday Ideas to Build Lasting Faith in Your Kids* (Grand Rapids: Zondervan, 2011).

[5]Smith and Denton, *Soul Searching*.

[6]Walter Brueggemann, *Biblical Perspectives on Evangelism: Living in a Three-Storied Universe* (Nashville: Abingdon Press, 1993).

[7]Brueggemann, *Biblical Perspectives*, 72–73.

Chapter Two—To Be a Parent Is to Be a Youth Minister

[1]Frederick Smith, *A Letter to Parents* (London: Darton and Harvey, 1806), 4–5.

[2]NPR Staff, "More Young People Are Moving Away from From Religion, But Why?" Morning Edition Losing Our Religion (series), NPR, January 15, 2013, accessed September 6, 2016, http://www.npr.org/2013/01/15/169342349/more-young-people-are-moving-away-from-religion-but-why.

[3]Suniya S. Luthar, "The Problem with Rich Kids," *Psychology Today,* November 5, 2013, accessed September 6, 2016, https://www.psychologytoday .com/articles/201310/the-problem-rich-kids.

[4]David Elkind, *All Grown Up and No Place to Go: Teenagers in Crisis,* rev. ed. (Boston: Da Capo Press, 1998).

[5]For more resources on youth and family ministry, see our website, www .teendisciples.org, under Youth and Family Ministry.

[6]Kara Powell and Chap Clark, *Sticky Faith: Everyday Ideas to Build Lasting Faith in Your Kids* (Grand Rapids: Zondervan, 2011).

Chapter Three—Disciples Learn from Disciples

[1]Spiros Zodhiates, *The Complete Word Study Dictionary: New Testament* (Chattanooga, TN: AMG, 2000).

[2]For more on Satan's specific attack on youth see Mike Taliaferro, *The Lion Never Sleeps* (Houston: Illumination, 2014).

[3]Karen Louis and John Louis, *Good Enough Parenting* (New York: Morgan James, 2015).

Chapter Four—What is a Youth Minister's Job, Then?

[1]For more detail about these ten roles of youth ministry, see: Houston Heflin, *Youth Pastor: The Theology and Practice of Youth Ministry* (Nashville: Abingdon, 2009).

Chapter Five—Building Faith at Home

[1]John Trent and Jane Vogel, *FaithLaunch* (Carol Stream, IL: Tyndale House, 2008), quoted in *Your Family Journey: A Guide to Building Faith at Home* (Colorado Springs, CO: Focus on the Family, 2009), 3.

[2]*Effective Christian Education: A National Study of Protestant Congregations,* (Search Institute, 1990), quoted in Mark Holmen, *Building Faith at Home* (Regal Books: Ventura, CA, 2007), 20–21. Much of this article was influenced by the work of Mark Holmen.

[3]George Barna, *Transforming Children into Spiritual Champions* (Ventura, CA: Regal, 2003), 78.

[4]Peter L. Benson, *All Kids Are Our Kids* (San Francisco: Jossey-Bass, 2006), 107.

[5]Marjorie Thompson, *The Family as Forming Center* (Nashville: Upper Room Books, 1996), 26.

[6]Watch the video clip (1:21) on YouTube titled "Jaws–Father and Son," https://www.youtube.com/watch?v=04mIMg4PTO8.

[7]Barna, *Transforming Children,* 84.

[8]Ibid., 85.

[9]Christian Smith with Melinda L. Denton, *Soul Searching* (New York: Oxford Press, 2005), 28.

[10] Martin Luther, "The Estate of Marriage, 1522," cited in Walther Brand, ed. , *Luther's Works* (Philadelphia: Fortress Press, 1962), 46.

[11] Jon Acuff, "The Problem with Halloween," *Work can be Awesome* (blog), October 5, 2015, accessed 8/1/2016, http://acuff.me/2015/10/the-problem-with -halloween/.

[12] Kenda Creasy Dean, *Almost Christian: What the Faith of Our Teenagers Is Telling the American Church* (New York: Oxford University Press, 2010), 142–43.

[13] For example, Ed Young, *The 10 Commandments of Parenting* (Chicago: Moody, 2004), 77–89.

Chapter Six—Discernment

[1] Adele Ahlberg Calhoun, *Spiritual Disciplines Handbook: Practices That Transform Us* (Downers Grove, IL: InterVarsity, 2005), 99.

[2] Nonna Vera Harrison, *God's Many-Splendored Image: Theological Anthropology for Christian Formation* (Grand Rapids: Baker Academic, 2010).

[3] Mark Powell, *Centered in God: The Trinity and Christian Spirituality* (Abilene, TX: Abilene Christian University Press, 2014), 187–97.

[4] David F. White, *Practicing Discernment with Youth: A Transformative Youth Ministry Approach* (Cleveland: Pilgrim Press, 2005), 37.

[5] Sally Gary, *Loves God, Likes Girls* (Abilene, TX: Leafwood, 2013), 220.

[6] Robert Audi, *Moral Value and Human Diversity* (New York: Oxford, 2007), 32.

[7] "Discernment is first of all a habit, a way of seeing that eventually permeates our whole life. It is the journey from spiritual blindness . . . to spiritual sight." Ruth Haley Barton, *Sacred Rhythms: Arranging Our Lives for Spiritual Transformation* (Downers Grove, IL: InterVarsity Press, 2006), 111.

[8] Michael J. Nakkula and Eric Toshalis, *Understanding Youth: Adolescent Development for Educators* (Cambridge: MA: Harvard Educational Press, 2006), 8–9.

[9] Ernest Larkin, *Silent Presence: Discernment as Process and Problem* (Denville, NJ: Dimension Books, 1981), 42–45.

[10] Individual discernment processes are described in: Barton, *Sacred Rhythms*, 110–129; Larkin, *Silent Presence*, 12–20; Calhoun, *Spiritual Disciplines Handbook*, 99–103; Elizabeth Liebert, *The Way of Discernment: Spiritual Practices for Decision Making* (Louisville: Westminster John Knox, 2008). Elaine Heath has created a method of discernment that I have enlarged and described in: Ron Bruner, "Living Deuteronomy 6 Today: Parenting as a Spiritual Discipline," in *Along the Way: Conversations about Children and Faith*, eds. Ron Bruner and Dana Kennamer Pemberton (Abilene, TX: Abilene Christian University Press, 2015), 47–60.

For discernment with adolescents, see White, *Practicing Discernment with Youth* and Mark Yaconelli, *Contemplative Youth Ministry: Practicing the Presence of Jesus* (El Cajon, CA: Youth Specialties, 2006), 157–76.

Group discernment processes include: James D. and Evelyn E. Whitehead, *Method in Ministry: Theological Reflection and Christian Ministry,* rev. ed. (Chicago: Sheed and Ward, 1995), 3–22; this is a thoroughly tested and used practice. Danny E. Morris and Charles M. Olsen, *Discerning God's Will Together: A Spiritual Practice for the Church* (Nashville: Upper Room Books, 1997); this work is a synthesis of traditional Christian spiritual discernment practices and the previous separate work of Morris and Olson. It involves a ten-component process that is useful, but considerably more complex. Ruth Haley Barton, *Pursuing God's Will Together: A Discernment Practice for Leadership Groups* (Downers Grove, IL: InterVarsity Press, 2012). Elizabeth Liebert, *The Soul of Discernment: A Spiritual Practice for Communities and Institutions* (Louisville: Westminster John Knox, 2015). A description of the use of communal discernment in a specific context can be found in Ron Bruner, "Communally Discerning a Covenant of Hospitality for the Care of Children at Westview Boys' Home" (DMin thesis, Abilene Christian University, 2010).

[11] Barton, *Sacred Rhythms,* 117, 119. Barton refers to this as "interior freedom" or "indifference." "We generally think of indifference as a negative attitude that is characterized by apathy and not caring; in the realm of discernment, however, *indifference* is a very positive term that is rich in meaning." (119). See also: Barton, *Pursuing God's Will,* 189.

[12] Barton, *Pursuing God's Will,* 119.

[13] Ibid., 189.

[14] Frederick Aquino appropriately calls this "epistemological humility." Frederick D. Aquino, *Communities of Informed Judgment: Newman's Illative Sense and Accounts of Rationality* (Washington, DC: Catholic University of America Press, 2006), 62.

[15] White, *Practicing Discernment with Youth,* 126.

[16] Carson Reed, Twitter post, February 17, 2016, 6:51 A.M., http://twitter.com/CarsonReed.

[17] For a helpful explanation, see Nakkula and Toshalis, *Understanding Youth,* 17–39.

[18] Robert C. Roberts, *Spiritual Emotions: A Psychology of Christian Virtues* (Grand Rapids: Eerdmans, 2007).

[19] Martin Luther King Jr., "Remaining Awake through a Great Revolution," (commencement address, Oberlin College, Oberlin, OH, June 1965), accessed February 15, 2016, http://www.oberlin.edu/external/EOG/BlackHistoryMonth/MLK/CommAddress.html

[20] Aquino, *Communities of Informed Judgment,* 95.

[21] Larkin, *Silent Presence,* 21–24.

[22] John Kay, *Obliquity: Why Our Goals Are Best Achieved Indirectly* (New York: Penguin, 2011). Jennifer Garvey Berger and Keith Johnston, *Simple Habits for Complex Times: Powerful Habits for Leaders* (Stanford, CA: Stanford University Press, 2015).

[23] Louis J. Puhl, trans., *The Spiritual Exercises of St. Ignatius* (Chicago: Loyola Press, 1951). A detailed explanation of the practice can be found in: Timothy M. Gallagher, *The Examen Prayer: Ignatian Wisdom for Our Lives Today* (New York: Crossroad, 2006). A much briefer description is in Calhoun, *Spiritual Disciplines Handbook,* 52–55. For a video that helpfully explains the practice to adolescents, see Phil Brookman's video at: https://www.youtube.com/watch?v=VspgLZSAk4E&list=PL78DACA582AE6D53D&index=30

[24] Adapted from Calhoun, *Spiritual Disciplines Handbook*, 53.

[25] Calhoun, *Spiritual Disciplines Handbook*, 57. Wilson McCoy explains journaling to adolescents in a video at https://www.youtube.com/watch?v=bNTjI7j3-PU&list=PL78DACA582AE6D53D&index=26.

[26] Emphasis by Merton. Thomas Merton, *Thoughts in Solitude* (New York: Farrar, Straus, and Giroux, 1958), 37.

Chapter Seven—Comfort with the Comfort We Receive from God

[1] 2 Corinthians 1:3–4 NIV.

Chapter Eight—Human Sexuality

[1] Scott Talley, *Talking with Your Kids about the Birds and the Bees* (Ventura, CA: Regal, 1990); *This Can't Wait: Talking with Your Kids About Sex* (Abilene, TX: HillCrest, 2000).

[2] Talley, *This Can't Wait.*

[3] "American Teens' Sexual and Reproductive Health," Guttmacher Institute, May 2014, accessed September 12, 2016, https://www.guttmacher.org/sites/default/files/pdfs/pubs/FB-ATSRH.pdf.

[4] Jim Burns, *Teaching Your Children Healthy Sexuality* (Bloomington: Bethany House, 2008), 37–43.

[5] Talley, *This Can't Wait,* 176–77.

[6] Twila Pearson, *The Challenging Years: Shedding Light on Teen Sexuality* (Bloomington: WestBow, 2012), 4–7.

[7] Talley, *This Can't Wait,* 194–202.

[8] Jonathan McKee, *More Than Just the Talk: Becoming Your Kids' Go-To Person about Sex* (Minneapolis: Bethany House, 2015), 157–69.

[9] Jim Burns, *The Purity Code: God's Plan For Sex And Your Body* (Minneapolis: Bethany House, 2008).

[10] Ritch C. Savin-Williams and Geoffrey L. Ream, "Prevalence and Stability of Sexual Orientation Components during Adolescence and Young Adulthood, *Archives of Sexual Behavior*, 36, no. 3 (2007): 385-94.

[11] Mark A. Yarhouse, *Understanding Sexual Identity* (Grand Rapids: Zondervan, 2013), 36–38.

[12] Yarhouse, *Understanding Sexual Identity*, 84.

[13] Francis S. Collins, *The Language of God: A Scientist Presents Evidence for Belief* (New York: Free Press, 2006), 260.

[14] Dr. Steven Gerali, *What Do I Do When Teenagers Question Their Sexuality?* (Grand Rapids: Zondervan, 2010), 52.

[15] Yarhouse, *Understanding Sexual Identity*, 129, 132.

[16] Gerali, *What Do I Do*, 123–30.

[17] Burns, *Teaching Your Children*, 85.

[18] Pearson, *Challenging Years*, 23.

[19] McKee, *More Than Just*, 96–108.

[20] Burns, *Teaching Your Children*, 25.

[21] Talley, *This Can't Wait*, 229–37, 241.

[22] Burns, *Teaching Your Children*, 52–53.

[23] Talley, *This Can't Wait*, 332–34.

Chapter Nine—Adoptive Parenting

[1] Ryan N. Fraser, *The Spiritual Narratives of Adoptive Parents: Constructions of Christian Faith Stories and Pastoral Theological Implications*, American University Studies VII, Theology and Religion, vol. 332 (New York: Peter Lang, 2013).

[2] For more information about these challenges, see Ryan N. Fraser, "A Fairy Tale with a Twist: Pastoral Counseling with Adoptive Families," *Journal of Pastoral Care and Counseling* 59 (March, 2005): 63–78.

[3] Nancy N. Verrier, *The Primal Wound: Understanding the Adopted Child* (Louisville, KY: Gateway Press, 2003).

Chapter Ten—Life among the People of God

[1] "Five Reasons Millennials Stay Connected to Church," Barna Research Group, September 17, 2013, accessed June 23, 2016, http://www.barna.com /research/5-reasons-millennials-stay-connected-to-church/#.UqpwJScyuRM.

Chapter Eleven—Life with Peers

[1] Alabama, "Mountain Music," in *Mountain Music*, RCA, 1982, http://itunes .com.

[2] C. S. Lewis, *The Lion, the Witch, and the Wardrobe* (New York: Macmillan, 1970), 75–76.

[3] B. Bradford Brown, "Adolescent Relationships with Their Peers," in *Handbook of Adolescent Psychology*, eds. R. M. Lerner and L. Steinberg (Hoboken, NJ: Wiley, 2005).

[4] Hillary Krantz, "Pressure from Peers Can Have Positive Influence on Teens," Youth Resources, Evansville Courier & Press, March 23, 2010, http://www.courierpress.com/features/family/youth-resources/pressure-from-peers-can-have-positive-influence-on-teens-ep-446764663-325799871.html.

[5] Samia Nawaz, "The Relationship of Parental and Peer Attachment Bonds with the Identity Development during Adolescence," *FWU Journal of Social Sciences* 5, no. 1 (Summer 2011): 104–19.

[6] I acknowledge here as some of the other writers in this book have, that the spiritual formation of children belongs to the parents first. We have confused public profession of faith/baptism as the beginning of our faith journey. It is but a step in the lifelong journey of discipleship. The first step of discipleship begins at birth, at home.

[7] Annette La Greca, M. Harrison, and Hannah Moore, "Adolescent Peer Relations, Friendships, and Romantic Relationships: Do They Predict Social Anxiety and Depression?" *Journal of Clinical Child & Adolescent Psychology* 34, no. 1 (2005): 49–61.

[8] Richard R. Dunn and Jana L. Sundene, *Shaping the Journey of Emerging Adults: Life-Giving Rhythms for Spiritual Transformation* (Downers Grove, IL: InterVarsity Press, 2012).

[9] C. Knoester, D. L. Haynie, and C. M. Stephens, "Parenting Practices and Adolescents' Friendship Networks," *Journal of Marriage and Family* 68, no. 5 (November 2006): 1247–60.

[10] Chris Segrin, Alesia Woszidlo, Michelle Givertz, and Neil Montgomery, "Parent and Child Traits Associated with Overparenting," *Journal of Social and Clinical Psychology* 32, no. 6 (June 2013): 569–95.

[11] V. Guilamo-Ramos, J. Jaccard, and P. Dittus, *Parental Monitoring of Adolescents: Current Perspectives for Researchers and Practitioners* (New York: Columbia University Press, 2010).

[12] Matthew 22:37–40 NIV.

[13] Rutger Engels, Maja Deković, and Wim Meeus, "Parenting Practices, Social Skills and Peer Relationships in Adolescence," *Social Behavior and Personality* 30, no. 1 (January 2002): 3–17.

[14] Karen Choi, "The Relationship between Youth Ministry Participation and Faith Maturity of Adolescents: Testing for Faith-Nurturing Characteristics in Youth Ministry as a Mediator Using Multiple Regression," *Christian Education Journal* 9, no. 2 (Fall 2012): 293–308.

[15] Ibid., 102.

[16] Ibid.

[17] "Peer Group Process and Guidelines: Comprehensive Guidelines to the Peer Group Practice for Friends Carrying Out a Ministry or Leading," Quaker Spiritual Formation, accessed June 23, 2016, http://quakerspiritualformation .org/sf-2/peer-group-process-and-guidelines/.

[18] "Spiritual Life," Hampshire College, accessed June 23,2016, http://www .hampshire.edu/spiritual-life/spiritual-life/.

[19] "An Introduction to the Peer Advisor Selection Process," Seattle Pacific University, accessed June 23, 2016, http://spu.edu/search-new/?cx =010768069351356013927%3Asnjgfukxg_g&cof=FORID%3A10&ie=UTF-8&q =An+Introduction+to+the+Peer+Advisor+Selection+Process%2C+Seattle +Pacific+University&sa.x=6&sa.y=5.

[20] "Five Reasons Millennials Stay Connected to Church," Barna Research Group, September 17, 2013, accessed June 23, 2016, http://www.barna.com /research/5-reasons-millennials-stay-connected-to-church/#.UqpwJScyuRM.

[21] Dunn and Sundene, *Shaping the Journey*.

Chapter Twelve—Friends, Mentors, Heroes

[1] Though various studies have approached this issue from different angles, nailing down a "hard statistic" is a challenge. For further reading on this estimate, please see "Deep Impact: Faith Beyond High School" in Kara E. Powell, *Deep Leadership: Training Onramps for Your Youth Ministry Team* (Fuller Youth Institute, 2010).

[2] The Appendix One questions on what has had the greatest impact on your spiritual journey, programming or people, may have already convinced you of the importance of adult involvement in student ministry. Before jumping into practical application, it is important to gather support for intergenerational student ministry programming from the Scriptures and current research (*Helpful hint:* programmatic change is difficult for any ministry because you are "correcting" the ministry practice ideas of someone else, living or dead. Demonstrating the need for change with passion without substance can lead to frustration and unnecessary pain. So, wade through the following information and take notes).

[3] The use of the word "love" in Scripture indicates much more than an emotive response. It indicates a person's willingness to follow the one he/she loves with loyalty and obedience.

[4] S. Dean McBride, "Yoke of the Kingdom: An Exposition of Deuteronomy 6:4–5," *Interpretation* 27, no. 3 (July 1973): 273–306.

[5] Moshe Weinfeld, *Deuteronomy 1–11, , Anchor Bible,* vol. 5 (New York: Doubleday, 1991), 351–54

[6] See Christian Smith with Melinda L. Denton, *Soul Searching: The Religious and Spiritual Lives of American Teenagers* (New York: Oxford University Press, 2005).

[7] *Encyclopaedia Judaica,* 2nd edition, s.v. "Education, in the Biblical Period"

[8] Weinfeld, *Deuteronomy 1–11*, 335. See also John T. Strong and Steven S. Tuell, eds., *Constituting the Community: Studies of the Polity of Ancient Israel in Honor of S. Dean McBride Jr.* (Warsaw, IN: Eisenbrauns, 2005), 277.

[9] *The Anchor Bible Dictionary*, s.v. "Education (Israel)"

[10] The following verses by no means represent an exhaustive list of references.

[11] By placing Deuteronomy 6:5 beside Leviticus 19:18, "love your neighbor as yourself," Jesus demonstrates how loving one's neighbor is made possible and highlights a person's devotion to God. See David L. Turner, *Matthew* in the Baker Exegetical Commentary of the New Testament series (Grand Rapids: Baker Academic, 2008), 537 for a full discussion.

[12] Victor H. Matthews, *Manners and Customs in the Bible*, rev. ed. (Peabody, MA: Hendrickson, 1991), 228–29.

[13] The Greek word used for "indignant" (Mark 10:13) indicates a physical reaction and violent irritation. See H. G. Liddel, R. Scott, and H. S. Jones, *A Greek-English Lexicon*, 9th edition (Oxford: Clarendon, 1940), 5–6.

[14] Leon Morris, *The Gospel According to Matthew* (Grand Rapids: Eerdmans, 1992), 461.

[15] There are many passages in which Paul calls his hearers to wholehearted devotion. This example does not represent an exhaustive list.

[16] William Hendriksen, *Commentary on I & II Timothy and Titus* (London: The Banner of Truth Trust, 1959), 362–63.

[17] See James D. G. Dunn, ed., *The Cambridge Companion to St. Paul* (Cambridge: Cambridge University Press, 2003), 21–22.

[18] John Stott, specifically referencing 1 Timothy 5:1–2, draws a number of powerful conclusions for church leaders, "The local church is rightly called 'the church family,' in which there are fathers and mothers, and brothers and sisters, not to mention aunts and uncles, grandparents and children. Leaders should not be insensitive and treat everybody alike. No, they must behave towards their elders with respect, affection and gentleness, their own generation with equality, the opposite sex with self-control and purity, and all ages of both sexes with that love which binds together members of the same family. John R. W. Stott, *The Message of I Timothy & Titus: God's Good News for the World*, Bible Speaks Today (Downers Grove, IL: InterVarsity Press, 1996), 126.

[19] Thomas C. Oden, *First and Second Timothy and Titus,* Interpretation series (Louisville: John Knox, 1989), 114–18.

[20] For this chapter's purpose, I will focus on only one research project. The work of Smith and Denton was chosen because it has been cited, supported, and addressed by both professional and "popular" speakers extensively. Also, in my opinion, the validity and breadth of their work is respected by scholars. Christian Smith and Melina Lundquist Denton, *Soul Searching: The Religious and Spiritual Lives of American Teenagers* (Oxford: Oxford University Press, 2005).

[21] Smith and Denton, *Soul Searching*, 4.

[22] Ibid., 265.

[23] Ibid.

[24] Ibid., 27.

[25] Ibid.

[26] Ibid., 28.

[27] Ibid., 117.

[28] In my experience, the same is true with students who come from families with strong parental support.

[29] Smith and Denton, *Soul Searching*, 170–71.

[30] Storytelling is crucial in helping people understand the need for the pain that often comes with the reorienting of church programming. Scott Cormode at Fuller Seminary has written significantly on this truth.

Chapter Thirteen—Bringing In the Outsider

[1] Grace Koelma, "Lawnmower Parents Are the Next Breed of Helicopter Parents," News.com.au, October 11, 2014, accessed February 11, 2016, http://www.news.com.au/lifestyle/parenting/kids/lawnmower-parents-are-the-next-breed-of-helicopter-parents/news-story/7e20d253be905aed08f1d93287078308.

[2] Jacques Derrida, "Hostipitality," trans. Barry Stocker and Forbes Morlock, *Angelaki: Journal of the Theoretical Humanities* 5, no. 3 (December 2000): 3.

[3] Luke 7:37—It is telling, I think, that three of the four Gospels find this story worthy of conclusion.

Chapter Fourteen—Maintaining a Holy Identity While Wholly Immersed in a Culture

[1] See the Pew Research Center studies on how quickly things are changing in this time in history compared to previous times at http://www.pewresearch.org/fact-tank/2015/03/19/how-millennials-compare-with-their-grandparents/.

In just fifty years education levels have increased tremendously, more women are earning bachelor's degrees, marriage ages are getting older, just to name a few.

[2] Christian Smith and Melinda L. Denton, *Soul Searching: The Religious and Spiritual Lives of American Teenagers* (New York: Oxford University Press, 2005). Smith is careful to note that this is evident not only in mainline Protestant and Catholic youth, but in most religious communities.

[3] Ibid., 162–63.

[4] Mike Yaconelli, *Messy Spirituality: God's Annoying Love for Imperfect People* (Grand Rapids: Zondervan, 2002), 42.

[5] Unfortunately, a cursory survey of any type of messaging that refers to adolescents, whether it be advertising, television characters, etc., provides one with an overwhelming majority of negative examples of imaging and attitudes that exist toward adolescents in today's culture.

[6] Perry Glanzer, "The Heart of Purpose: The Major Difference behind Student Answers to One of Life's Biggest Questions," in *A Faith for the Generations*, eds. Timothy Herman, Kirsten Tenhaken, Hannah Adderley, and Morgan Morris (Abilene, TX: Abilene Christian University Press, 2015): 29–48.

[7] David Kinnaman and Aly Hawkins, *You Lost Me: Why Young Christians Are Leaving Church—and Rethinking Faith* (Grand Rapids: Baker, 2011), 29.

[8] Andrew Root, *Unpacking Scripture in Youth Ministry* (Grand Rapids: Zondervan, 2012), 28.

[9] Dietrich Bonhoeffer, *Life Together* (New York: Harper & Row, 1954), 97.

[10] Richard H. Niebuhr, *Christ and Culture* (New York: Harper, 1951).

Chapter Fifteen—Dreams, Visions, and Real Life

[1] "Speaking the truth in love" is the accepted translation of verse 15, but the verb in Greek is the verb form of "truth." "Speaking" is supplied by translators because we have no verb form for "truth" in English. The phrase, "Truthing it in love" would better capture the writer's intent. All words and actions by the believer should represent the purposes of Jesus Christ.